Call no: VM 331 B36 1994

California Maritime Academy Library (CSU)

D0382352

DATE DUE

WITHDRAWN

VOYAGING
UNDER POWER

VOYAGING
UNDER POWER

THIRD EDITION

by Captain ROBERT P. BEEBE

Revised by JAMES F. LEISHMAN WITHDRAWN

LIBRARY
CALIFORNIA MARITIME ACADEMY
P. O. BOX 1392
VALLEJO, CA 94590

International Marine
Camden, Maine

Published by International Marine®

1 0   9   8   7   6   5   4   3   2   1

Copyright © 1994 International Marine®, an imprint of TAB Books. TAB Books is a division of McGraw-Hill, Inc.

All rights reserved. The publisher takes no responsibility for the use of any of the materials or methods described in this book, nor for the products thereof. The name "International Marine" and the International Marine logo are trademarks of McGraw-Hill, Inc. Printed in the United States of America.

Library of Congress Cataloging-in-Publication Data
Beebe, Robert P.
   Voyaging under power / Robert P. Beebe.—3rd ed. / revised by James F.
  Leishman.
     p. cm.
  Includes bibliographical references and index.
  ISBN 0-07-158019-0 (alk. paper)
   1. Yacht building. 2. Naval architecture. 3. Passagemaker (Yacht) 4. Ocean travel.
  I. Leishman, James F. II. Title.
  VM331.B36 1994
  623.82'31—dc20   94-4555
                          CIP

Questions regarding the content of this book should be addressed to:
  International Marine
  P.O. Box 220
  Camden, ME 04843
Questions regarding the ordering of this book should be addressed to:
  TAB Books
  A Division of McGraw-Hill, Inc.
  Blue Ridge Summit, PA 17294
  1-800-233-1128

Voyaging Under Power is printed on acid-free paper.

Unless otherwise noted, illustrations are by Jeff Leishman.
Printed by Arcata Graphics, Fairfield, PA
Design by Ann Aspell
Production and page layout by Janet Robbins
Edited by Jim Babb, Don Casey, Pamela Benner

To my wife, Linford, best of shipmates.
And to the first crew of Passagemaker:
Ralph Arndt, Ev Bibb, and Connie Curts.
They have been there.

CONTENTS

FOREWORD

It was June 5, 1967. PASSAGEMAKER was moored to a marina dock in Rondout Creek, a few hundred yards from New York's Hudson River. It was our first night's stop on a 400-mile inland passage to Expo '67 in Montreal. The other three in *Passagemaker*'s crew had gone off in the dinghy to explore the creek, leaving Bob Beebe and me alone on the afterdeck.

Our pipes were lit and we were drinking *Passagemaker* tea (tea sweetened with Tang and laced with a shot of rum—ideal to lubricate one's conversation machinery). In the previous five days my view of cruising had been turned topsy-turvy, as if someone had spun me around so I could see it from another perspective. I was mesmerized.

The experience that led to this new outlook was a 400-mile run up the Atlantic coast from Norfolk, Virginia, to New London, Connecticut, and three days at home, thinking constantly about all I had seen and learned from Bob on the offshore passage. Some 30 miles off the Atlantic coast we had motored steadily at 7.5 knots, the same speed that had carried the motorboat three-quarters of the way around the world, from Singapore westward to California. Not only was I stirred by this vision of a new way of cruising, but I felt strongly that Bob was sitting on a story the boating world was waiting for. (Interestingly, when this book was first published, the noted ocean-racer Carleton Mitchell wrote in his Introduction: "This is a book whose time has come.")

So, sitting in the fading sunlight, sipping tea and smoking my pipe, I said, "You know, Bob, you really have to write a book about the entire *Passagemaker* experience—the theory, the plans, the boat, and the long cruise that *proved* the theory."

He sort of grunted and waved dismissively, saying that he had *already* told the story in eight or ten articles, published in four or five magazines, over a span of six or seven years.

I pointed out that the number of owners and would-be motorboat owners with ocean-crossing ambitions who had seen, read, and *saved* that scattered batch of articles must be small indeed. Then I brought up the idea that had been growing in my mind since the offshore passage.

What if, I asked him, I started a publishing company? Would he consider writing *that* book for me? His answer—after more sips and more puffs on his pipe—was yes, and Bob's yes, I learned, was a promissory note. It's a tribute I take pleasure in paying to a very special and now-departed friend that he never wavered in his promise, though any major publisher would have leaped at the chance to publish the book.

The story ends this way. Three years passed before Seven Seas Press came into being—with capital enough for paperback books only for the first few years. A full seven years after the Rondout Creek conversation I finally wrote Bob and asked him to start writing what became the first edition of this book. Of the 28 titles that appeared during the early years of Seven Seas Press, *Voyaging Under Power* was its publisher's proudest achievement. It became a Dolphin Book Club main selection and the "bible" of long-distance motorboat cruising.

I have always believed that "VUP" (as Bob always termed it) would remain in print for a lifetime—or be, at very least, the starting point for anyone's serious consideration of a cross-ocean passage in a motorboat. So credit is due to those who brought this new edition into being: Jim Babb of International Marine, who recognized the book's enduring value; Jim Leishman, whose enthusiasm and equally high regard for the book were matched by an impressive amount of oceangoing experience over many years; and my longtime friend Linford Beebe, who has revised her original galley chapter for this new edition and joined me in providing these recollections of how the book began.

This impressive technical update, which retains all of Bob Beebe's vital material from the original, gives today's reader the opportunity to study the Beebe design principles and discover how those principles led to the successful ocean-crossing motorboat against contemporary state-of-the-art technical developments. He will discover anew, I believe, why an earlier generation of long-distance motorboat owners dubbed this book the "bible."

STEVE DOHERTY

Shelter Island, New York
March 1994

PREFACE

It WASN'T UNTIL HALFWAY ACROSS the Atlantic that I began to realize the enormity of the task I had taken on. Crossing the ocean under power? No, not that; that's the easy part. What I'm referring to is the update of Robert Beebe's classic, *Voyaging Under Power*.

Some time had passed since I'd agreed to update the book, but there had been so many distractions with family and business that I looked forward to this month-long cruise to make significant progress on the manuscript. As each day of our voyage passed, I read and reread each chapter and made pages of notes, pursuing various ideas that showed promise of being the best approach to revision. There was plenty of time to devote to the project during the idle hours aboard ship, but my progress was slow and discouraging. The original book had been so well done, was so interesting and so correct that despite two decades of progress, its important content was essentially still as current and useful as when originally published.

On this passage from Fort Lauderdale to England, using the same routing and fuel stops as Beebe's own yacht *Passagemaker* had used 25 years earlier, I realized that to revise much of this classic work with an honest dedication to improvement would not be as easy as I had thought. In retrospect, I should have been well aware of how superb Beebe's original work was. I had been so impressed after reading *Voyaging Under Power* that I persuaded the shareholders of our own company to defer a new sailboat design and to authorize the design of an ocean-crossing powerboat that adhered to most of the formulas and ratios laid down within the book. The end result, designed by my brother Jeff Leishman, with me acting as co-designer and project manager, was the Nordhavn 46, and it was aboard the tenth hull built that I was now crossing the Atlantic. Beebe had influenced me so much and the advice given within his book had proven so valuable that I concluded my contribution must be, with minor exceptions, the addition of material to this classic work. It is in this vein that I present to you the revised *Voyaging Under Power*.

As the late Robert Beebe proclaimed, there *is* an alternative to sail for the cruising enthusiast. He knew it and proved it to himself and many others. A proper motorboat of moderate size can be cruised anywhere—with equal economy, greater comfort, greater security, less effort, and greater dispatch than a comparably sized sailboat. Sound outrageous? Read on. The pages ahead will lend credibility to these claims.

Cruising of the serious variety is an activity most people pursue as the fulfillment of a dream. They seek adventure, travel, and challenge, and in today's complex, controlled, and densely populated world, a high-quality experience that's unique and really special is not as easy to find as it once was. The sea has tremendous appeal. It is vast, challenging, ever-changing, and perpetually beautiful. The allure of ocean voyaging and of destinations that are unlimited in number and variety is truly what dreams are made of. Cruising on one's own yacht offers an experience and adventure that is unrivaled.

Over the past 20 years an entire industry has produced seaworthy boats (mostly sail) by the thousands to meet the demand created by people's desire to cruise. I have made my living designing, building, and selling these offshore vessels and have been witness to both successes and failures in individual pursuits of this dream. While most long-range voyaging has been done under sail, I am convinced that for numerous reasons a proper power yacht is a better choice for a significant percentage of both the experienced and the inexperienced.

In this revised *Voyaging Under Power* we will explore the reasons for choosing power, and we will immerse ourselves in the technicalities of the proper passage-making powerboat. Our goal is not only to provide the latest technical information on the subject of powered cruising but to continue Robert Beebe's work of introducing current and future cruising sailors to this logical and exciting alternative to sail, which he pioneered with his worldwide travels aboard the renowned *Passagemaker.*

Somewhere Bob Beebe is cruising a better *Passagemaker* on a bigger and bluer ocean, but he wanted his work to go on. With the encouragement of Bob's devoted wife, Linford, and Bob's close friend Bob Sutton . . . off we go.

JIM LEISHMAN

Dana Point, California
March 1994

ACKNOWLEDG-MENTS TO THE THIRD EDITION

SPECIAL THANKS MUST GO TO Robert Beebe himself. The archives he left behind contained invaluable work, some of which was done after the original publication of *Voyaging Under Power*.

I'm grateful to Jim Babb of International Marine and to Linford Beebe for giving me the opportunity to work on this project, and to my two business partners of 20 years, Dan Streech and Joe Meglen, who supported my efforts, even on company time.

Jim and Susy Sink's narrative of their experiences while circumnavigating in *Salvation II;* the update of Chapter 16, "Cruising in Europe," as well as their contribution of Chapter 17, "Inland Voyaging"—all are greatly appreciated.

Customers who have become friends, fellow shipmates, owners of our own designs—many of them have supplied the performance data and experiences that have served to shape my opinions on the many aspects of powerboat voyaging. I'm indebted to Bruce Kessler, who unselfishly shared his knowledge and experience, gained while circumnavigating in his 70-foot *Zopolote.* Thanks also go to David Hamilton for his pioneering work on the bulbous bow and his contribution to our progress with "flopperstopper" stabilizing systems. Thanks to all the others—too many to mention—who have enthusiastically shared their experience, which collectively amounts to hundreds of thousands of oceangoing miles while voyaging under power.

Finally, I thank all the designers who have contributed their designs for the revision of Chapter 12. Particular thanks go to my brother, Jeff Leishman, who has tolerated thousands of hours of my over-the-shoulder review and proven his superior design skills to me over and over again.

ACKNOWLEDG-
MENTS TO THE
FIRST EDITION

Because yacht design and naval architecture form the basic structure of this book, I owe a considerable debt to those practitioners of the art who have helped me with advice and encouragement from my early beginnings to the present day: William Atkin, Howard I. Chapelle, L. Francis Herreshoff, Weston Farmer, William Garden, and Philip C. Bolger. This does not imply that any of them would necessarily agree with what is in this book. In fact, yacht designers being the individualists they are, I am quite sure they would not. Nevertheless, their dedication to excellence and the integrity of their work have always been an inspiration to me.

I am also especially grateful to the designers who contributed their work, which makes up the bulk of Chapter 12. Without exception, those asked responded with enough designs to make up a most interesting, instructive, and diverse chapter, one that should be of continuing interest both to the informed amateur and to the student of boat design.

The experiences of many seamen, too many to acknowledge, have been incorporated into this book—experiences from many sources. But I am particularly grateful to two men, among the few with long-range motorboat experience, who have made special contributions: Avard Fuller, with his experience in long, light vessels; and Jerrems C. Hart, whose comments on Chapter 6, "Technicalities of the Seagoing Motorboat," and review of its drafts were particularly helpful.

Thanks are also due to several magazine editors who have given permission to use, in whole or part, articles originally printed in their publications: Monk Farnham of *Boating* for "*Passagemaker* Across the Atlantic," which makes up the greatest part of Chapter 15, and "Seagoing Boats for the Canals of Europe," which appears in Chapter 16; Bill Robinson of *Yachting* for "Once Over Heavily" and "Once Over Lightly," excerpts of which are used in Chapter 5 (and special thanks to Norris D. Hoyt, author of both articles); Pete Smyth of *Motor Boating & Sailing* for "Flopperstoppers for Seagoing Motorboats," portions of which are found in Chapter 8; and Joe Gribbins of *Motorboat,* who published "The Passagemaker Experience," a shortened version of material that now comprises Chapter 4.

Thanks are also due to Robert P. Sutton whose story of *Mona Mona* was so good we persuaded him to let us use it in Chapter 13. My special appreciation goes to my wife, Linford, who not only contributed Chapter 19, "The Long-Range Galley," but also acted as my long-suffering sounding board for innumerable drafts of the entire book, much of which was written on long freighter voyages.

I have been helped significantly in the production of this book and want to express my gratitude to: Donna Doherty, who after cooking and cruising aboard *Passagemaker* on passages to New London and Montreal in 1967, contributed her considerable art talents to the design of this book; Margaret Joyce, whose copyediting contributed so much to clarity and precision; and John Stephen Doherty, editor and publisher of Seven Seas Press, who occupies a special position as the original push behind getting this book started some years ago, subsequent to his having qualified as crew on *Passagemaker*.

CHAPTER 1

A LITTLE BIT ABOUT ROBERT BEEBE

*B*ORN IN 1909 AND RAISED as an "Army brat" (his own description), Robert Beebe was introduced to his lifelong passion as a young child. His interest and love for all things nautical began with his experiences in a dugout canoe given to him by his father, the commanding officer of a garrison on the island of Zamboanga in the Philippines.

Recalling his childhood, Captain Robert Beebe states:

> *I don't think one day passed that we were not out on those marvelous, clear, tropic waters right out in front of our quarters. I have never forgotten those days and have been a tropics buff ever since, and a boat nut as well. In a dugout canoe my brother and I, together with some of the neighboring kids, fought more pirates, found more buried treasure, and raised more mysterious shores than any kid today possibly could in the present-day curse of outboard-driven dinks.*

Throughout adolescence, Beebe's experience and skill grew, and he began to develop an appreciation for the technical aspects of the various sailing dinghies and small cruisers he had sailed aboard. He studied the few periodicals of the day and paid particular attention to the "How to Build" articles by William Atkin that appeared in *Motorboating*. As he neared completion of his primary school education, aviation caught his interest, and he was faced with a decision of studying aeronautical engineering at MIT or entering the Naval Academy at Annapolis. In the end his lifelong love of the water drew him to Navy service and Annapolis, where the Academy offered, along with a degree in aeronautical engineering, plenty of opportunities to hone his already keen sailing skills.

Graduating in 1931 and becoming a naval aviator in 1933, Beebe spent his first fleet tour in the San Diego/Long Beach area. It was here on the West Coast that he began to think of an ocean-going cruising sailboat for himself and his new bride. When it became apparent to the Beebes that his next tour of duty would be in the Hawaiian Islands, they searched for a vessel capable of crossing the Pacific and suitable for cruising the islands. They located a partially completed 30-footer that seemed perfectly suited for the voyage. Beebe later related:

1

Figure 1-1.
*Philippine canoe
Robert Beebe owned
as a boy.*

*We inspected the boat. She was set up in her own
building shed in what is now Newport Beach. The hull was practically complete and all the
material for her rigging and interior was present. All the workmanship was beautiful, all
fastenings the best, lead keel, bronze hardware, and so on. She was an Atkin design, number
311, and had never been given a name. She was one of his double-enders. Many vessels of
this size go to Hawaii every year, but in 1936 we didn't get much encouragement.*

*The problem was getting her done in time. We checked everywhere and had several
builders in to give us an estimate, more of time than money. We reluctantly had to conclude there was practically no chance for us to get her in time for a proper shakedown and
passage before I had to report to Hawaii. So we let her go. I've often wished since then we
had been a little bolder. She was really an exceptional vessel. The next year a member of the
services did sail out for duty in Hawaii—the (then) Colonel George S. Patton, U.S. Army,
in an Alden schooner.*

Stationed at Pearl Harbor in 1936, Beebe found himself piloting the biplane flying boats of the
era over the waters west of Hawaii. The Pearl Harbor Yacht Club had a fleet of eight Herreshoff
S-class sloops, two of which belonged to the commanding officers of the air station and navy yard.
Beebe became sailing officer, responsible for all maintenance of the two vessels, which allowed him
to participate in almost every one of the weekly races. What he learned from competitive sailing in
the rugged sailing conditions around the island of Oahu would be formative: "I developed a profound admiration for the Herreshoff S and, by extension, a liking for heavy keelboats in general."

His continuing desire to own a cruiser with liveaboard accommodations was as strong as ever,
and his experience with the S boats caused him to develop his own ideas about a suitable design.
"I started sketching my own ideas, and it was soon apparent I didn't know beans about how to go
about it."

Beebe ordered up a copy of a newly published book called *Yacht Designing and Planning* by
Howard I. Chapelle.

*I must have read through that book a half-dozen times.
It certainly changed my life. Where formerly I had been content to sail in what I could find
without much thought as to whether the boats were really good or not, now the fundamentals
explained in Chapelle's book led my thoughts to how things could be improved, the advantages
of certain shapes, and the influence of various factors.*

Beebe continued to develop his own rough sketches, and when time permitted he read the published works of other designers. He began to correspond with William Atkin about his ideas. When his tour of duty in Hawaii ended, he returned to Annapolis for postgraduate studies, where he developed a friendship with his mentor, Howard Chapelle. Chapelle's sharpie designs greatly appealed to Beebe for sailing in shallow Chesapeake waters, and after a visit with the designer in Ipswich, Massachusetts, Beebe returned to Annapolis with a set of Chapelle plans in hand. He commissioned a local Annapolis yard to build the 34-foot sharpie, christened *Sara Reid* after his mother.

Beebe sailed his new ketch every chance he got and was so impressed by her performance that he wrote numerous articles about her, the first of which appeared in the August 1939 issue of *Yachting.* The next 40 years saw many articles by Robert Beebe in the most popular boating magazines, and not all of a purely technical nature. Beebe developed the skills of an excellent storyteller, and his adventures gave him a constant supply of new material. He tells of a particular experience aboard the *Sara Reid* that undoubtedly influenced his lifework:

> *Working to windward once in the company of a 40-foot
ketch, we were in the center of the bay (Chesapeake) with a south wind of 22 knots blowing
against an outgoing tide. Naturally we could not hold the ketch under those conditions. We
started our borrowed two-horsepower outboard and ran it at half speed. The* Sara Reid *caught
and passed the ketch both pointing and footing—the best illustration I have ever seen of the
effect of a bit of power in windward work.*

As 1939 marked the beginning of World War II, Beebe found himself called to Florida as a training officer, producing much-needed carrier pilots. He found time to sail the *Sara Reid* south, and it was while sailing aboard his agile sharpie on the north end of Biscayne Bay on a beautiful winter's day that Beebe learned of the attack on Pearl Harbor. There was no time now to think of yachting.

With his accumulated experience and training, Beebe was given command of an air squadron in the Pacific. But then the unexpected happened.

> *Well, we did go west and I did get command of a dive-
bombing squadron. Unfortunately, just as our air group was ready to proceed to the South
Pacific, I had to be hospitalized for some necessary surgery. My squadron went off and left me,
and by the time I returned to duty, I was sent to the USS* Saratoga *as a ship's officer, where I
became navigator of this aircraft carrier, one of the world's largest ships, and served in her the
rest of the war.*
>
> *Regardless of how I might have felt at losing my squadron, from the point of view of yacht
design, no job could have been better. The navigator's duties, while extremely important, are
not overwhelmed with the details of a department with hundreds of men. He does have some
free time. In addition, he has at hand an excellent source of drafting paper as so many of the
ship's charts are made obsolete by later ones, a process that went on with amazing speed as we
probed deeper into the South Pacific. In addition, while the ship was underway, which was*

Figure 1-2. *Aircraft
carrier USS* Saratoga,
Beebe's wartime ship.

*most of the time, the navigator was on the bridge and in his charthouse. This kept him out
of such mundane distractions as bridge games in the wardroom and encouraged industry.
The result was the production of a good bit of work in several fields.*

It was this sequence of events that likely sealed Beebe's fate—that of becoming a designer/
authority whose expertise would ultimately equal those for whom he had such great respect.

At the war's end, Beebe had amassed a considerable amount of design work on cruising sailboats, particularly sharpies similar to the *Sara Reid.* Beebe's now close friend Howard Chapelle
admitted that he could not justify working on the sharpies for clients who were so value con-
scious that they were unwilling or unable to pay a reasonable designer's fee. Beebe, considering himself an amateur and with a primary income paying his bills, took referral work of this type from
Chapelle for a number of years.

Robert Beebe proved to be a very modest man. Even in 1980 he continued to refer to himself
as an amateur, but note how he qualifies the term and considers it an important ingredient in his
success in the field of long-range seagoing motorboats:

> *Certainly I have sold plans from time to time since the
earliest days of learning the art. But at no time have I been under any compulsion to try to
make designing my principal source of income. I think this is the key. A professional yacht
designer then is anyone who intends to make designing his primary source of income. He may
fail, of course, but if he does have this intention, he is under certain constraints that do not
affect the amateur. He must, for instance, seek out the most active and popular field of design
of his day and try to carve a niche there. Recently this field has been the so-called cruiser-racer
sailing vessel. And here he must work in the restrictions of the rules in vogue, regardless of his
own ideas. However much he may wish to experiment and advance the art, he must judge his
work not on whether it is, in fact, a new breakthrough, but on what is saleable. An amateur
does not labor under any of these restraints. He is free to go where his interest leads him.*

Figure 1-3. *Robert P. Beebe.*

Beebe's experience and enthusiasm for sail and his extensive design work in the field were all a solid foundation for his developing concept of passage-making in specially designed motorboats. The thought process could not have evolved without the sailing experience and possibly the "amateur" association with naval architecture. It should be remembered that in the late '50s when Beebe was developing his Passagemaker concept, long-range cruising in small motorboats was almost unheard of.

Let's move now to Robert Beebe's introduction to his vessel *Passagemaker* and some of the history that led up to her design.

CHAPTER 2

HISTORICAL BACKGROUND OF POWER VOYAGING

IT WAS THE LAST DAY. As I came on deck for the 0400–0800 watch, a faint light in the east showed the horizon clear, with brilliant stars overhead. There would be a good fix on this, our landfall day. The bow wave chuckled softly.

Sipping a mug of coffee while waiting for sight time, I had much to think about: the years of research and theorizing, the days and weeks of drawing plans, the months of watching the vessel grow in the builder's yard—a vessel whose highly unusual makeup we hoped would prove my theories—the sea trials, the first miles of our cruise, the ports we visited, the weather. Everything. Now, just ahead lay Rhodes, one of the fabled islands of Greece.

My thoughts went back even farther, to World War II when, like so many other armchair long-cruise planners, I found myself transported to the South Pacific under circumstances that had never entered my wildest dreams. There, as navigator of the aircraft carrier *Saratoga,* I observed at firsthand the conditions small cruising boats would meet after the war. It was this experience that first turned me toward a vessel distinctly different from traditional long-range types. Now, as we neared Rhodes, the work begun on the bridge of the old *Saratoga* had passed from dream to reality, and the reality was carrying me and my crew northward across the Mediterranean on this clear, calm morning toward the castle of the Knights Hospitalers.

For the yacht *Passagemaker* was about to complete her first voyage. In six weeks *to the day* we had made the passage to Greece from Singapore. Almost 6,000 miles of calms, brisk breezes, and gales lay astern. And through it all our ocean-crossing motorboat had chugged steadily along, averaging exactly her designed passage speed of 7.5 knots.

I knew now that crossing oceans in owner-operated small craft in the 40- to 50-foot range, under power alone and using crews by no means made up of rough and tough seamen, worked and worked well. I had also learned what I'd only suspected before—that a very good case could be made for the power approach over sail for all long voyages.

To generations of seamen brought up on tales of long voyages in small sailing craft, such statements must sound like heresy. Some years ago I, too, would have counted myself among those seamen. But certain experiences, certain selective reading with a critical eye, and certain designing in new directions had finally convinced me that it was possible on long voyages to do better. It is the evolution of the theory, its testing with *Passagemaker,* what we learned and what can be recommended for the future that this book is all about.

The book, then, is about voyaging under power as contrasted with voyaging under sail. While a vast literature exists about deep-sea cruising under sail, there is little in print about long-range power voyaging. Of course, many of the problems encountered at sea are similar in both cases. But the power approach does differ from sail in several important ways that need consideration. To cite just one example: the naval architecture rules that govern the speed and range of a long-range motorboat are quite rigid and must be thoroughly understood before selecting such a craft or operating it to the limits of its ability. On the other hand, the sailing cruiser, with its "free" propulsion power, is largely independent of these rules.

Of course, I have nothing against cruising under sail. The long sailing cruises I have made have all been great fun. But, as will appear, there are certain conditions and certain groups of sailors for whom the power approach has definite advantages. It is for those sailors this book is written.

It was the search for a retirement boat that led me to consider power as an alternative to sail. The more I looked into it, the more interesting it became, until the years spent pursuing the matter finally led to the building of our 50-foot *Passagemaker.* Some 60,000 miles of deep-water cruising in her, including three ocean crossings, a round trip to Hawaii, and two East Coast–West Coast passages, taught me much that can be safely passed on to those who share this interest. Of course, during those years I exchanged experiences with the few others who had background in this narrow field, considered the features of other ocean-crossing motorboats, and studied the work of other designers.

One of the first things I undertook when I decided to embark on the design of a long-range motorboat was research in the history of the boat type. It is a scanty field, but useful lessons can be learned from what material is available.

There were two early small-boat voyages across the Atlantic under power; both were made to demonstrate the reliability of the internal combustion engines then coming into use in boats. The first voyage was by the *Abiel Abbot Low,* using a kerosene engine. In 1902 she crossed from New York to Falmouth, England, in 38 days. The second voyage was by the motorboat *Detroit* in 1912. She used a gasoline engine to cross from New York to Queenstown (now Cobh), Ireland, in 28 days. What lessons can we learn from these two pioneer efforts?

My first impression after reading the logs of the *Low* and the *Detroit* was that the voyages were excellent examples of what *not* to do. With due regard for the guts of the crews, it is clear that the designers and builders had a lot to learn. This is understandable, of course, as no one had attempted such a voyage. Possibly more important, the men involved in these projects had their major training in sail.

It must have been this sail background, for instance, that produced the astonishing layout of *Detroit.* She was 35 feet long with a 9-foot beam and a 4-foot, 6-inch draft. She was double-ended and resembled a lifeboat in that she had high shelters bow and stern. Amidships she was low-sided, and in the center of this deck space was the steering station—a stand-up wheel with no shelter whatever. The watch-stander was supposed to stand there with no handholds and steer the vessel while waves washed across the deck from either side. Fantastic! Here was a station well laid out for the watch to keep an eye on the sails—but no sails!

Understandably enough, this feature caused a good deal of discontent among the crew of four

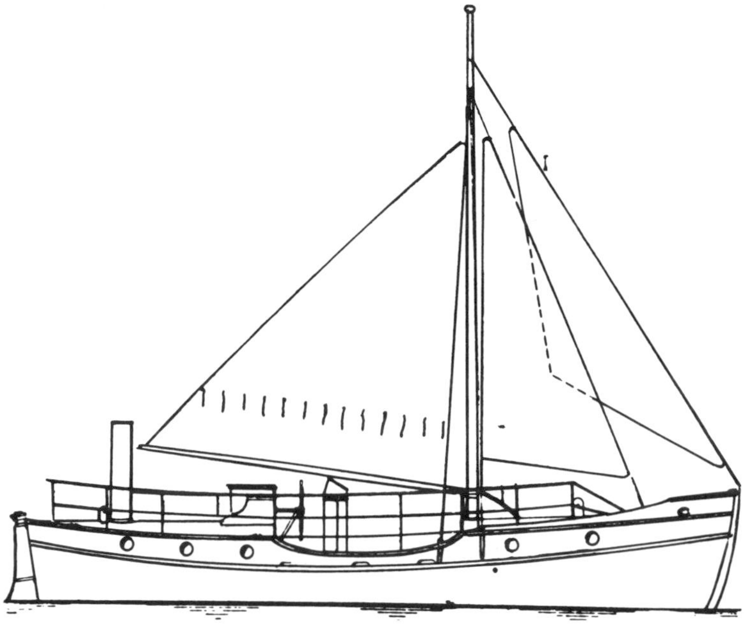

Figure 2-1. *The* Detroit. *Note the
steering arrangement and the low
side amidships. The* Detroit *crossed
the Atlantic in 1912 in 26 days.*

when *Detroit* entered the open Atlantic. However, the engine performed flawlessly, and *Detroit* arrived in Queenstown in good order.

The *Low* was not well laid out for the crossing, either. She was 38 feet long with a 34-foot waterline, 9-foot beam, and 3-foot 8-inch draft, double-ended, with a trunk cabin forward and cockpit aft. Instead of providing some shelter by putting the wheel against the trunk cabin forward, it was placed aft as on a sailing vessel and was wide open to the elements.

Low's principal problem was crew trouble. Her skipper, having been hired to make this engine-demonstrating voyage, chose to take his 16-year-old son as his only crew, then tried to do every-thing himself. With no relief from the tyranny of continuous steering, he soon became exhausted. This produced all sorts of crises. *Low* was also unfortunate in her weather, spending a good deal of time hove-to or riding to a sea anchor. When this was compounded by her copper fuel tanks spring-ing numerous leaks due to the pounding of heavy seas, by kerosene getting into everything below

Figure 2-2. *The* Abiel Abbot
Low, *the first motorboat across the
Atlantic. She crossed in 1902 in
38 days.*

decks, and by a constant battle to bail as much oil as possible back into the tanks, her crew was reduced almost to survival conditions. But they toughed it out and made it. The engine ran perfectly all the way.

Nobody felt impelled to follow in the wake of these two vessels, and the way these voyages tested to the limit the endurance of hardened professional seamen makes this reluctance understandable.

Commencing in 1912, annual motorboat "races" were held from the U.S. to Bermuda. These died after three runnings from lack of entries. I do not think the designs of the vessels that participated show any developments of particular interest to us today.

It was not until 1937 that the next crossing of the North Atlantic by a small motorboat took place. This voyage is of great interest as it was the first in a craft incorporating features found in modern ocean-crossing motorboats. The voyage was made by a Frenchman named Marin-Marie, who was the official marine painter to the French government. Marin-Marie had been a small-boat sailor all his life. In 1933 he built a double-ended cutter and sailed it singlehandedly across the Atlantic from France to New York. He enjoyed this adventure so much that he wondered how the voyage would go under power. He certainly did a good job of researching the project and made up a specification designed to correct the flaws of earlier boats and to add features permitted by modern developments. His book, *Wind Aloft, Wind Alow* (Scribners 1947) is maddeningly vague about details, but it appears his *Arielle* was about 42 feet 6 inches long and drew 4 feet 6 inches. She was equipped with a 75-horsepower four-cylinder diesel and carried 1,500 gallons of fuel, a steadying and emergency propulsion rig, an enclosed steering station, a primitive form of photo-electric autopilot, and a vane steering gear that antedated by many years the models popular today on sailing cruisers. In fact, I think the only thing missing from *Arielle*'s equipment was some method of stabilizing against rolling. She did use her steadying rig for this purpose, but it was ineffective for the usual reasons (see Chapter 8).

In spite of dire predictions of disaster, to the point that the elders of the Club de Yachts de France considered having Marin-Marie restrained legally from such a foolish venture, *Arielle* left New York on July 22, 1937, and arrived in Le Havre, France, 19 days later, essentially with nothing to report—the way any well-conducted cruise should end.

Marin-Marie's voyage was met with devastating silence on both sides of the Atlantic. The fact that a yacht of *Arielle*'s size, under

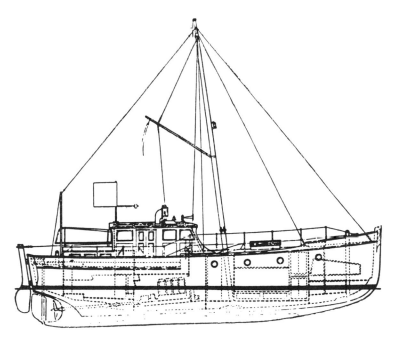

Figure 2-3. Arielle, *profile. Note the covered steering station, steadying rig, and general air of competence in this excellently planned 43-footer.*

Figure 2-4. Arielle *at sea, a photo
taken from the deck of a steamer.
Despite her seamanlike crossing in
1937, the feat was met by a
"devastating silence."*

the command of a well-known yachtsman, had crossed the Atlantic to where she could now cruise the fascinating waters of Europe and had done so in less time and for less money than would have been required to prepare the boat and ship it across (and probably arrived in much better shape than if she had been shipped) didn't seem to make *any* impression. Marin-Marie and *Arielle* were far ahead of their time, and I want to pay tribute here to their successful pioneering effort.

In 1939, the first crossing of the Atlantic from east to west was made in a 31-foot motorboat named *Eckero*. One might say this voyage presaged things to come—*Eckero* was not designed for the voyage, nor specially fitted, nor was her crew trying to prove anything.

Eckero's owner was Uno Ekblom and he lived on the Åland Islands in the Baltic. In 1939 he decided to visit the United States, but for some reason he couldn't get a visa—and no visa, no steamship ticket. Not one to let such a detail upset his plans, Ekblom decided to go anyway, in the motorboat *Eckero* which he had designed and built for himself 10 years previously. She was 31 feet long with a beam of 9 feet 10 inches and had a single-cylinder diesel of 10 horsepower—like thousands of fishing vessels in the Baltic.

Ekblom got together a crew of two friends, gave the diesel a factory overhaul, fitted a small steadying rig, and away they went on May 3, 1939.

They stopped in Copenhagen, Denmark, and Göteborg, Sweden, had their worst weather of the trip in the North Sea, and arrived in Rotterdam, Holland, on May 28. They then motored to Dover, Southampton, and Falmouth, England, following Ekblom's rule of spending only one night

Figure 2-5. Eckero, *the first powerboat to cross the Atlantic from east to
west. She crossed in 1939 in 34 days.*

in a port—a rule he observed scrupulously to the end of the voyage. On June 9 they left Falmouth bound for Horta in the Azores, arriving at the end of a passage of 1,260 miles in nine and a half days. After a day in port they were off for Bermuda, 1,800 miles away. They entered St. George on July 7, refueled, and left the following day. When they arrived in New York on July 13, they had covered no fewer than 3,725 miles in 34 days, with only two in-port days.

All of these details are from Humphrey Barton's book, *Atlantic Adventurers.* Barton called this ". . . an amazing distance to cover in 34 days," then went on to say, "I believe this to be the most outstanding voyage that has ever been carried out by a small motorboat and great credit is due to Uno Ekblom and his crew for their seamanship and endurance. Nor must the little diesel engine which served them so faithfully be forgotten. It must have run like a clock."

I certainly agree with Barton that credit is due to the ship, her crew, and her engine, but not necessarily with his comment that the performance was "amazing." Perhaps it seems so to a long-time sailor with several Atlantic crossings under sail to his credit. But the fact is, judging her voyage by the technical yardsticks to be developed later in Chapter 6, *Eckero* didn't do too well. Her time underway—if compared to standards that seem reasonable—should have been 24 to 26 days, not 34.

What conclusions can we draw from these voyages? In the first place, they made such demands on the endurance of their crews that these enterprises obviously were not suitable for inexperienced seamen or their families. The greatest complaint was about rolling. A reliable and consistent means of reducing rolling appears to be the prime factor necessary for popular participation in long-distance power voyaging. Crew comfort is a must. Such absurdities as exclusively outside steering stations, absence of steering assistance, and hulls too small to carry the required load and still provide decent room for the crew reduce this sort of voyage to the stunt level. Singlehanded ocean passages prove nothing, either: not many people are interested in such feats.

On the other hand, the perfect record of the engines involved shows this part of power passage-making is a solid base on which to build. By correcting the objectionable features noted, a vessel of unique qualities can be produced with capabilities for a new sort of cruising.

Aside from the pioneering efforts that concentrated on crossing the Atlantic, a major portion of the development of true seagoing motorboats has taken place on the West Coast. This development was dictated by the characteristics of the area. From San Francisco northward, the year-round weather off the coast is, on the average, worse than that of any other area except the high latitudes of the Southern Ocean. This coastal area not only has winter storms but also is bedeviled in summer by very strong winds caused by differences between pressure over the cold ocean waters and pressure over the hot interior valleys. The worst gale *Passagemaker* ever encountered, for instance, was off Cape Mendicino in the middle of August. It was not a storm, just a gradient wind.

Yet fishing vessels operate off the coast and in the Gulf of Alaska the year round, so it is possible for well-found craft to cruise these waters. It gradually became clear in the postwar years that a type of vessel was required that was not an advertised stock item.

The early examples were modified fishing boats. Designed first by Seattle designers Edwin Monk and William Garden, a type of boat began to evolve that was lighter and more economical than a true fisherman yet offered adequate seaworthiness. "Northwest Cruisers" they were commonly called at first, though this term has about died out today.

As more and more of these boats were built, their reputation gradually became widespread

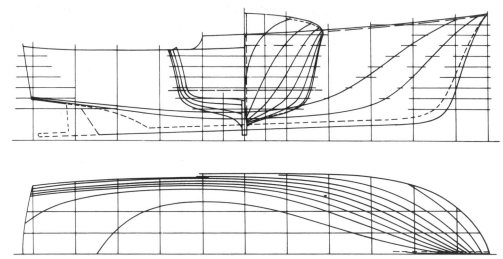

Figure 2-6. *Lines of a "Northwest Cruiser" by William Garden, showing the evolution of the early fisherman-shaped cruisers to a lighter model. (Retraced by R. P. B.)*

and led to the sudden proliferation of vessels that today are called "trawlers." There will be a good deal to be said on that subject later.

This was the background, then, for the design of *Passagemaker,* and we turn now to the development of the Passagemaker concept and the design, building, and testing of the vessel herself.

CHAPTER 3

EVOLVING THE PASSAGEMAKER CONCEPT

TURNING TO PASSAGEMAKER *AND* how she grew, I mentioned earlier that the first idea of such a boat came to me during World War II when I was navigator of a large aircraft carrier in the Pacific. Years before, like so many small-craft sailors, I had built up a library of cruising tales—from Joshua Slocum on. During prewar duty in the Pacific, there had been ample opportunity to keep an eye on the activities of the comparatively few long-range sail cruisers at sea in those days. So I was reasonably well aware of their problems, and my developing designer's eye noted how few of these vessels seemed suited to their intended work.

As the war ended and we cruised through waters hitherto forbidden to small craft, it became apparent to me that the cruising routes would differ sharply from the "standard track" so often described in cruising yarns: from Panama to the Galapagos, the Marquesas, Tahiti, and on.

For one thing, cruising among the islands the United States occupied during the war leads one into areas having long periods of little or no wind, so considerable range under power would be useful. My own idea of a postwar cruiser, as I sketched and designed boats on the backs of old charts (as duty would allow), gradually evolved into a long, slim hull of 54-foot length overall (LOA), easily driven under power, with fuel for 1,500 miles, and carrying a three-masted-schooner rig. It was interesting later to see L. Francis Herreshoff's ideas of a postwar cruiser published in *Rudder.* He had come to the same conclusion I had, producing the 55-foot *Marco Polo,* another three-masted, long, slim vessel. While comparison of our vessels ended there, I found it nice to be in such distinguished company.

But nothing came of all this at the time except the publication of my thoughts on "Postwar Pacific Cruising" in *Rudder* for August and September of 1946. Here the case for more range under power was stated as follows:

> *The chief difference from cruises of the past is that the voyager may venture into waters where for long periods there is hardly any wind at all. He will also make passages that do not lie entirely within the tradewind belt. It would seem*

therefore that good power is essential, coupled with cruising range well above what we are accustomed to. Whether this is to be achieved by a large craft or one that achieves range from being easily driven is a matter of opinion. Personally I favor the latter, as it ties in with my ideas of a small crew and easily handled sail plan. Draft is not a problem unless one wishes to explore off the beaten track, away from islands that have been used for war purposes.

To my mind the editor of Rudder *has done the prospective cruising sailor a great service by bringing forth Herreshoff's* Marco Polo. *Not only is this model a good sailing machine, adapted in every way to the use for which it is intended, but its basic design is ideally suited to the conditions to be met in a Pacific cruise. It also permits a new type of cruise, one that will fill the needs of the sailor who, however much he may dream of spending months lying under the shade of a palm, watching sarong-clad native girls dance for his amusement, must limit his cruise to a definite time and get back to the old grind, where he may happily accumulate enough of the wherewithal to go cruising again.*

This statement, made in 1946, was my first step away from the conventional sailing cruiser, a step that, it will be seen, was subject to further modification. In particular, the last sentence contains the germ of an idea that was destined to grow, the idea of concentrating on passage-making.

In 1957 I jumped at the chance to be navigator of the first Herreshoff 55-footer to be completed—Joe Newcomb's *Talaria*—on a November trip from New York to the Bahamas. This rugged trip under winter conditions (described in *Rudder* for February 1958) raised certain questions about the concept evolved during the war, and was more grist for the mill—a mill now shifting into high gear as my retirement from 30 years of Navy service drew closer.

Three years before *Passagemaker* was designed, I wrote a story about the subject, mainly as an exercise in lining up my thoughts on what I was trying to do. The editor who requested the story had not published it by the time I knew *Passagemaker* would be built, so I asked that the manuscript be returned to me, promising the editor a report on the finished boat and its performance at a later date. Now that *Passagemaker* has proved all the story's points—and more—the story has become something of an historical document, a statement of basic principles. The early developmental work that led to the concept on which *Passagemaker* was built can be illustrated by excerpts from this story.

At the suggestion of the editor, I wrote the story in the form of a conversation among three friends at a yacht club. The characters were: Tubby Watson, a dedicated ocean-racing man; Don Moore, an experienced amateur yacht designer; and Bob Reid, a "dedicated boat nut from way back who had also done some designing." Here's a condensation of the article:

Tubby Watson walked out onto the yacht club porch in company with . . . Don Moore. Moore was a tall, spare man with the look of the sea about him. Under his arm he carried a roll of blueprints. Moore had recently moved to the West Coast and was thinking about a retirement boat that would not only be suitable for local cruising but something more. Tubby had invited him to bring his plans over to the club.

Moore said, "Suppose I give you a little background first. I find it helps. When I moved to the West Coast and found I had more time for cruising, I started thinking about all the places I hadn't covered—parts of the East Coast, the Bahamas, Great Lakes, and so on. And out here, British Columbia and Mexico. The question was how to do it?"

"Why not fly there and charter?" offered Tubby.

"That has its points, of course. But I've owned boats all my life and would feel lost without something to putter around on and fix up. My first idea was a trailerable cruiser, so you could make the long jumps by car. This is probably the cheapest way, and the boat is reasonably able. But it would be nice to have a genuine liveaboard boat when you got there. So I looked into the problems of making the trips by water."

"That's quite a project," Bob Reid said, "going from here east by boat."

"Most people think so," Moore responded. "But the more I worked on it, the more I began to see you could do a good deal to cut it down to size. The problem, of course, is making the passages. In fact, I call the final result a 'Passagemaker'."

"It seems to me," Reid said, "there are a lot of boats that could qualify as passage-makers."

"Actually, there aren't," Don replied. "Let's really look at passage-making for a minute. Of course, many people do make long passages. But the general idea seems to be to take a well-found sailboat of some sort and start out. They get there, of course; but what most of them are really doing is *ocean cruising*. I'm not interested in that— I've been to sea. What I like to do is go to a nice area like Puget Sound and poke around from port to port. The quicker I get there, the more time I'll have for cruising. Speed and dispatch is what I want. By speed I mean to keep *average speed* as high as possible. And by dispatch I mean to meet some sort of *schedule*. It is much easier to find a crew if they can be told with reasonable certainty when they will get home—"

"You mean if their wives can know—" interrupted Tubby.

"That's right! Why not face it?" replied Moore. "All these considerations *do* affect the basic idea. If you read accounts of 'voyaging' with a critical eye, you will soon pick up hints that it's possible to do better. . . ."

(This exchange was the first use of "Passagemaker," the word I coined to describe the type of yacht that was evolving from my thoughts on the subject.)

The group went on to discuss Moore's idea that any of the boats should be capable of singlehanded operation. Tubby didn't think much of doing that, so Moore explained that with a crew, you can singlehand by turns, so to speak; that is, run with a one-man watch. *(This remains a fundamental point.)* Tubby then suggested that Moore needed a long-range diesel motorboat.

"I considered that, of course," said Don. "The fact that so many of them are being built out here is a tribute to the good sense of some yachtsmen. The trouble is they are too expensive for me. I ran through a preliminary design of one to see how it would go in the 50-foot size. Here is the sketch I drew. She is about as 'houseboaty' as you can get and still be really seaworthy. And she has a feature I like—lots of unobstructed deck space."

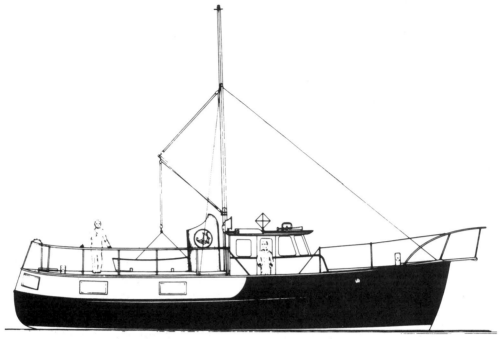

Figure 3-1. *Profile, Beebe Design 50—a 52-foot "oceangoing motorboat," sketched in 1959.*

"Looks nice. Too bad you couldn't swing it," Reid said.

"Well, what we are doing here is facing facts, and that's one of them. But the interesting thing about these boats is the performance you can get out of them."

The group next had a thorough discussion of the significance of "hull speed," "speed/length ratio," and range. *(As all these technical matters are thoroughly explored in Chapter 6, we will hold them until later.)*

Moore said, "Now let's look at the sailing cruiser. She shows up worst of all: she is not adapted to singlehanding, she can't guarantee speed or dispatch, and she must have a full watch-standing crew of experienced sailors before she can leave the dock."

Tubby demurred. "It's not as bad as all that!"

"Well, let's go back to the concept. In the passage to and from the East Coast, the leg from Acapulco to Panama is particularly well known for its calms and light airs. This is where the ordinary cruiser falls down on the job. You end up wishing you had a motorboat with more fuel than the auxiliary can carry so you can meet your schedule. In fact, it was considering this aspect that first turned my ideas toward what I call a 'motor-all-the-time' boat."

"What sort of a craft is that?" Reid inquired.

"The original idea came from a designer friend of mine," Moore answered. "He pointed out, in considering ocean racers, that by having something less than 5 horse-power available continuously for propulsion, and using only a simple rig of two or three lowers, you could lick the best of the lot carrying their load of spinnakers, jibs, genoas, mizzen staysails, and the rest—and do it a lot cheaper."

"The Race Committee wouldn't like it," Reid offered.

"The Jib Tenders Union would *never* allow anything like that," said Tubby with quiet confidence.

"Of course, it's not a practical proposition," Don answered, "and my friend hasn't done anything with it. But the principle involved looks good for what I've already called a 'Passagemaker'—where you want an assured average speed. Basically the question was this: Would it be possible to shrink the seagoing motorboat down closer to the size and shape and accommodations of the sailing cruiser, with a great reduction in cost, and still get the performance desired?" He looked around the table. "Well, it turns out that you can. And then I put a rig on her suitable to the sailing you would do while singlehanded."

"So you settled on a motorsailer," said Tubby.

"No, *sir!*" said Don Moore emphatically. "I don't consider my boat a motorsailer. To me a motorsailer is something different. It has a rather large rig and is expected to use sail alone whenever the wind is at all favorable. Most of them do not carry much fuel, though more than the ordinary auxiliary, of course. And they usually compromise on propeller/hull efficiency in an attempt to provide a reasonable sailing potential. I guess you could call my boat a 'motorboat with rig'."

"Aren't you quibbling a bit?"

"Not really. What I am referring to is the underwater body—it is wholly dedicated to efficiency under power. It is a matter of prismatic coefficient."

(This discussion reflected a tremendous amount of research and calculation. It is, of course, no great trick to take a large, burdensome hull, load it up with fuel, and achieve a very long range. What was not readily apparent in the beginning, from the available technical data, was whether this "shrinking down" process was feasible. If you don't want to be burdened with a large, heavy vessel, or your budget won't build it, shrinking down must be the answer. I recall vividly the sense of discovery and pleasure I felt when I finally found I could have Moore honestly say, "Well, it turns out that you can." There are many technical matters involved— matters such as stability when fuel is almost gone, for instance. A good deal of the research done appears again in Chapter 6 in the discussion of "displacement/length ratio.")

The three men spoke at length of the significance of the "prismatic coefficient" *(another matter covered in Chapter 6).* Moore explained that he was trying to achieve the required range with the least fuel possible. This led to a discussion of what the range should be.

"What range are we talking about?" Reid asked.

"In the San Diego–Key West voyage, with stops at Acapulco and Panama, the longest leg is 1,400 miles. But, returning from the East Coast you might want to head out to sea from Acapulco on the starboard tack and power-sail up the old sailing-ship route to California. It's rather hard to pin down, but I decided a 2,400-mile 'still-water' range would be about right, and stuck to that. That would be useful coming back from Honolulu, too."

"What size boat do you need to achieve that?" Reid asked.

"I worked her up in several sizes," said Moore. "The ideal would be 48 feet overall, with a 42-foot 6-inch waterline, and a 27,000-pound displacement—with 600 gallons of diesel fuel. Here are the lines of that boat. She actually weighs about half of that 50-foot motorboat I showed you and costs a great deal less to build. She has the correct prismatic coefficient for a speed of 8 knots and will do the 2,400 miles at that speed, using about 30 horsepower. A lot of people won't believe that, but it's true. If you back off on the speed, the range takes a tremendous jump. For instance, she could make San Diego–Panama nonstop at 7 knots without stopping in Acapulco for some of that good Mexican beer."

"No nonstop for me," Tubby said fervently.

"It doesn't appeal to me, either," said Moore, "but I can think of several trips where the extra range would be useful. Unfortunately this 48-footer proved too expensive, too, so I settled for a final design that is 40 feet 6 inches long, 36 feet on the waterline, and some 20,000 pounds displacement. She will make the 2,400 miles at 6 knots on 300 gallons of fuel. For shorter passages, she will do 1,400 miles at 7 knots and 900 at 8."

(This discussion was the end result of a great deal of work that finally made it apparent that the project—designing specifically to make the desired passage—could be accomplished and made sense.)

Moore pointed out that his vessel could go from San Diego to Key West in 28 days,

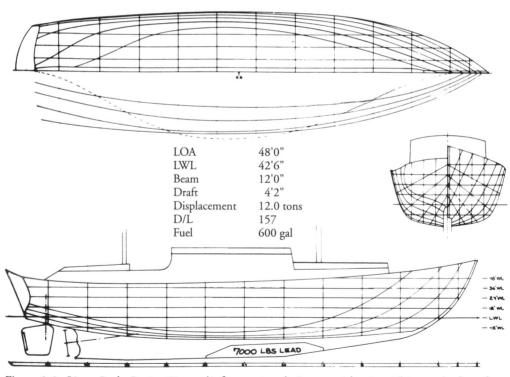

LOA	48'0"
LWL	42'6"
Beam	12'0"
Draft	4'2"
Displacement	12.0 tons
D/L	157
Fuel	600 gal

Figure 3-2. *Lines, Beebe Design 53—a 48-footer using the* Presto *midsection. This was the first of Beebe's designs called a "Passagemaker."*

LOA	40'6"
LWL	36'0"
Beam	12'0"
Draft	4'0"
Displacement	9.4 tons
D/L	201
Fuel	300 gal

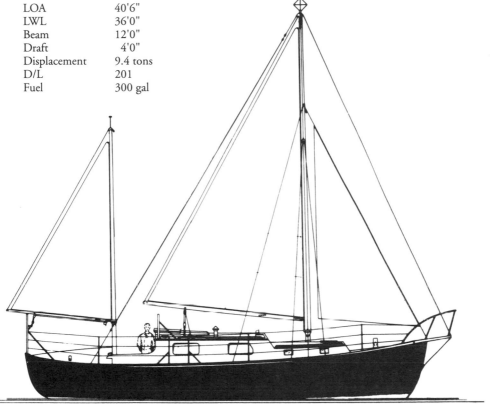

Figure 3-3. *Profile, Beebe Design 57—a sailing Passagemaker of 40 feet LOA. This is the design Don Moore was having built in the story in Chapter 3.*

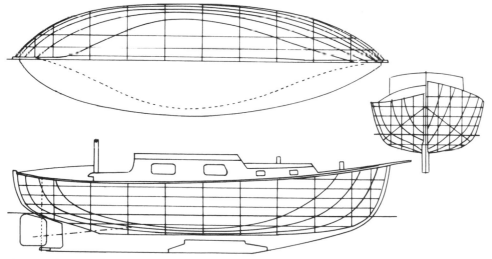

Figure 3-4. *Lines, Design 57.*

with 4 days off—2 each in Acapulco and Panama. Thus, a cruise to the desired area on the East Coast and return could be accomplished in less than a year.

(I still believe that a 2,400-mile range is a figure that makes a lot of sense. But, as will be brought out in Chapter 6, range figures must always be qualified by the speed that the operator expects to use.)

Moore then explained why it was impractical to design a boat that would do what he wanted and also be capable of Tubby's ocean racing. Moore did mention that if the big propeller were removed, sailing performance might be surprising.

"Ah, ha," exclaimed Tubby, "so you do want to race her!"

"Well, no," replied Moore, "I don't think my budget would stand two or three spinnakers, genoas, and all the rest. But someone might want to outfit my design with racing sails and try it. I was all through with the design before I suddenly realized that she should do very well in some of these West Coast downwind races, like the ones to Honolulu and Acapulco."

"Why do you say that?" Reid inquired.

"Because any race off the wind, with no windward work, should go to the boat that needs the least push to exceed the speed required to win on her own rating. The instant the first boat finishes, every following boat has an average speed it must exceed to place first on corrected time. The less actual horsepower a boat needs to attain that speed, the more chance she has that prevailing conditions will provide it. As I concentrated on this, I saw my design should have an advantage over the round-the-buoy racers with their emphasis on windward ability. Here are two pictures of a model test I made. This one is at her hull speed

Figure 3-5. *Model test of Design 57 showing her being towed at her hull speed of 8 knots.*

Figure 3-6. *Model test of Design 57 showing her being overdriven to a speed/length ratio of about 1.6 (10.19 knots). Note minimal wave hollow amidships.*

Figure 3-7. *A CCA-rule-type ocean racer. Note how the over-driven hull has developed an extreme wave hollow amidships. (Photo by Rosenfeld)*

of 8 knots, while this one shows her being overdriven to a speed-length ratio of about 1.6. She has a good deal less wave hollow amidships than most Cruising Club of America (CCA)–type cruiser/racers under these conditions, yet she weighs about the same."

Moore's photos showed graphically the effect of prismatic coefficient on efficiency under power. The friends then moved on to discuss the interior of the vessel.

(In the design's accommodation, I had the chance to emphasize features that I felt, from research in long-range cruising tales, needed a new direction. As can be seen from her accommodation plan, she is laid out for singlehanded convenience, though she has bunks for four. The Root berths in the main cabin can be replaced with an ordinary transom berth/settee for local cruising.)

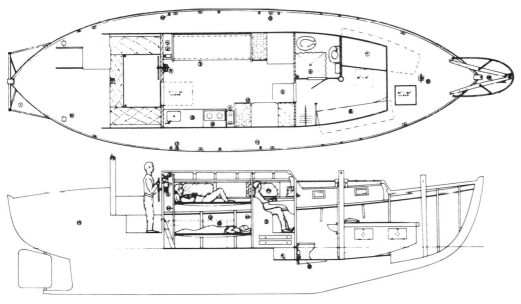

Figure 3-8. *Accommodation plan, Design 57.*

"Now, how about her cabin?"

"The main cabin is very carefully designed for the work to be done in it. It is as high as it is because all the space below the waterline is taken up by tanks. Everything in this area is dedicated to singlehanded convenience. Personally I think it is a great advance over anything that has been used for this kind of cruising before. For instance, the skipper's bunk is up in line with the ports so he can look out while resting."

"The officers of the deck are a bunch of drunks. They stand their watches in their bunks!" chortled Tubby.

"*Mister* Watson!" Don said with mock severity. "You know very well I never touch the stuff underway. But seriously, I fail to understand why *not one* singlehander has ever done this. If you read the cruise accounts, you will be struck by how many times the skippers leap from below to see what's going on. If they could just open one eye for a look around, many vague dangers would evaporate."

"How about the cockpit?" Tubby asked. "Isn't it a bit unusual?"

"Yes, it is," Moore answered. "But I made a cruise years ago in a Francis Herreshoff yacht, the *Marco Polo* type, that had one like this. That spoiled me—I never want to go very far to sea again in a conventional cockpit cruiser where you sit way aft on deck without any shelter. The deep, standing-room, athwartships cockpit—with seats all around—was just wonderful. In this case the wheel is on the forward bulkhead at stand-up height as you only use it for maneuvering."

"How do you mean?" asked Tubby.

"Why, she uses an autopilot, of course," said Don. "This is basic to the concept, and one of the great advantages of an engine-running-all-the-time vessel—you always have power for it. That's what makes a singlehanded passage not only feasible but enjoyable. Your crew steers all day and never talks back, never gripes about the chow, never gets seasick. Steering a motorboat day after day can be a terrible bore."

The three men finished their discussion with an examination of Moore's boat's proposed delivery trip. She was being built in Europe, and an interesting point developed when Don said he intended to go to the Canary Islands about September 1, then cross the Atlantic via the Cape Verde Islands.

"Why, that's right in the middle of hurricane season," protested Tubby.

"That's right. But I can't sit around the Canary Islands until the middle of November like the sailing cruisers do before starting for the West Indies, and my 'Passagemaker' doesn't have to. We'll start out from the Cape Verdes, trying to get in a little tradewind running with twin staysails and self-steering, but continually slanting south toward the Equator. Then, when we get down to latitude 5 or 6 degrees north, we'll head due west, getting what help we can from the winds, but prepared to go all the way under power. There's never been a hurricane recorded that far south.

"We'll stop at Port-of-Spain in Trinidad for fuel and some rum, then head west along the coast of South America, still south of the hurricane belt, to Panama. From there to Acapulco I'm sure we will use a lot of power. After a couple of days ashore, we'll be off on the last leg. We'll head directly for Cabo San Lucas, the southern tip of Baja California. When the wind comes ahead, I'll put her on the starboard tack with power and head out to sea. As the wind shifts around, we'll gradually come to a more northerly course and end up where the clippers used to, about 600 miles west of San Francisco. Then it's due east on a reach till she slides under the Golden Gate Bridge, and there we are! How about it, Tubby, want to come along? I'll make a real cruising man of you yet."

"I'd sure like to. Maybe I could make at least one leg of it—or two."

"Your ideas are very interesting, Don," Bob Reid said. "It will be fun to watch how she works out. As far as I can see, you have everything you need for your 'Passagemaker'. Count me in with Tubby for part of your voyage, if you can. I'll do my best to make it."

"I'll do that, Bob," replied Moore, rolling up his prints. "You and Tubby will be hearing from me one of these days. Keep your seabags packed!"

They sat for a few minutes, thinking about Don Moore's story. Bob saw Tubby had a faraway look in his eye, a look that said he was running through the trades with Don— blue water and a fair wind, with the 'Passagemaker' chugging quietly along. Finally he sighed and looked around for a waiter.

"George," he said, "bring me the check—."

That was the end of the story. Looking back on it now, from the actual years of operating at sea that followed it, I can see that it extended the ideas first expressed in the 1946 *Rudder* article to encompass the requirement that range under power should be complete; that is, fuel for continuous motoring for any contemplated passage should be carried. Not only is that necessary for speed and dispatch, but it permits the continuous use of the autopilot. The "APE," as Carleton Mitchell calls it (for autopilot extraordinaire), is not simply a convenience for the crew, it is a necessity. It permits the use of a one-man watch, makes it possible to use inexperienced watch-standers, and, by taking the most onerous task off the crew's shoulders, contributes a great deal to establishing passage-making as a relaxed and pleasurable way to cross oceans.

The boats discussed in the story were full-sail vessels that could be used for sail cruising upon reaching their destinations, after exchanging their passage propellers for two-bladed sailing types. It is obvious now, though it was not then, that placing increasing emphasis on power would bring great changes to the status of the sailing rig, as will be seen.

This story was the origin of my use of the term "Passagemaker" and the "Passagemaker concept," the words I coined to differentiate my type from other classes of yachts. (The correct version of this word when applied to voyaging is passage-maker or passage-making.) In fact, the whole discussion was pointed toward why the vessels discussed could not be classified as of any existing type, but were really a new concept.

Before then, the terms "motor-all-the-time boat" or "motorboat with rig" were used when I had to describe this craft, one that could not properly be called a motorsailer.

In fact, what to call long-range motor cruisers still causes trouble today. In his book *Sea Sense*, Richard Henderson calls *Passagemaker* a "modified MFV Type," which she certainly is not. The term "trawler yacht" started out to mean just that—a yacht patterned after a fishing trawler. Today "trawler yacht" is used to describe boats that never in one's wildest dreams could be called true trawlers.

Let me set down here what I conceive *my* Passagemakers to be now:

1. She may carry sail or not, but in any case must carry at least enough fuel for an Atlantic crossing under power. The quantities of fuel and speeds involved are discussed in Chapter 6.

2. Her layout and equipment must be primarily for the comfort and efficiency of the crew on long passages. In-port convenience must be secondary. For some items that bear on this, see Chapter 4: What We Learned.

3. Her seaworthiness, glass areas, above water/below water areas ratio (A/B), ballast, and other factors must clearly mark her as capable of making long voyages in deep water in the proper seasons for each area. These factors are discussed in Chapter 6.

In retrospect, it is surprising but quite true that the designs I worked on were considered solely in the light of their suitability to make the San Diego–Key West passage. It was not until the work was near completion that it occurred to me to think, "If it will do that, why not extend your ambition to cross the Atlantic and cruise the Mediterranean? Or the South Seas? Or around the world?"

This was the prospect before me while I labored on the last of the series of designs. When this vessel was built and launched to test my ideas, she could hardly be called anything else but *Passagemaker*. How she was designed and built and how she worked out comes next.

CHAPTER 4

PASSAGEMAKER: DESIGNING, BUILDING, AND TESTING—AND THE LESSONS LEARNED

THE DESIGN FOR THE BOAT that was finally built and christened *Passagemaker* was drawn in a hectic six-week period beginning in January 1962. Innumerable sketches and six designs taken through the lines and layout stages preceded her. Each one of these provided something for the next—it is surprising how much can be learned from a design that is never built. When *Passagemaker*'s turn came, she went together with ease, involving only the combining of concepts that had previously been tested and refined on paper.

By now the original concept had been expanded. Due to a drastic change in my personal situation, it became desirable to have a vessel that not only filled the requirements of the Passagemaker concept discussed in Chapter 3, but also had room for full-time living and working aboard. Sketching with this in mind, I soon realized that the 50-foot size was best to fill this specification along with the basic Passagemaker concept—especially as the contemplated vessel would have no "double-decking"—a term that will become familiar later.

The drawings on pages 26 and 27 show what *Passagemaker* looked like. Later we will discuss what we learned from her.

The lines show a hull of moderate deadrise with constant deadrise aft and a perfectly straight run. The quarter-beam buttock aft is literally straight. And thereby hangs a tale. Howard Chapelle, designer and marine historian, has helped me extensively over the years by criticizing my designs and admonishing me when I needed it. One day at the Smithsonian Institution I showed the plans for *Passagemaker* to Howard.

Looking at the lines, he nodded and said, "Not bad." Then, pointing at the quarter-beam buttock aft, he added, "But that should be straighter."

That gave me the opening I was looking for. "Damn it, Howard," I said, "I *knew* you would say that. That line was drawn with the straightest straightedge I could find!"

He merely answered, "Humpf."

The high stern was needed to preserve the room inside the stern cabin by providing the last 7 feet with an area where the sole could be raised. The bow was the same height as the stern, which is unusual and made her look a bit like a dhow. The entire hull shows the influence of my previous

LOA	50'0"
LWL	46'6"
Beam	15'0"
Draft	5'4"
Displacement	27.0 tons
D/L	268
Fuel	1,200 gal

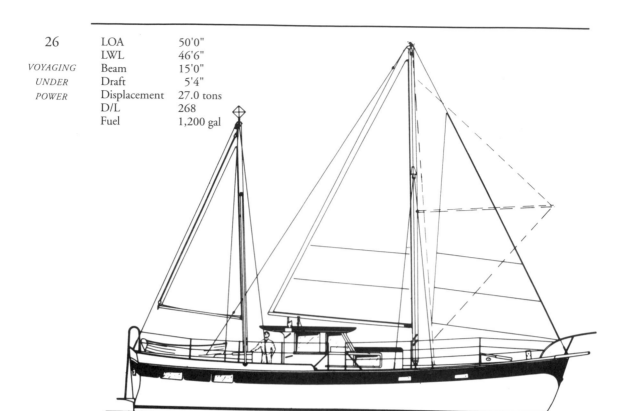

Figure 4-1. *Profile of* Passagemaker, *Beebe Design 67.*

sailing experience. *PM* (my abbreviation of her name) certainly ran nicely, with no wake to speak of, at her ocean-crossing speed of 7.5 knots. When completely built, she was somewhat overweight, and the significance of this will be discussed in Chapter 6 as an example of the technicalities of the business. The long keel and skeg with large rudder made her run before a gale as if on rails, and effectively handled the broaching problem so often exhibited by ordinary motorboats.

The arrangement shows the big stern cabin that was originally wide open—a combined drafting office and social center. Forward of this was the cockpit, on the same level as the pilothouse. It was designed to ensure the single watch-stander a secure place to go outside and observe—something that has to be done as it is impossible to keep the pilothouse windows salt-free all the time. The pilothouse was kept small but had all required space, including a chart table and a raised settee with a good view all around. Forward of this and down three steps was the combined galley/dinette. The six-person dinette was raised 18 inches to put diners' eyes at the level of the ports while eating—a much appreciated feature. The space under it provided 21 bins for canned goods—stores for six people for 60 days. Forward of this was the owner's quarters, with head and shower. In the stern a convertible sofa made two berths, with a third on top of the drafting table. In this way there were four berths for the passage-making crew, the number we had on the first voyage from Singapore to Greece. Later a pipe berth was fitted up forward, increasing crew berths to five—until the aft cabin was further modified as described under "What We Learned."

27

PASSAGE-
MAKER:
*DESIGNING,
BUILDING,
AND
TESTING*

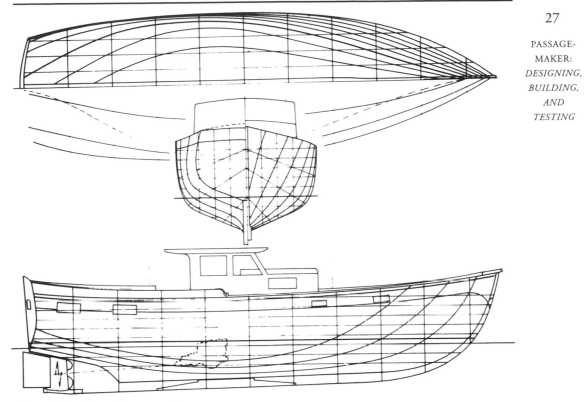

Figure 4-2. *Lines of* Passagemaker.

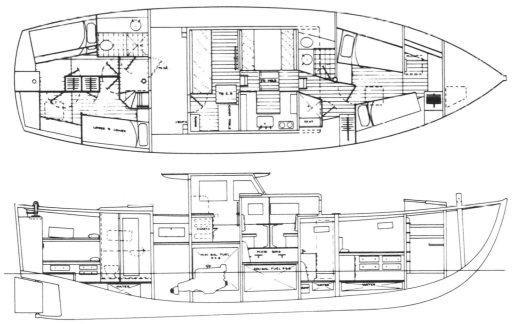

Figure 4-3. *Accommodation plan of* Passagemaker.

The profile shows the rig. It was quite short. Originally I had planned to have a much taller mainsail so I could attempt to sail in fair winds—motorsailer fashion—with the aid of a Hyde feathering propeller. But when the Hyde people told me they did not approve of their propeller being used in this manner, that is, on what was essentially a motor-all-the-time-boat, the rig was reduced and considered as emergency propulsion only. At that time there was no other feathering propeller I would trust. It would have been hopeless to try to sail well with her 32-inch, three-bladed prop. We did have plans to carry and rig all the gear necessary to remove the prop at sea but never did it. The mizzen was wholly dedicated to carrying the stabilizing rig, and its bit of sail was rarely used.

The single Ford 330 six-cylinder diesel, a Thornycroft conversion with heavy flywheel—a must with Fords—and capacity for 1,200 U.S. gallons of fuel were selected to take us the required 2,400 miles. Due to doubts raised in researching the problems of attaining maximum range—let alone estimating it—I made allowances everywhere I could to ensure we got the range desired. These included drawing the hull to the prismatic coefficient suited to a speed of 7.5 knots; providing an oversize propeller for greatest efficiency at cruising speed—but without the ability to use all the power the engine could provide—and providing an excess of fuel over what was theoretically necessary. As a result of these precautions she attained a range well in excess of that desired, showing on a run from San Diego to Panama without fueling a reserve of some 400 miles, for an all-gone range of 3,200 miles.

BUILDING

My research on the building problem showed the family budget could stand the cost if she were built abroad of wood and with very simple equipment. The plans were sent out for bids, and a contract for the construction was ultimately awarded to John I. Thornycroft & Sons of Singapore. Work commenced in July 1962.

I spoke of being able to swing the cost if the boat were built abroad. I planned to take advantage of all the money-saving possibilities of such a project. There are a number of steps involved that can lead to the greatest possible economy. Not everyone will be able to take advantage of all these, but here is how they worked for me:

1. The construction bid itself was lower than those from yards in the U.S.
2. I designed her myself and avoided that cost.
3. I went to Singapore and superintended the job. Not only did I live more cheaply than at home, but I feel some form of supervision is essential on a foreign contract. It is impossible to draw the details of everything, and if any solutions are left to the yard, differences in building practice are bound to make you unhappy over some of them.
4. The vessel came home under her own power. This is a saving two ways. First, you save the considerable freight bill, which includes many hidden expenses. Second, you save on duty since the boat is secondhand on arrival. *Passagemaker* arrived in the U.S. 17 months after completion. The duty was reduced by 20 percent, that reduction covering the expenses of the trip. And we had a fine cruise in the bargain.

29

PASSAGE-
MAKER:
*DESIGNING,
BUILDING,
AND
TESTING*

Figures 4-4, 4-5, and 4-6. *Three views of* Passagemaker *during construction at the yard of John I. Thornycroft & Sons, Singapore.*

Figure 4-7. Passagemaker *at Thornycroft's fitting-out dock, with flags flying in celebration of the christening.*

Figure 4-8. Passagemaker *during her trials in Singapore harbor. The stabilizer poles are swung out for the first time, but the stabilizers are not in the water.*

Experience since 1963 shows steadily rising building costs in the Orient, reducing the differential in bid costs. But it still appears possible to save money if the boat comes home under her own power. One thing more: Supervising is not easy. I worked seven days a week all during the seven months I was there.

Thornycroft did an excellent job on the boat, using teak planking over triple-laminated chengal frames and plywood decking topped by Cascover sheathing. With spruce spars and English sails, and now properly christened *Passagemaker,* she lay alongside the Thornycroft pier ready to go—tanks full of fuel, provisions stowed, and crew aboard—on March 18, 1963, eight and a half months after construction began.

PASSAGEMAKER*'S CRUISING*

I mentioned earlier that Marin-Marie's voyage in *Arielle* resulted in his crossing the Atlantic with essentially nothing to report; this is the way it was with *Passagemaker.* Although we passed through the fringes of two hurricanes and had some gales, we always made our ETAs, suffered no damage we couldn't fix, and had the engine start when the switch was turned on and run until we stopped it.

But it will be appreciated that when we left the builder's yard in Singapore on March 18, 1963, none of the crew knew what to expect. Two of us, Captain Ralph Arndt, USN, Ret., and myself, had considerable sailing experience; Colonel Everett Bibb, USA, Ret., had extensive coastal motorboat experience; Congdon Curts, my old friend from service in Alaska, was the only man qualified as a novice. But the vessel and the ideas behind it were wholly untried. There was at that time no other vessel that could even attempt what we were trying to do.

31

PASSAGE-
MAKER:
DESIGNING,
BUILDING,
AND
TESTING

Any anxieties we may have felt turned out to be completely groundless. *Passagemaker* soon showed she would do all we expected and more. The log of that first voyage essentially went like this: We hurried our departure because the boat was late being completed, as is usual with yacht builders. We feared the beginning of the southwest monsoon in the Indian Ocean that would have effectively barred our way to Aden. We finished storing supplies late one night and left at dawn the next day. The three days spent running up the flat-calm Strait of Malacca were used to shake things down, get the rigging in shape, and so on, before entering the Bay of Bengal, headed for Ceylon. In the bay we found favorable winds, the remnants of the northeast monsoon, and made excellent time to Colombo (Ceylon, now Sri Lanka), arriving before dawn on the seventh day. We had to jill around for several hours before we were able to enter port.

After a stay of four days we were off on the 2,200-mile passage to Aden. We touched the southern tip of India at Cape Comorin to get a good navigational departure, then headed for Minicoy Island and the passage through the Maldive Island reefs. From there it was a straight shot to Cape Guardafui, the northeast tip of Somaliland, and another run of 400 miles to Aden. That section took 12 days—in a flat calm most of the way. We were lucky—the southwest monsoon must have set in just a few days after we passed this critical point.

After three days in Aden we left for Suez, experiencing the usual blow from the south at the south end of the Red Sea and from the north at the north end. In the middle it was quite nice. Bucking the norther at the north end convinced us that we rated some time off, so we stopped for two days at Endeavour Harbour on Tawilla Island at the entrance to the Gulf of Suez. At the Canal they were kind and efficient, and we started through at the stern of a convoy the next morning and made the usual one-night stopover at Ismailia. The next afternoon we let our pilot off with a running jump to the dock in Port Said and headed out into the Mediterranean for Rhodes, taking care to pour a libation to Poseidon as we entered his domain. The *meltemi* from Russia to Egypt was blowing pretty hard, and we had to buck it most of the way. It took us four days, but we finally arrived in Rhodes—in a flat calm.

In a total elapsed time of six weeks we had made some 6,000 miles to Greece, averaging underway *exactly* our designed ocean-crossing speed of 7.5 knots. We knew then that in *Passagemaker* we had something. And subsequent cruising in her has shown how right we were. There we were, 42 days from Singapore, ready for cruising in the fascinating waters of the Mediterranean. It's difficult to determine the records of sailing vessels that have made the same trip, but we had certainly arrived ahead of any of them by a matter of months! Even the cutter *Beyond,* mentioned in Chapter 18, would have trailed us by at least 30 days despite her

Figure 4-9. Passagemaker *at anchor in Endeavour Harbour, Tawilla Island, at the entrance to the Gulf of Suez, where we took a well-earned rest.*

range under power of 1,500 miles. Our record was achieved not only by keeping up a high average speed but also because the crew was rested and relaxed enough to be ready to leave port again in a matter of days. That was the start of our kind of passage-making.

For the rest of the summer we cruised in Greece and Yugoslavia. The next spring we cruised to Malta and Italy, then moved eastward along the Riviera to the mouth of the Rhone River. There we prepared to test another of *Passagemaker*'s features—her ability to go into the French canals (see Chapter 16). With her masts down and her engine turning at the maximum permitted rpm for a speed of about 9.4 knots, our vessel went up the Rhone to Lyon in two days. This was followed by an idyllic meander through France to Strasbourg on the Rhine River, then down the Rhine and across the North Sea to England for some work at the Thornycroft plant, which lies three locks up the Thames River past London.

On departure day from London we dropped down the Thames in the middle of the night to catch the tide, put up our masts in the Medway, went to Plymouth for fuel and supplies, and crossed the Atlantic via the Azores and Bermuda to Newport, Rhode Island, in 21 steaming days.

Singlehanded, I then took her down the Inland Waterway to Miami. With a new crew, we went from Miami through the Bahamas to Panama, then up the coast to San Diego, California, in 29 days—not bad, considering we took three days off to cruise in the Bahamas. (How well I recall my earlier concern about this east-west passage in the planning and theory-stage years!) After San Diego, a crew of two took *Passagemaker* up the coast to her home port of Monterey to end a delivery cruise of some 21 months that had been fun all the way.

After that, *Passagemaker* made a cruise to Hawaii and return via the Pacific Northwest. She also made a trip to the Pacific Northwest straight up the coast, nonstop, in seven days—our most rugged cruise.

Figure 4-10. Passagemaker's *dinghy was patterned after the Herreshoff Columbia model, and sized to fit the raised poop deck. Here she takes a capacity "liberty party" ashore at Delos, Greece.*

In 1967 she went east to Expo '67 in Montreal and was stored on the East Coast preparatory to sailing to Europe the following summer. Some months later a gentleman who had made a long cruise with me bought her, on the condition I would help him take her to Europe in 1969, which I did (see Chapter 15).

It was a wrench to let her go, but I felt I had learned all I could from her and wanted to take the next step. *PM* happily cruised in Europe from April to October for the next five years, covering beautiful cruising grounds from Norway to Turkey. After passing through several other owners, *Passagemaker* was last spotted cruising off Trinidad, in the early 1990s.

WHAT WE LEARNED

33

PASSAGE-
MAKER:
*DESIGNING,
BUILDING,
AND
TESTING*

The lessons learned comprise such a big file that I can only give the conclusions here. But believe me, there is much data to support every point, even if some of the conclusions sound dogmatic. So here is a list of the major items, emphasizing those that affected future design:

Layout. The highly specialized and personal layout of *Passagemaker* would not be anyone else's cup of tea. As a matter of fact, it did not work out and was never used for its designed purpose. We finally converted the stern cabin into two double cabins with a head. While this layout was highly satisfactory at sea, it was not a success in port.

The reason for this layout failure was that I had been so concerned about *Passagemaker*'s seaworthiness and ability to perform at sea to the required concept that other facets of the whole-boat problem were neglected or ignored. For instance, to keep her above water/below water areas ratio as low as possible, she was not "double-decked." This concentration on performance contributed to making her a seagoing machine. I would be hard put to find some feature of her performance at sea that could be changed to advantage.

But in port her lack of lounge space, except the galley/dinette area and the pilothouse settee, was a distinct drawback to her having any wide appeal. The fact is, such a large and expensive vessel does not make sense unless she is used the greater part of the year. This leads to the requirement that such a vessel should have good in-port living space for the owner and his wife, with all the amenities of a shore apartment if they can be fitted in. When you get right down to it, such a vessel is most suitable for a retired couple who use it as a home afloat. The problem is to combine living space with the necessary seaworthiness for ocean voyaging. I believe now that a better balance of such qualities is feasible.

I spoke above of "double-decking." This means to have one full-headroom compartment under another full-headroom compartment. *Passagemaker* was not double decked, nor is such a popular model as the Grand Banks 42. As an example of double-decking, the Grand Banks 50 takes it about as far as you can go. It is clear the amount of double-decking largely determines how much living space a vessel can have, a matter explored in depth in Chapter 9.

Cockpit. At sea, *Passagemaker*'s cockpit—4 feet deep—was one of her best features. It enabled the watch-stander to go outside to observe all around while remaining securely *in* the boat, with no possibility of falling overboard. This is a very serious problem on the seagoing motorboat. We found that the single watch-stander was alone much of the time, day as well as night. The consequences of someone falling overboard while alone, with the ship running on autopilot, are not pleasant to contemplate. On *Passagemaker* there was only one absolute

Figure 4-11. *Beebe,* left, *talks with Dr. James Kergen in British Columbia. Note the deep cockpit, so useful at sea.*

Figure 4-12. *Aboard*
Passagemaker. *Beebe,*
left, *with Dr. John
Gratiot at Mykonos
Island, Greece. Note the
lifelines that are 40
inches high forward
and 30 inches high aft.
They are slack,
preparatory to
launching the dinghy.*

rule: The watch-stander was not allowed to go on deck without someone watching him. The captain was always available for this duty. But the 4-foot-long cockpit, subtracted from the overall length, certainly hurt the accommodations. In subsequent designs I have felt it necessary to dispense with this feature.

With a pilothouse placed on deck where the watch-stander can gain access to the side of the vessel, I feel it is necessary that the rails should be not less than 4 feet high and solid in any area the watch-stander is permitted to go. The presence of sailing-racer-inspired, 30-inch-high lifelines on seagoing powerboats is shocking. They make sense on a sailing vessel because higher ones interfere with sails, the crew wears safety harnesses, and there is more than one watch-stander on deck. But for the single watch-stander of the oceangoing motorboat they certainly are not adequate, being a height only sufficient to trip you overboard. On *Passagemaker,* the lifeline stanchions forward were 40 inches high, and on the raised afterdeck they were 30 inches. It was surprising how much difference the 10 inches made in the feeling of security.

Sailing Rig. This feature is hard to justify by the facts of our cruising. It is not a good emergency propulsion system for this reason: If the engine should fail, sail would get you somewhere, but the chances of its being where you wanted to go are pretty slim. Consequently, your cruise would be pretty well ruined, while an alternative power system would allow the cruise to continue. In addition, an efficient sailing rig is expensive—*more* so than another diesel engine.

Sail has two things to recommend it. It gives the crew something to do and is fun from this point of view. (But with an assured speed of 7.5 to 8 knots, it is surprising how often the wind is so far ahead that the sails won't draw) And sail gives the vessel the aspect of a motorsailer, making it more acceptable to proceed at hull speed or below without embarrassment when passed by faster coastal motorboats. I'm not being facetious here: I am convinced this is the real reason for the existence of the so-called "motorsailer." I have never seen one with its sails up in coastal waters. This is certainly a legitimate reason, but an expensive one. For vessels with sail, I now recommend they *also* have alternate engine-driven emergency drive.

35

PASSAGE-
MAKER:
DESIGNING,
BUILDING,
AND
TESTING

Figure 4-13. Passagemaker
spreads her downwind
running sails by backing
down for the photographer.
Note the wake at the bow.
(Photo by Norris D. Hoyt)

Stabilizing Rig. *Passagemaker*'s rig, the West Coast Anti-Roll Stabilizer, familiarly called "flopperstoppers" (F/S), changed the whole aspect of our cruising in ways we could not imagine before we started. For one thing, it made ocean crossing by motorboat an activity that could be thoroughly enjoyed by persons without any seagoing experience. This aspect turned out to be such a vital contribution to the success of our Passagemaker concept that there is a whole chapter devoted to it later. Now I'm sure it is a *required feature* of the ocean-crossing motorboat, so important that in the larger and more expensive vessels, an alternative means of stabilizing should be provided.

Freeboard. The bow was too low. We found that the measure of speed possible against the sea depended very much on the height of the bow. When encountering seas from ahead, it is mandatory that you slow down until green water does not come over the bow. If you do not, you will eventually damage the vessel. We often wished our bow was higher by a foot or so, as it could have been without aesthetic damage to the profile.

Stern. Some people expressed concern about our broad stern in a following sea, a concern I did not share, feeling that the shape under water, not above, was the criterion. I was pleased to observe that in gales from astern we never had more than a foot or two of water over the stern platform.

Steering Comfort. *Passagemaker* was built with a sprocket on the wheel to provide eventually for an outside steering station. This was never installed as we felt no need for it, piloting around docks and through the canals from inside with no difficulty. While the flying bridge has its points in local cruising of the weekend variety, one must remember that the tropical sun cannot be faced day in and day out on a long voyage. In *Passagemaker* the watch-stander could go outside as much as he pleased when there were others on deck.

Handholds. Although our stabilizing gear cut rolling by two-thirds, which made ordinary rolling around 5 to 10 degrees at most, we found *Passagemaker*'s pipe handholds in the galley were one of her best features. At the corner of each counter and at the inboard edge of the dinette table there were brass pipes to the overhead. These were constantly in use as handgrips, particularly by the cook in passing hot plates to the table, which could be reached with one hand while the other securely held a pipe.

If handholds were so useful in the intimately related galley and dinette of *Passagemaker,* it's clear that a greater separation between galley and dining table with no handholds would be quite dangerous. If a person loses his balance and starts to move across the ship, this movement must be stopped before it can accelerate to the point of injury. That is the reason why, in the days of trans-

Figure 4-14. *Beebe's stepdaughter, Gael Donovan, in* Passagemaker's *galley. She is holding two of the galley handholds, and the third one is visible.*

atlantic passenger steamers, storm-wracked ships used to reach port with extraordinary numbers of injured passengers. Yachts with wide saloons must be careful about this.

Propeller. *Passagemaker* was fitted with an oversize prop. That is, she could not turn up the maximum permitted rpm for continuous duty. The reason for this was to get her long-range speed of 7.5 knots at a lower rpm, 1,750, which placed the engine at its most efficient fuel-consumption rate. While this provided a percent or two of better range, I feel now it would have been better to use the conventional prop for maximum continuous horsepower at maximum continuous rpm. You would then not have to worry about overloading the engine and would have a somewhat higher top speed and be allowed a higher local cruising speed.

Equipment. While simplicity of equipment is an ideal given much lip service, oceangoing motorboats are often found with amazing amounts of equipment for amazing amounts of money. This is discouraging to those with small budgets.

It doesn't have to be that way; *Passagemaker* proved it. We left Singapore with hardly more equipment than one would expect to find on a 30-foot sloop making the same voyage. We did have an autopilot—but this is a necessity on an oceangoing motorboat. We had a compass, a sextant, a radio for time ticks, a small radio direction finder (RDF), a 100-foot depthsounder, a two-burner Primus stove, hand pumps for water, and a box for ice—when we could get it. That was the lot. And we had a ball all the way, ate very well, and were able to fix any small item that went wrong.

We did not have radar, radio transmitter, watermaker, hot water, gas ovens, air conditioning, pressure water system, or any of the multitude of items so often installed today, and we never missed them. I recommend this approach, though I think it is pretty much a lost cause today. Basically you must be sure you have an answer to the question, "What will I do when that quits?" Not *if* but *when,* as it will. For instance, there is the incredible story of the all-electric yacht that went to the South Seas where its *single* generator gave up the ghost. They couldn't even flush the heads. End of story—and end of cruise.

Of course I have no objection to owners installing as much equipment as their budgets can stand. It makes sense to provide space for the later installation of equipment by building in everything possible in the construction phase. But you don't really *need* this stuff. Get underway with-

37

PASSAGE-
MAKER:
*DESIGNING,
BUILDING,
AND
TESTING*

out it and enjoy the cruise. Once you convince yourself that warm beer is just as good as cold, refrigeration is a waste of time and money, in my opinion—but not that of my wife!

Night Vision. One thing I completely forgot to provide for was night vision in the pilothouse. If a light was on in the galley, the watch-stander couldn't see a thing. And the galley was the only space available for the navigator to work up his evening stars. In Ceylon we tried to fix this with a hatch cover and curtain. This helped, but a real light lock with a door is a necessity. This problem should be well up on the list in the design stage.

Fuel Tanks. *Passagemaker*'s fuel tanks were fitted with a draw-off sump that trapped all contamination. We opened a tank after five years to see how it was doing. It was perfectly clean and free of corrosion. I feel, then, that it is permissible to build tanks without clean-out plates if a sump is used. This gets rid of a potential leak source.

Guardrail. *Passagemaker* had a guardrail 6 inches wide outside, with full-length scarfed and glued timbers. It was considered an external sheer clamp. Inside, the frames were blocked and, with the internal clamp, there was a solid 12 inches of timber at the sheer. Knocking around ports overseas as we did, with no yacht-type moorage to speak of, we were *very* glad we had this rail. It took with aplomb some incredible knocks. It also furnished a dividend we didn't anticipate. The 6-inch, flat-top surface of the rail made a convenient and safe place to run around outside the lifelines when setting fenders, lines, etc. I recommend the arrangement. Most American yachts are flimsy in this department.

Noise. In the planning stages I was concerned about the possible effect of noise and vibration on the crew over long stretches. Some information on this subject indicated that noise alone can cause cumulative fatigue if the level is high enough. Consequently, as much as possible was done to suppress noise. Two inches of fiberglass insulation was used both in the engine room and in the overheads. The entire vessel from end to end inside also had acoustic tile on the overhead. The aft bulkhead of the engine room, which opened on the aft living spaces, was also heavily insulated.

No fatigue from this source was evident. In fact, the steady noise of the engine soon became a part of life and was ignored. The comment often made by sailing men that noise would drive us crazy turned out to be wishful thinking on their part.

I believe the acoustic tile did more to suppress noise than anything else as it stopped reflection

Figure 4-15. Passagemaker *arriving at the dock in Monterey, California, in 1964, at the end of her passage three-quarters of the way around the world, proudly flying the flags of the 18 nations she visited.*

back and forth from sole to overhead, a potent source of noise. In addition, the insulation and tile kept the interior of the boat cool on the hottest days.

Hot Salt Water. Something I thought up and tried out proved to be the most popular and appreciated feature on the ship. This was to have hot salt water from the engine cooling system piped into the galley to furnish, when the engine was running, an unlimited supply of very hot water for rinsing plates and pots. The cooks and cleanup crew really missed it when the engine was shut down in port. To avoid unbalancing the engine cooling system, the water ran all the time. A two-way valve either dumped it into the sink drain or turned it into the faucet. As an added dividend, the temperature and volume of the running water gave the watch-stander a quick check on the cooling system.

Summary. Finally we, and by "we" I mean all of the people who cruised aboard *Passagemaker,* discovered how much fun even long passages could be in a vessel that made no demands on one's endurance nor required skills developed over years of experience under sail. This was something new, something worth emphasizing as we will see in Chapter 15. ". . .with speed and dispatch," the concept stated. Well, we achieved this and it does make for a different sort of cruising. On our voyage to Hawaii and return we went out in 12 days and returned in 13. By contrast, a sailing vessel that at speeds comparable to ours should have come back in 16 days left about the same date—and took 70 days!

CHAPTER 5

THE PHILOSOPHY OF POWER PASSAGE-MAKING

THE STORY OF PASSAGEMAKER'*S* voyages certainly illustrates the vessel's capability, but a skeptic might point out that her captain was a man of extensive experience. It could be argued that Captain Robert Beebe could cross the ocean in anything and make light of it.

Every year we see examples of incredible voyages: Atlantic crossings in tiny sailboats, outboard-powered trimarans transiting the entire Pacific Ocean, even rowboats laboring from one continent to the other. These stunts prove nothing but the expertise, determination, and endurance of the individuals involved. Let's face it, Thor Heyerdahl sailed a bale of hay across the Pacific, but that doesn't mean we should design and build hay boats—it simply says something about Thor Heyerdahl.

While there's no question about Robert Beebe's expert seamanship, what really excited him most about voyaging under power was how easy and comfortable the experience was compared to his previous voyages under sail. This is where the appeal lies, and it is more important today then ever before because of the increasing popularity of offshore cruising aboard personal yachts.

This is not to say that voyaging under power is easy or effortless or without great reward. It requires the same planning and attention as cruising under sail, but most would perceive the comfort level higher and the physical and mental demands reduced when operating offshore under power. These differences can have a very positive effect on continued and ambitious cruising.

Within this chapter we review three examples of successful passage-making under power. The first two accounts contrast passages aboard heavy- and light-displacement vessels and are excerpts of articles that originally appeared in *Yachting* in August and September of 1966. The third account is more recent and is offered as inspiration to the ambitious yet inexperienced enthusiast.

ONCE OVER HEAVILY by Norris D. Hoyt

Thirty times a year, for the last 10 years, I've made speeches to Power Squadrons about crossing the Atlantic in sailboats. As I ate their dinners and drank their laughter, the slow suspicion leaked through the keelbolts of my habituation to sail that all these pleasant people must have some reason for liking motorboats. If not looks, utility; if not excitement, economy; if not complexity, stability; if not exercise, company. Awash with burgeoning curiosity, I last spring made the great decision and signed on for not one but two crossings of the Atlantic in two different motorboats. The two boats were as unlike as boats can be: One was a massive Scottish seine-netter built from fisherman molds as a yacht; the other was a sweetly subtle product of a lifetime of design development in modern powerboats. Both were superb executions of their owners' basic intentions. . .

Kytra (LOA 54 feet, beam 17 feet, draft 7.5 feet) . . . was superbly built, eloquently seaworthy, sound, round, and fully packed when we got 50 friends aboard at Newport for a final party . . . and shoved off on June 12, in the opening westerly of a large high-pressure system, for Cobh, Ireland. We hadn't a worry in the world, for the boat had come over under her own power . . . On top of that, every member of the crew had made at least one transatlantic trip, four were navigators, all were good cooks, and there were three conversationalists and two listeners.

. . . At 0020 we left Race Point and the United States and set course due east. It would take us 100 miles south of any known ice. With one man at a time on watch, watches were 4 hours, and one man was off, on rotation, to help the cook for 24 hours and sleep through an unbroken night. Hasty calculation will reveal that an average of 20 hours a day was ours to use as we would. For the next 2,600 miles!

So many people cross the ocean in sailboats, and sailors are so inclined to write about it, that the world sees sailboats as passage-makers and motorboats as coastwise cruisers. Nothing could be less true. The fact is that a well-designed motor vessel makes a cinch of a passage and offers no opportunity for heroic postures. I suspect that motor passage-makers arrive casually for lunch and move on to the next port, unnoticed—no baggywrinkle, no tattered canvas, no ragged beards, no stormcloths. There are reasons why motor passage-making is safe and easy, and there are techniques for keeping it that way.

In the first place, it is easy because progress is constant. . . . In a sailboat, about one-fourth of your time is spent in near calms, and about a fourth of your time in headwinds—even in a traditionally downwind crossing of the Atlantic. . . . A good motorboat averaging 8 knots can start on the eastern edge of a high and cross the Atlantic in stable weather. Yet if you're in a sailboat, you average 8 knots only when there's fresh weather from astern; and if a storm's coming, you'll wait for it, because it will either have contrary winds or no winds in front of it. . . .

Weather control, within limits, is the first great safety factor of motorboats. The second is comfort. We made a round trip of the Atlantic without getting wet or cold; in fact, Beau Wood came and went without getting out of his carpet slippers. . . . Because you're operating behind glass, and with only one man on duty at a time, you have reserve energy for emergencies.

The third factor in safety on motor passages is the variable: crew and boat preparation. If you're going offshore for long passages, the engine room and the engine must be given the same knowledgeable attention that rig and sails get from the offshore sailor. An engine tucked into a cramped space almost as an afterthought, minimal fuel tankage, and a crew that only knows how to start and stop the engine—this sailboat approach to power does not fit the ocean-crossing motorboat picture. The more sophisticated the engine room, the more sophisticated the engineer must be.

But once you truly are master of your vessel, the joys of passage-making on a motorboat are great—of them I sing.

It takes a little time on a passage to get used to the new tempo of sea time and sea life. When sailing, the watches change in herdlike shifts from cabin to deck, punctuated in midshift by meals, and delayed by dish wash-up. The boat's motion, the constant sail trimming, steering, sail shifting, and variation of speed give a sense of involvement in the enterprise. . . . At first it's mainly busy and tiring. Then you get the rhythm, and the duty watch periods are filled with cheerful talk, instinctive activity, and the changing spectacle of the vessel heeling and running through the tireless seas.

The motorboat passage is entirely different. From the frantic business of loading, storing, fueling, checking equipment, and last-minute calls, parties, and purchases, you're abruptly off into the great silence of the sea—shore, telephone, and family astern, horizon ahead, nothing much to do, and less inclination to do it. Necessity has just been turned off and the silence is deafening. The autopilot clicks erratically, the diesel mumbles, the bow pushes through the yielding sea, and the duty watch-keeper sits alone, lightly clad, in a warm cabin, on an upholstered settee, half-reading a book and half-watching the edge of the horizon rock gently through the pilothouse windows. For the first day or so you do almost nothing—make your bed, experiment with the best place to put a box of cameras, drink a beer every now and then, read, sleep, eat, wash up, wander around the deck looking at the gear, sunbathe, mess with watch and sextant, check WWV, read, sleep, and eat again.

The first night watch introduces you to passage-making. Out of a warm bed and into pants, slippers, and a sweater in the black pitch of midnight, you wander up to the wheelhouse, share a leisurely cup of coffee with the man you're relieving, have a little aimless conversation, and take a reluctant parting from his pleasant voice in the darkness.

Then you're alone on the pulsing, pushing boat on the dark ocean and under the open, luminous sky. You check the compass for a while, and she's hunting about four degrees across the course. You go out on deck, gaze carefully around the horizon, see nothing Creation didn't put there, and gaze in silence at the stars. Your fellow rovers are breathing trustfully in the darkness below, and you're absolutely alone in the absolute middle of peace. It's an expansive sensation.

You watch the bow wave for a while, check around the horizon every half hour, make a sandwich, check the compass again, think about important things, and go inside to repeat the process. A sensation of enormous well-being fills you. As the watch runs out, you wake your relief and talk with him for 15 minutes or so before you wander peacefully to bed.

. . . like me, everyone somehow found amiable jobs to do and whistled away at them while *Kytra* ran along at about 8 knots, string-straight across the Atlantic. For no apparent reason at all we felt euphoric.

It's been years and years since I've had 20 hours out of 24 to do exactly as I pleased, and *Kytra* gave them back to me for the first time since college vacations. Yet motor passage-making is a delicately balanced idleness, with enough event and opportunity for effort to flavor the day.

We ate voraciously. In fact, for the last four days we had to. The deep freeze broke down. It was good duty—I gained 11 pounds.

On Friday, June 26, our luck broke, our idyll ended. We'd been having such a good time that we were rather shocked to see Fastnet Rock blinking, right on course, at 2308. The next morning all hands came on deck at dawn, Beau Wood in a purple silk dressing gown and slippers, to take down the steadying sails, break out the lines and fenders, and get ready to dock in Cobh—14 days from home. The passage was over; Beau had made it in his slippers. It had been a delightful

Figure 5-1. Kytra *in a lock of the Crinan Canal, Scotland. (Photo by Norris D. Hoyt)*

milk run and, I suppose, no more than I should have expected. We were thoroughly rested, full of excitement for the land, and quite pleased with the world. Our passage had increased all our dimensions, and we were ready for Dublin the next day, the Crinan Canal the day after, and the variegated fleshpots of the Continent that stretched ahead of us.

ONCE OVER LIGHTLY by Norris D. Hoyt

Our pleasant voyage to Scotland aboard that solid craft *Kytra* had in no way prepared me for the trip home in a 50-foot diesel motorboat. The most exciting motorboat of my experience, *Passagemaker* was built in Singapore and brought around to England via the Suez Canal. She was the end product of Bob Beebe's years of planning the perfect boat.

My connection with her was of long standing. After being privileged to watch *Passagemaker* develop in letters, plans, models, and photos, I was eager to settle myself on her for the return voyage. . . .

As a matter of fact, I was a little apprehensive. Our trip east had been such a milk run I had premonitions of averaging out with a blast of meteorological excitement. Furthermore, though *Passagemaker* was only 4 feet shorter than *Kytra,* she weighed less than half as much. A couple of years of messing with *Hoot Mon* had taught me that light displacement, though seaworthy, is violently active.

My apprehensions were, of course, completely groundless. She was not lightly built . . . planked with inch and three-quarters teak, and all copper riveted, it was an impressive job of building. . . .

Bob is not dedicated to the proposition that he should take everyone on the block to sea with him. The boat, therefore, sleeps five in 50 feet. You could squeeze in a sixth, if he didn't mind sleeping on the duty-helmsman's seat. Still, that's not the idea, and why be subversive? Reflect, rather, on the blessings of space to spare from bow to transom. . . .

Passagemaker is an exceedingly stable boat. Her stowage patterns assert her stability everywhere, ashtrays, bowls, books, and binoculars reclining casually here and there. She'd come a third of the way around the world, and nothing had dents in it. *Passagemaker,* as the eye and mind rove over her, is superbly planned for exactly what she's intended to do... move comfortably and safely anywhere. Like her owner, she exudes an orderly sense of leisurely inevitability. And she does well exactly what she's supposed to. . . .

The trip down to the Azores was comfortably uneventful. After a long swell came in, we dumped the flopperstoppers in the water. Her rolling stopped entirely; the side effects were remarkable. We puzzled the local fishermen more than a little. They wander about with great wooden boats with long outriggers trolling for tuna. Boat after boat saw us steaming much too fast, looking much too new, and trailing two steel wires at the end of the booms. From three miles away they'd swing to intercept, steam suspiciously across our bows or alongside, and then line the rail and peer. The whole crew would raise their shoulders and make the Gallic gesture of bafflement with upheld palms. We puzzled the porpoises at least as much. As Bob already knew, the harmonic whine of the flopperstopper wire magnetizes schools of porpoises from afar, and they leaped after us to curvet flirtatiously alongside the singing vanes. . . .

We were not idle, however; Bob Beebe was an instinctive schoolmaster. Navigation class met each morning at 1000. Bob produced pads, notebooks, printed worksheet forms of his own design, and diabolical exercises and ideas at any hour. Our fires banked in slumber, we were poked up for a dawn starsight; dawdling over postprandial coffee, we were snatched to sextants and the moon. Each of us had his own plotting sheet, and by the fourth day we were checking our results against the skipper's. Without comment, he observed and lay in wait.

Figure 5-2. Passagemaker's
"hurricane" off Bermuda. The rain
was so heavy it flattened the waves.
(Photo by Norris D. Hoyt)

We were eager to try our passage sails in fresh tradewinds, but we were doomed. We slid over an oiled sea. On Friday, August 7, we plotted Bermuda on our charts, two days away, altered course northwest for it, and picked up a large glass fishing ball. As the day wore on it degenerated into a full gale. We carried sail and went north of the course. The gusts were hitting 55 knots. It rained torrents—visibility less than 100 yards in the midst of Niagara Falls. The barograph, reacting two hours behind the side effects, tilted over and went down at 45 degrees. In the late afternoon it dropped a vertical quarter of an inch, and abruptly the air cleared and the wind went northwest. We took the sails down, went on course, and thanked the Lord for the flopperstoppers. . . .

On August 9, Bermuda was 60 miles away. Bob had gotten an early star fix and our sun lines were north of it. We figured and refigured, little realizing he had villainously and feloniously doctored his sights to test our self-confidence. Bermuda finally showed up where it always was. . . .

We poked off for Newport the next day, had a pleasant trip home, coming in, I'm vain to say, from two days out on my fix, and sliding neatly past Block Island in the rain and haze. When we tied to the *Constellation* dock at the Newport Naval Base, we put on oilskins for the first time in a round trip of the Atlantic, had a last meal together at the Officer's Club, and disbanded. The simple casualness of our arrival matched the plain pleasure of our experience. Motorboats are safe, economical, comfortable (by design), companionable, and fit vehicles for Nature's noblemen as they cruise the seven seas.

TRANSATLANTIC ABOARD SALVATION II
by Jim Leishman

Contrary to what some may think, most people successfully cruising their own vessels are careful, conservative, and quite sensible, and more often than not, of retirement age. They seek adventure but have no desire to take unnecessary risks. For many already cruising, experiencing the ease and comfort of cruising under power in an appropriate vessel could lead to a broadening of their cruising horizons. For others the power alternative can allow successful cruising that might not otherwise be possible.

One example of which I'm quite proud involves a newly retired couple from Houston. I first met Jim and Susan Sink at a boat show on Clear Lake, Texas, while displaying one of our company's 44-foot sailboats. Winding down a successful architectural career and with grown children leaving home, the Sinks were focusing their efforts on the pursuit of a dream conceived almost 30 years earlier.

The Sinks' preparation for this adventure actually began with the dream's conception. While not able to gain experience aboard yachts at sea, they spent thousands of hours reading of others' travels. Their library also contained dozens of technical volumes and references, including the original edition of this book. Jim became convinced that a proper motor yacht, designed within the parameters outlined by Robert Beebe, would best suit their needs.

Accustomed to their beautiful 6,000-square-foot home, the Sinks wanted their new home afloat to have a relatively high level of comfort, yet it had to be of a size two people could handle in all conditions. Jim and Susan recognized their limitations and felt that to meet their comfort requirements, crew limitation, and experience level, a sailboat would not be practical.

The Sinks were aware that our company was designing a long-range 46-foot motor yacht, and the three of us spent the afternoon talking about powerboats of the ocean-crossing variety. After a year of correspondence, telephone calls, and meetings, I found myself northbound as both delivery captain and teacher aboard *Salvation II*—the 10th Nordhavn 46 built—headed for the Pacific Northwest. Jim was aboard from Dana Point, California, northward, and Susan boarded in Coos Bay and continued on with us to Bellingham, Washington, where the delivery crew departed. The three of us spent the next three days further reviewing the basic operation and the handling of their new home. I must admit that upon bidding these eager but very inexperienced owners a fond farewell, I had concerns over their ability to fulfill the incredibly ambitious cruising plans to which they had committed themselves.

A week later I received the first phone call from the Sinks, and to my relief, it was an enthusiastic report of successful dockings, overnight anchoring, and unwavering confidence in their own ability and the capability of *Salvation II*. Somewhat to my surprise, these glowing reports continued to come in all summer, and in the fall, after exploring Alaskan waters, Jim and Susy steamed into Dana Point, having logged over 6,000 miles in three months of cruising.

After reprovisioning and adding GPS, *Salvation II* headed south in December for Mexico, Costa Rica, and a passage through the Panama Canal. She crossed the Caribbean to her home port of Houston and, after a short stay, ran to Florida and up to Maine for the early summer. Thoroughly enjoying their brief Downeast cruise, they turned *Salvation II* southwest and entered the Hudson River, making their way to the Great Lakes and ultimately down the Mississippi River and back home to Houston (this inland leg is described in Chapter 16) to wrap up personal business. After a haulout, the able little ship headed back to Fort Lauderdale for a continuation of what the Sinks had then decided would be a world circumnavigation.

Jim and Susy asked if I'd assist in the transatlantic leg from Florida to London via Bermuda and the Azores. I agreed but made it perfectly clear that any number of business commitments might force me to cancel prior to departure. As the weeks went by, things seemed to fall into place to allow me to firm up the commitment. Jim finally advised me that he would cancel the voyage without my help (I don't believe he would have), and I formally signed on to the crew list.

Hank Schuette assisted in the original Dana Point–Bellingham delivery aboard *Salvation II* and was also asked to join us in Florida for our May 15th departure. With four aboard, loads of food, and 938 gallons of clean fuel, we headed east across the Gulf Stream for the south end of Great Abaco Island. There we would pass through the Bahamas and turn northeast for Bermuda and the wide Atlantic.

At the beginning of any long voyage, everyone aboard feels some apprehension. After many thousands of miles aboard *Salvation II*, Jim and Susy trusted her completely. I, too, knew the boat well enough to have absolute confidence in her capability, but Hank had only our word that this was no ordinary motorboat.

Hank is a longtime member of the San Diego Yacht Club and has thousands of miles of offshore experience—mostly under sail. A dozen or so years earlier I had sold Hank a new 49-foot

Figure 5-3. *Jim and Susy Sink aboard* Salvation II *on the Mississippi River. (Photo by Barbara Gerard)*

ketch—the largest in a line of sailboats he had owned—which he used extensively between San Francisco and Acapulco, Mexico. After nine years he sold it to take delivery of a popular new production 49-footer, a commodious motor yacht with the above-water shape of an offshore cruiser and the underbody of a standard semidisplacement coastal cruiser. He kept the powerboat less than two years, replacing it with a 38-foot sailboat. His inability to gain confidence in the motor yacht's offshore ability was the reason for its sale.

An ex-Marine jet-fighter pilot, Hank doesn't scare easily. A year before this trip, he and I sailed one of our Mason 53s in the Transpacific Yacht Race, and he wouldn't hesitate to cross an ocean in his small sailboat, but the motion and behavior of his previous motor yacht when offshore had left him apprehensive about powerboats. His experience running up the West Coast aboard *Salvation II* almost two years earlier offered only delightful summer conditions with no gales or significant weather to test the vessel's ability, and I had to assure him that, unlike his previous motorboat, this little ship had the capability to handle almost anything the Atlantic would likely throw our way. The *Pilot Chart* of the North Atlantic for the month of May showed we could expect about 15 knots of breeze from the east, which is exactly what we experienced. We all settled down for this 925-mile first leg and anticipated a little uncomfortable going with the wind and sea on our nose. As we closed on Bermuda we expected the wind to shift more to the south and offer some assistance.

Early on the fourth day, the wind began to freshen and shift more to the northeast. The weatherfaxes showed a fast-developing low-pressure system brewing to the southeast of Bermuda, and soon gale warnings were issued for the entire area. Bermuda was only 300 miles ahead, but the low was building strength and moving to the northwest—directly across our path.

During the evening we made radio contact with *South Bound 1* (an amateur weather forecaster in Bermuda) and were warned that this fast-developing storm was building in intensity and headed in our direction. Our weather briefer, Herb, somberly suggested we turn to the southwest (almost a 180-degree turn) and try to run across the storm's path and into its southern quadrant where wind speeds would be less. Concerned and plagued with a poor SSB connection, we inquired as to the anticipated strength of the storm and learned that wind speeds of around 40 knots were anticipated but with considerably stronger winds likely. Since we had already seen gusts to 50 mph on our anemometer (an mph-calibrated home unit), we decided to press onward directly toward Bermuda. Our little ship was performing perfectly, experiencing little difficulty, maintaining headway of about 5.5 knots, and still steering under autopilot. We had taken the precaution of installing our port-side storm plates on the saloon windows, and we spent the night riding out the storm in relative comfort. It didn't take Hank long to figure out that this stout

Figure 5-4. *Installing saloon window storm panels in building seas near Bermuda.* Salvation II's *asymmetrical saloon makes this an awkward job on the port side.*

little motorboat was "an entirely different kettle of fish" from his previous 49-footer, and he expressed his confidence in the vessel's ability to handle seas significantly worse than what we were encountering.

Dawn broke and the Force 8 conditions continued with a steady barometer. By midday we were picking up Bermuda on the radar, and by 1900 we had passed the first channel marker at the entrance to St. George. Interestingly, we had come in just behind a 100-foot-plus motor yacht, the *William I*. Dockside conversations with her captain revealed that they had experienced the same conditions we had, but the larger vessel did not fare as well. The semidisplacement design was not well suited to open-ocean conditions, and storm damage to her forward saloon windows and some to her interior forced her to heave-to for repairs. When underway again, her progress into the rough seas was very difficult, and despite her great horsepower she could not maintain the speed of *Salvation II*. Hank boasted to the captain that we rode out the gale in T-shirts and stocking feet and never had to alter course or reduce speed. We were quite proud of our able little ship.

There was little time to enjoy Bermuda as our stay was only about 40 hours. Two dinners ashore, an oil change, fueling, light provisioning, and a little touring of St. George by foot were all we had time for. I was sorry that we could spend so little time in such a pleasant place; Bermuda offers beautiful beaches, perfect weather, friendly people, and a tremendously interesting history.

I promised myself I'd return, but we were all anxious to get underway. We departed under bright sunny skies and with an exceptional weather forecast. The gale that roughed us up coming into Bermuda had dissipated and moved to the northwest, and we were finally seeing the overdue development of a high-pressure system around the Azores—commonly referred to as the Azores High. This was a relief as the area had been plagued by constant gales prior to our Fort Lauderdale departure and throughout the first leg of our voyage. This high-pressure system is a necessary ingredient to a pleasant transatlantic crossing, and we were happy to see it forming.

This second leg—sailing a great-circle course—calculated out at just under 1,800 nautical miles. The Nordhavn's range graphs show this to be an easy undertaking, but considering the possibility of a long duration of adverse weather and potentially unfavorable currents, we decided on a very conservative approach. Departing Bermuda with a maximum load (1,072 gallons) of diesel aboard, the initial governor setting allowed 1,650 rpm, which propelled the heavily laden *Salvation II* along at a leisurely 6.5 knots with a fuel burn of 2 gallons per hour. As we progressed and burned fuel, the speed would increase, but at this initial speed we were guaranteed a calm-water range in excess of 3,200 miles.

A "How-Goes-It" fuel curve was developed for this leg of the trip, and we decided upon a target fuel reserve of 20 percent at our arrival in Horta on the Island of Faial. In retrospect, Beebe's recommended 10 percent reserve is probably sufficient, but we were taking no chances. By the beginning of our sixth day our speed had increased to about 7 knots, and with 873 miles to go and 747 gallons remaining, our fuel curve indicated that we would have a reserve of about 1,000 miles, or 55 percent—well above our target.

The beautiful weather that greeted us on the east side of Bermuda somehow got better each day: air temperatures in the low 80s by day and the 70s at night, low humidity, and a breeze going from light to absolute calm. For two days the ocean looked like undulating glass, without a zephyr-induced ripple to be found. The sea surface mirrored the sky with such duplication of color that it was difficult to make out the horizon. We all agreed that we had never seen a more beautiful combination of sky and sea.

Figure 5-5. Salvation II *taking on fuel in Bermuda in preparation for the next leg of her transatlantic passage—1,800 miles to the Azores.*

The water temperature was 78 degrees, and Hank and I decided to go for a swim. In the absolute middle of the Atlantic Ocean, in over 15,000 feet of water, we left the security of the ship and dove into the deep. We actually justified the stop to shut down and check the engine fluids, and after five minutes in a 110-degree engine room, the dive from the boat deck into the cool, blue Atlantic was one of high points of the trip.

Fair weather continued with some wind filling in, but hardly enough to drive a sailboat. I paid particular attention to this as the "Atlantic Rally Cruise" fleet was gathered in Bermuda and scheduled to depart the day after we left, also bound for the Azores. Without a deck-load of diesel-filled jerry jugs, the usual 17- to 24-day passage considered normal for cruising sailboats in the 45-foot range would be wishful thinking in these windless conditions. *Salvation II*'s effortless and economical 170-mile days were looking pretty good.

As we closed on the Portuguese island chain, we increased engine rpm to 1,925, and our daily distance made good increased to more than 180 nautical miles with a fuel burn of about 3.4 gph. *Salvation II* is equipped with Koopnautic hydraulically activated stabilizing fins, and while they extract a cruising-speed penalty of about three-eights of a knot, the added comfort is well worth the price. On our tenth day at sea we sighted the 7,700-foot peak of the island of Pico, the highest peak in the Azores and, in fact, in all of Portuguese territory. Soon we began to see the closer but lower island of Faial on radar. We arrived in the Harbor of Horta just before dawn with 350 gallons of diesel remaining—representing more than 1,000 miles of reserve range (almost 60 percent) running at 155-mile days.

Like Bermuda, Horta proved to be a delightful place worthy of weeks of exploration. At 38 degrees north latitude, the climate is not really tropical but still warm and comfortable with little humidity. The terrain is mountainous, and the town has great character, reminding me of Avalon on the Island of Catalina off the California coast. Whitewashed, red-tile-roofed buildings line well-kept narrow streets rising from a quaint but primarily commercial waterfront. An interesting feature of the harbor area is the extensive but tasteful graffiti on the surfaces of the seawalls and surrounding rocks and concrete walkways. Yachts from around the world leave behind bright and carefully painted murals indicating the ship's name, hailing port, date, and sometimes crew names. This mural has become a tradition in Horta and is encouraged but controlled by the Portuguese government. The quality of the artwork must be guaranteed and a background of white paint is required.

After far too little time but with full fuel tanks, fresh fruit and vegetables, and a case of excellent Azorean wine, *Salvation II* departed Horta and took up a course direct for England, steering around the Islands of São Jorge and Terceira. Only 1,300 miles remained, but we had to climb over 12 degrees of latitude, and these last seven days proved the toughest of the trip. Air and water temperatures dropped as we cleared the Azores, and the barometer began to fall. Weatherfaxes indicated numerous lows descending from the Arctic and far North Atlantic, and soon *Salvation II*, with storm plates in place, was again running into rough and uncomfortable weather. We endured two Force 7 gales with some discomfort but little reduction in speed. Our little ship progressed confidently and on schedule, arriving in Falmouth, England, at dawn on June 13. Following a brief champagne celebration and after clearing customs, Hank and I bid Jim and Susy farewell, and boarded a train for London and home.

At 110 miles per hour on the tracks of British Rail, Hank and I reflected on our adventure. Personal commitments had made it difficult enough to take the four weeks necessary to undertake this voyage, and we agreed that without *Salvation II*'s ability to reliably maintain reasonable speed in all weather conditions, neither of us could have committed to the voyage. With short layovers planned in both Bermuda and Horta, we didn't have the option to reduce our stay ashore to catch up on lost transit time, but we still confidently scheduled return flights to the U.S. months before our departure, and we arrived in England with two days to spare to catch our flights home.

It had been a pleasant, relaxing, and quick trip without incident. While we were prepared to deal with significant mechanical breakdowns, our only problem was an autopilot motor. With more than 3,000 miles on the little DC motor, we anticipated its failure and carried a replacement. We made the change in a matter of minutes, and the off watch never knew of the problem. *Salvation II* required no service in Falmouth other than an oil change and departed two days after her arrival to continue on with her summer's cruising. We had crossed the Atlantic burning a volume of diesel fuel that cost little more than four one-way airline tickets over the same route—economy class. But without question, we had traveled first class.

Figure 5-6. Salvation II *arrives in Falmouth, England, with a happy, rested, and relaxed crew.*

CHAPTER 6

TECHNICALITIES OF THE SEAGOING MOTORBOAT

IN TURNING NOW FROM what *Passagemaker* proved to applying this experience to future vessels, the first step must be a solid grounding in the technical side of the business. The figures and how they are arrived at are not difficult—but they do require some study.

The reason why technical calculations are so important is that small, long-range motorboats must press every factor that affects performance if they are to achieve the desired results. It is one thing to design a racing sailboat and hope it will make a shambles of the opposition—all sorts of "ifs" can affect that. It is quite another thing to say, "I want a motorboat to take my wife and me, with a crew of friends, across the Atlantic. A range under power of 2,400 miles at a speed/length ratio of 1.2 is about right." Here there is only one measure of success—that the vessel *does* achieve your goal.

It is the whys and wherefores of figures like those given above that concern us here. If your vessel is to be an original design, the naval architect will gladly discuss these matters with you. If you are interested in an existing boat, a knowledge of the factors involved in performance will give you a gauge of whether such a vessel will fill your needs, whether it will do what its builder says it will.

A case in my files is an example of the confusion caused by the advertisements for motorboats billed as "seagoing," or "trawlers," or "go-anywhere boats." A husband and wife bought a popular brand of 42-foot "trawler" with the expectation of cruising in the South Seas, an expectation amply reinforced by the salesman who sold them the boat. It was my sad duty after much work on their project to tell them their vessel could not possibly do the job, and no feasible modification would help.

A wider understanding of the technicalities has become even more necessary because of the recent great increase in the number of designs for what are called "trawlers." What is needed is a summary of the naval architecture rules involved in the selection of *any* seagoing motorboat. The rules are not complicated when compared to designing an ocean-racing yawl. But they must not be ignored! What follows is as simple an exposition as I can make, but it does take studying. My advice to a prospective owner is to approach salesmen and advertising with your calculator in hand—ignoring Madison Avenue blurbs—and check out their figures against what is said here. If the figures are not made available, demand them. If you don't know how to make the necessary calculations, learn; you will certainly need this ability later to run your long-range cruiser.

A further consequence of the expansion of interest in seagoing motorboats is that they come in such a range of sizes and performance characteristics that one term can hardly be used to cover all types. For our purposes here, let's call vessels "ocean-crossers" if their performance is roughly comparable to *Passagemaker*'s. Of course this does not mean they are useful solely for ocean crossing. Rather, they have the range and seaworthiness to do it, the equipment and comfort at sea to make such a cruise safe and enjoyable, and are ready to cross an ocean if the owner is. You can see such characteristics are also desirable for shorter cruises. Let's apply "trawler" to lighter vessels with some seagoing capability but with neither the equipment nor the range to qualify for full status as ocean-crossers. And we will use "seagoing motorboat" to cover all types when such a general term is needed.

There is one thing more that needs to be said about "trawler." As we are going to use the term here to designate a class of motorboats that has sprung up lately—a class that has solid virtues in itself—we must first understand that the majority of today's "trawler yachts" have not even a nodding acquaintance with a real seagoing fishing trawler. Such statements as one printed in a recent article on "trawler-yacht design," saying ". . . designers went to work and developed a type of hull that had none of the faults of the commercial trawler yet retained all the desirable features and the general trawler look," are pure nonsense. Don't misunderstand me. There is nothing wrong with these yachts if they meet your needs. But just because they are called "trawlers," don't imagine that the seaworthiness of the true trawler has rubbed off on them.

Now, naval architects judge hulls mostly by using *coefficients* or *ratios*. There are many of these, but we will limit ourselves to four. They are:

Displacement/Length Ratio (D/L)
Speed/Length Ratio (S/L)
Above Water/Below Water Area Ratio (A/B)
Prismatic Coefficient (PC)

And we might add one I just invented. It is called the *trawler/truth ratio (T/T)*. A trawler is and always has been a fishing vessel designed to tow a *trawl* (or net) that is pulled along the bottom to trap fish. To do this, she needs a husky hull with a good grip on the water and aperture space for a large, slow-turning propeller. She is expected to work the sea, winter and summer, and some of the best trawling grounds have the worst weather. Hence the seaworthiness of the North Sea and Icelandic sea trawlers made "trawler" the symbol of seaworthiness; that is, until Madison Avenue got hold of the term. Thus the need for this T/T ratio—how near to a true trawler is the boat? There are yachts that would score quite high, as they were patterned after true trawlers. But today we see advertised as "trawlers" designs that would score, if one were charitable, 1 or 2 percent.

Let's first consider the common way of comparing relative *heft*, or weight, in boats. This is important because a relatively heavier boat must have more volume underwater to provide that weight. Hence she has more space for accommodations, fuel, stores, and the like.

What we use to measure this is called the *displacement/length ratio (D/L)*. This is the displacement *in long tons* (2,240 pounds) divided by the *cube* of the waterline length *(LWL)*, divided by 100. The division by 100 is merely to keep the number small.

$$D/L = \dfrac{D}{\left(\dfrac{LWL}{100}\right)^3}$$

The ratio is useful for this reason: If you take a certain yacht and make a second model of it, *twice as big* but with the same lines exactly, its D/L will remain the same, although the bigger vessel will weigh *eight times as much*. But if you take another vessel that is not the same shape or the same length, comparing its D/L to the first model's will tell you if the new model is relatively heavier (greater D/L), or lighter (lower D/L). It is also, from experience, a good way to separate the men from the boys, so to speak. For instance, checking the D/Ls of coastal motorboats that are designed to use considerable power to attain quite respectable speeds in local cruising, you find their D/Ls range from, say, 160 to 220. Of course these types are not expected to cross oceans.

So, taking the ocean-crossers first, what D/L should they have? This question is open to argument. But I have had certain experiences in this matter that are a good basis for my thoughts on the subject. First let's define what we are talking about in relation to space required for crew, fuel, stores, and so forth—a space requirement that must eventually be reflected, in part, by cubic feet under water, which of course is displacement.

Take my client who wanted to go to the South Seas in his 42-foot "trawler." To make that cruise, in my opinion he needed a vessel with a range of at least 2,400 miles under power, permanent bunks for five or six, 60 days' supplies, and, ideally, full-time liveaboard space for owner and wife. The vessel he purchased did not meet any of these requirements and could not be modified to have them—the cubic space simply was not there. In other words, her D/L of 230 was too small.

My own *Passagemaker*'s design was supposed to be on the light side compared to the heavy diesel motorboats of the 1950s and 1960s, which were mostly fishing boat models. The idea behind her relative lightness was economy in construction and powering. The lines were drawn with a D/L ratio of 230. But when she was built and loaded, ready to go with all the gear required for long-range cruising, we found her draft had increased, so her D/L rose to 270. There was some overweight in construction, but most of this increase was in disposable load. Obviously she should have been built to a D/L of 270 to begin with.

This and other data led me to the following conclusions: A satisfactory ocean-crossing vessel—a vessel to meet the requirements of the gentleman who wanted to go to the South Seas—cannot have a D/L less than 270 in the 50-foot overall size, and a bit more is desirable. A specialized vessel such as a long, slim aluminum yacht could prove me wrong. But for a conventional hull, carrying good accommodations for living on board and not stinting on equipment, supplies, and ballast, this rule is a good guide.

The shorter a vessel, the larger its D/L should be. In fact, you *must* increase the D/L in smaller vessels to carry the load. I see in two of my recent designs that the 50-footer has a D/L of 300, while the 42-footer has a D/L of 375. There is no particular rule here—the proportions just look right to me. Contrast the D/L of my 42-footer with that of the 42-foot "trawler" discussed above. Their respective displacements are 24 tons and 15 tons—a difference of 9 tons! This essentially shows a difference in the requirements to which the boats were drawn, for I am sure the *designer* of the light 42-footer did not expect his boat to head for the South Seas.

If your demands for range, accommodations, and seaworthiness are less than those of a well-equipped ocean-crosser, you may find a "trawler type" acceptable. In the 40- to 43-foot size their D/Ls run from 156 to 230, the difference largely concentrated in the amount of fuel they carry. Naturally these D/Ls seem low to me, but I admit to limited experience with the type. My suggestion would be to investigate these craft very thoroughly as to motion at sea and storage area, in addition to tests to be described later. Keep in mind there is a great deal of difference between a vessel fresh from the builder's yard and one fully loaded for a long cruise. I have not seen a long-range cruiser yet that did not fill every nook and cranny with stores and spares. There was absolutely no vacant space under the cabin soles of *Passagemaker,* for instance.

We have talked about low limits on D/L to emphasize the importance of enough cubic capacity to carry the loads the cruiser requires. What about high limits?

The highs, of course, would be the true fishing trawlers. Studying the three volumes of *Fishing Boats of the World,* published by the F.A.O. branch of the United Nations, which are absolute gold mines of information applicable to long-range motorboats, we find the D/Ls running from 450 for a 40-foot waterline, to 400 for 50 feet and 350 for 60 feet. Yachts that have some relation to true trawlers in their design, say a T/T ratio of 80 percent or more, run somewhat less—about 20 percent. This makes sense because a yacht does not have the load problems of a fishing boat. The yacht essentially does not vary its "payload," while the trawler has to handle loads from zero to several tons. For this reason it is not at all good practice to slavishly copy a fishing boat model for a yacht.

The suggested figures for D/L must not be taken too rigidly, especially those given in relation to length overall. As the waterline length is cubed, slight variations can have a good deal of effect. In addition, the varying weights of fuel and stores are constantly changing a vessel's D/L. One must check for just what condition the displacement figures are given. Our suggested figures are for all-up weights, ready to depart on that long cruise.

So much for displacement, or heft, and for the D/L ratio. We will talk more about D/L after we take up the *speed/length ratio (S/L),* as the two become quite intertwined when you talk about power, range, and speed.

The speed/length ratio is the speed of the vessel in knots, divided by the square root of the waterline length in feet:

$$S/L = \frac{V\,knots}{\sqrt{(LWL)}}$$

This is a very important ratio and has a powerful effect in many ways. At the same time let me define *hull speed.* Strictly speaking, this is the speed at which the hull makes a wave as long as its waterline. It is an S/L of 1.34. If you find salesmen using S/L ratios of 1.4 or even 1.5 as hull speed, or telling you their pride and joy has a hull speed of *x* knots that is clearly *over* an S/L of 1.34, you have an excellent indication that they don't know what they are talking about. And if a salesman does the unspeakable and gives you speeds in *statute* miles per hour, laugh in his face and walk out! You are surely being conned.

To appreciate the importance of the S/L ratio, look at a typical speed/power/range curve. The curve in Figure 6-1 was made for a 50-footer and is based on one of the estimating formulas used by naval architects. In practice it seems to be a bit on the conservative side in the area that is

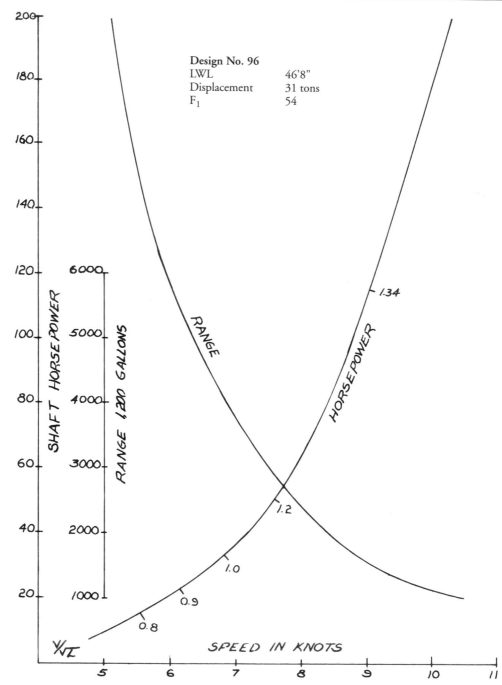

Figure 6-1. *Speed/power/range curve for Beebe Design 96.*

useful, from S/L 1.0 up. Below that it becomes too optimistic as the formula used would produce zero power at zero speed, where, as a practical matter, at around S/L 0.6 your engine would be idling and you couldn't go any slower.

Although the ordinate is shaft horsepower at the engine, what we are really interested in here is gallons per hour so it can be combined with speed to give range, as the curve shows. A consumption of 0.06 gallons per horsepower per hour is a good average figure to use here.

Note how the horsepower required starts out relatively low at the slow-speed end and curves up rapidly to an S/L of about 1.2 where it becomes a straight line that continues on up. Marked on the curve are the speed/length ratios from 0.8 to 1.2 and then the hull speed of 1.34. So this curve can represent the relative changes for any craft by using S/L ratios instead of speed in knots. In fact, when discussing the performance of seagoing motorboats, it is better to speak in terms of S/L ratios than in knots so differences in size will not affect the results. We can also say that this curve illustrates the *cost of speed*. For instance, in this particular craft, doubling the horsepower from 100 to 200 will produce 1.7 knots more speed.

The region between S/L ratios 1.1 and 1.2 encompasses the practical speeds for long-range voyaging under power in small craft and hence is of greatest interest to us. Note how for this particular vessel the range is 2,800 miles at 1.1 S/L and 2,200 miles at 1.2. Thus she can do the Bermuda–Azores run of 1,850 miles easily at 8.25 knots, or S/L 1.2. But to cover the 2,240 miles to Honolulu she would have to slow to 8 knots—with a 200-mile reserve. And let us say you are running at an S/L ratio of 1.15. If you start to worry about fuel, dropping the speed to 1.0 will produce *50 percent more range on what remains!* In other words—and this is important—small changes in speed make large changes in fuel consumption. In fact, the whole secret of the long-range boat is that it goes slowly, using small S/L ratios. It has to; there is just no way to lick this.

The type of curve shown, taken from mathematics, is useful in planning a boat of a certain weight, but as soon as possible the new craft should be actually tested carrying the weights with which she will start a cruise—to develop a curve that is more useful. In fact, the careful skipper will add his experience to his curve as he goes along. Salesmen of stock boats must also be ready to furnish such a verified curve.

The simplest way to check cruising ranges is to use a calibrated standpipe that will allow accurate measuring of fuel used while the vessel is running a measured mile.

The third ratio we will consider is the ratio of area of the side view of the vessel *above* water to that *below* water (A/B). That is:

$$\frac{Area\ Above\ Water}{Area\ Below\ Water}$$

Obviously, the smaller this ratio the better. Thus fishing trawlers may get as low as 1.0 to 1.5. It is difficult to get below 2.0 in a yacht because of the pressure for more and better accommodations. And it is this demand for more space and comfort that has gradually pushed up this ratio in contemporary yachts, with an accompanying loss of seaworthiness. Several vessels that meet my ideas of being qualified as ocean-crossers range from 2.1 to 2.6. In the light "trawler" group, this ratio tends to run higher. It has to, of course, with less hull under water. In one case it ranges as high as 4.6, which scares me, particularly as a large part of this increased area is usually glass, and thin glass at that. Steps that can be taken to hold the line after such increases are greater beam and conversion of the largest possible proportion of the side area to watertight-integrity portions of the hull.

The last item for us to consider is the *prismatic coefficient* (PC). This must be calculated from the lines and is not ordinarily available from salesmen. But it is well worth inquiring about the PC of any vessel you are considering.

The prismatic coefficient compares the actual volume of the hull below the waterline in cubic feet to what the volume would be if the body were a *prism* composed of the largest section from the lines carried the full length of the waterline. In effect, it is an expression of how much you sharpen the ends.

Tank-testing of hull models has shown that for each S/L ratio there is an ideal PC. That is, at each S/L a vessel designed with the correct PC will need less power to make that S/L than a vessel with an incorrect PC. It so happens that the correct PC varies most widely from one S/L to another in the very range we are interested in, S/Ls from 1.0 to 1.34, and on into the area where the light types try to drive past hull speed for local cruising, say to S/L 1.6. The table below, from D. Phillips-Birt's *Naval Architecture of Small Craft,* shows this clearly.

S/L	PC		S/L	PC		S/L	PC
1.0	0.53		1.4	0.64		1.8	0.70
1.1	0.54		1.5	0.66		1.9	0.70
1.2	0.58		1.6	0.68		2.0	0.70
1.3	0.62		1.7	0.69			

After S/L 2.0, dynamic lift becomes a major factor and the hull becomes a *planing* hull. Nobody is going to go very far at sea in such a vessel. As Bill Garden said once in an article on this type of boat, "A planing hull can't carry enough fuel to get out of sight."

In heavy seagoing motorboats, the effect of the PC can be dramatic. The British Fisheries Board actually built three 62-foot waterline coastal fishing boats of exactly the same length and displacement but differing PCs. The results, from *Naval Architecture of Small Craft,* were as follows:

PC	Hp Required for S/L 1.14, 9 Knots
0.645	123 (Many fishing boats have this PC.)
0.612	105
0.537	75 (This is the correct PC.)

We should not be too hard on the fishermen. The requirements of the trade may demand a larger than ideal PC. But yacht builders do not have this excuse for choosing the wrong PC.

If you are interested in maximum range with minimum fuel, there is no question that you should have a vessel with the PC set for the desired cruising speed. If you desire to cruise somewhat faster in local cruising, however, a compromise position might be better. You would use a little more fuel but have a hull shape designed for a slightly higher speed.

If the PC of a vessel you are interested in is more suited to higher speeds, say from an S/L of 1.5 to 1.9, this suggests that the hull is really better suited to local use than to long-range cruising. We might say then the PC indicates the designer's (not the advertiser's!) intentions and is worth checking.

So much for the four formulas that have the most effect on seagoing motorboats. We will look later at how to apply them to specific design problems. But first let's go further into the differences between the *true* trawler yacht and the lighter types we are calling "trawlers" for convenience, the name having been preempted by this type.

Long-range passage-making essentially is aimed at reaching the desired cruising ground *with dispatch* so you have time to enjoy the local area. Once there, there is no problem of range or fuel availability (we hope!) so you can run at any speed you wish. On *Passagemaker* we habitually ran at hull speed in local cruising. This was 9.1 knots on a 46-foot waterline. Would it be possible to do better—that is, cruise even faster locally and still have a vessel seaworthy enough for ocean passages?

A true trawler yacht is so heavy there is no question of driving her over hull speed. It simply wouldn't make sense to carry the machinery to do it. Their owners must therefore content themselves with thinking, when faster boats pass them, how their fuel bill is peanuts compared to the types that drink up hundreds of gallons per day. The hull offers enough room to be a real home afloat and the solid feel that makes for comfort at sea. This type's domain is the open sea, and if they are not used there, but stick to local cruising or coastal waters, they don't make much sense. In addition, a real trawler would, at 50 feet, have a draft of around 7 feet. This is excessive in many cruising grounds, particularly on the east coast of North America. It was this draft problem, for instance, that turned me away from considering one for myself.

On the other hand, the light "trawlers" have their own advantages and drawbacks. One of their chief virtues is their ability to run somewhat over hull speed. Now, hull speed is pretty low by U.S. standards. It takes enormous increases in waterline length to get hull speed up to the speeds ordinary coastal motorboats can achieve. In fact, to have a 12-knot hull speed takes a waterline length of some 80 feet! Yet 12 knots is an ordinary top speed for coastal motorboats. Is there a way to lick this?

What the designers of the light "trawlers" have done is to compromise between the heavy, extremely seaworthy true trawler on the one hand and the coastal type on the other—so light everyone would agree it should not go to sea. In effect, they have opted for a lower trawler/truth ratio. They say it is possible to design a hull that can exceed hull speed by a certain amount and still retain the basic seaworthiness required at sea. The steps in this process lead to lightness (relative lightness, that is) to hold down power demands and a flat stern aft to avoid squatting at higher speeds. They contend that the resulting hull form has ample seaworthiness for any reasonable cruising and cite impressive statistics to prove it. They also say that most clients who buy this type will not actually make long trips, but will be content with coastal cruising and island hopping, and be happy to have a vessel for this purpose that is clearly superior in seaworthiness to the ordinary motorboat. All of this is perfectly true, and it is not the designers who write those ads that imply these craft are fit to "go anywhere." Our quarrel is really with the advertisers and salesmen who produce the unhappy situation of our gentleman who wanted to take his 42-footer to the South Seas.

Obviously, the further above hull speed a light "trawler" is driven, the closer she will approach the coastal motorboat in lightness and use of large amounts of horsepower. So claims in this matter must be approached with a *really* critical eye. Taking the advertisements of seven yachts that are touted as "trawlers" or "go-anywhere boats," yet also claim they "cruise" at *x* knots *over* hull speed, we find they range from S/L 1.44 to 1.67, with D/Ls from 156 to 234. As "cruising speed" has no definition in naval architecture, it really would be better to check their claimed maximum speed to see how much over hull speed they are being driven.

At the same time, these vessels claim ranges from 900 to 1,500 miles. While boats with these ranges may be sufficient for many skippers' needs, it is surprising to see them advertised as go-anywhere-your-heart-desires boats when they can't even cross the smallest ocean, the Atlantic. But nothing is impossible in the advertising world, apparently. And a little calculator work shows they achieve these ranges not at their "cruising speed" but right down at S/L ratios around 1.1, where we would expect to find them. To improve these ranges you would have to add fuel capacity. And, as I found out working over the 42-footer for the gentleman who wanted to go to the South Seas, there isn't any safe place to put it; the space just isn't there.

All of these craft have the broad, flat stern necessary to exceed an S/L of 1.6. Characteristically, this type of hull steers badly with seas from the quarter or aft. As the true long-range motorboat *seeks out* these conditions, keeping the wind aft as much as possible, this point is important. I recall a client who really went into this motor passage-making business, including a long trip with me, and who was talking about being able to run over hull speed locally. He took the opportunity to make a delivery trip from San Francisco to Puget Sound as crew on a fine, custom-built, twin-screw, flat-stern yacht. Off Cape Mendocino they had a gale from astern and had a wild night, handing the throttles continuously to keep her from broaching. He came home and said to me, "Forget it. From now on I'm a hull-speed boy."

Now it will be noted that this yacht made it, even if it was uncomfortable. And, in fact, the problem with this boat was not hull shape per se but was connected with her being twin screw with small spade rudders behind each prop. These perform well at normal smooth-water speeds. But when you slow way down, they don't have enough area to take command properly. A single-propeller craft with deep skeg and large rudder would not have this trouble. So it's possible to avoid this steering problem.

Another problem with "trawlers" is they do not carry any ballast. Now I may be supercautious, but to me, whether a seagoing yacht carries some ballast is what distinguishes the true seagoer from a vessel that is not really serious about it. My *Passagemaker* (46-foot LWL, D/L 270) carried 5,000 pounds of lead on her keel, with more inside. I doubt if we needed it 98 percent of the time, and we paid good money to carry it around. But believe me, when we got into gales and the fringes of the two hurricanes we managed to find, we were delighted to have it aboard. A quotation from L. Francis Herreshoff's *Common Sense of Yacht Design* captures this even more graphically:

> It is, though, interesting to note that several designers at various times have thought they had discovered the secret of designing a V-bottom launch that went smoothly in a seaway, and this reminds me of an incident that happened to Bill Hand about 1915. Mr. Hand was one of the early big game fishermen to use high-speed gasoline launches for that purpose. Well, one fall he was fishing for tuna somewhere southeast of Block Island. It was probably pretty rough and probably Mr. Hand was quite proud of the good weather his V-bottom launch was making of it when all of a sudden it became very much rougher (which it can do suddenly in that region). To make a short story of it, Mr. Hand finally got back to New Bedford okay, but after that he made a specialty of designing heavy

*auxiliary schooners much after the fashion of Gloucestermen, and this is the type he subse-
quently used himself for fishing southeast of Block Island, and, gentle reader, I am under the
impression you will do the same thing after you have really been caught out in the same kind
of weather.*

CONCLUSIONS

Now that we have reviewed all this material, what have we got? All of my recommendations are
arguable. Naval architects are by no means in agreement on the levels of the figures I have given. So
in your quest for a vessel that meets your needs, you can expect to hear rebuttals of what is offered
here. But with your calculator in hand and a knowledge of the basics, you are much better armed
to check what they say.

One of the first things to check is range. You simply have to decide for yourself what range
you require. A realistic decision on how your boat will actually be used, not how you would like
to use it, is the first step. Then the cruises you expect to take must be checked for their maximum
legs. In this connection the capabilities of the seagoing motorboat can be exploited to improve on
conventional ways of doing things. For instance, instead of departing from Miami direct against
wind and current to the Virgins, it would be much easier on the crew and the vessel to go north
far enough to get out of the trades, then go east until you can head south to your destination. It
even appears attractive (if you plan to spend the winter cruising the Islands) to make your first
hop a passage east, then south clear to Grenada to cruise up the entire island chain.

A decision on size and relative heft is next. Size is much influenced by one's budget. Any
naval architect will tell you any vessel would be better if longer. But size has to stop somewhere.
The number of persons to be carried is also a factor. With comfortable full-time accommodations
for owner and wife, I do not believe it is possible to have more than four permanent bunks until
the length reaches 46 feet, or even better, 48 feet. Long passages can be made with a crew of four,
of course, but we found it easier with five or six.

If your vessel is to be an original design, the designer would now be in a position to come up
with preliminary sketches and a speed/power/range curve like that shown in Figure 6-1. If you are
investigating stock boats, the seller should be able to produce this curve together with certification
that the vessel has been tested and will do what the curve says. If he does not have it, walk out.

Some designers make this curve at full load and half load of fuel and water. I prefer to make the
curve for *full load only.* This gives you a safety factor in range from the vessel becoming lighter as
she goes along. My own experience with this type of curve has shown a 10 percent reserve is
ample to take care of adverse conditions, provided you are running at S/Ls from 1.1 to 1.2. If you
are thinking about stretching range to the limit for some unusual passage by running at S/L 1.0
or even 0.9, you need a larger reserve as you haven't got the leeway to slow down—you would be
too close to running the engine at idle. The curve should show the fuel rate used.

As an example, consider a vessel designed to cross the Atlantic and cruise in Europe. I would
recommend for this a range of 2,200 miles at S/L 1.2. It is true the longest leg is 1,850 miles
from Bermuda to the Azores going east. This track can be used both ways. Returning by this
route in the fall, however, you are squeezed between the hurricane season and the winter storms.
It would be more fun and more comfortable to return over the usual track of sailing vessels. They

leave Gibraltar for the Canary Islands not later than the end of September, go to Las Palmas to drink the excellent local wines until November 15, then take off like a flock of ducks for Barbados, 2,800 miles downwind, and spend the winter in the Caribbean. You can see in the curve we used as an example that a vessel that can do 2,200 miles at S/L 1.2 can do the 2,800 miles at 1.1. And if you get nervous, say at the two-thirds distance mark, you can drop the S/L to 1.0 and gain another 300 miles of range, as the curve shows. This is the sort of figuring you do for range.

Analyzing the ads for the "trawlers," you can sort out the "cruising speed" and the "range" figures with the aid of the curve. Usually you will find "cruising speed" is well above the speed required to achieve the range claimed; that is, the boat will not actually "cruise" the "range." This is acceptable as long as you understand it.

Regarding statements of top speed, check the curve to see if top speed requires more horsepower than the maximum continuous rating of the engine. If it does, forget it. Diesels ordinarily have three ratings: block, which means engine block only, without any accessories, not even a water pump; maximum intermittent rating, which means for one hour only—a rather useless exercise; and maximum continuous rating—the only one worth considering in a boat. It is a sad thing, really, to see manufacturers advertising diesels as 120 hp when this is the useless block rating and the engine has a continuous rating of 102 hp. It didn't used to be this way before Madison Avenue got into the act.

If the top speed is within the continuous rating of the engine, think about it a bit. Take a 46-foot waterline boat, about 50 feet overall. If it has a top speed of 12 knots, it would be running at an S/L of 1.77. This is pretty high and requires a flat stern and a low D/L, not to mention lots of horsepower. Would you be willing to settle for 10 knots instead? This lowers S/L to 1.48. With this small excess over 1.34 you can have a reasonably high-deadrise, parallel-in-the-aft-sections, flat-run hull that steers like it was on rails with the seas aft, carries fuel for more than 2,800 miles at S/L 1.1, and has a D/L of 270. I know this is so because it describes my own boat. We didn't get *Passagemaker* up to 10 knots because her oversize prop (for range) limited her to using 85 hp. With this she reached an S/L of 1.4, or 9.4 knots—which means she could have done 10 knots on 98 hp.

If your range demands are more modest, say from 800 to 1,500 miles, and you really want to cruise faster in local waters than S/L 1.48, I would certainly recommend the lighter types, particularly for their first-cost economy and lower running expenses, provided consideration is given to two items not ordinarily considered in stock boats: First, remember their motion at sea—with their smaller T/T ratios—will be worse than in the heavier boats and certainly demand some type of stabilization to make satisfactory long voyages; and second, if it is a twin-engine type with spade rudders, adding a large central rudder will correct steering faults exhibited by these types when running off slowly before a sea.

As for the above water/below water ratio, this is pretty much of a lost cause today. I can only say again and again, *hold it down.* But perhaps it would be better to urge prospective owners to consider what they will do when each large window is broken. What is their second line of defense? I have seen some light "trawlers" that were very well equipped for this contingency and others where this danger had not been given a thought.

Certainly *areas of operation limitation* should be considered. For instance, in one of my designs destined for full-time living afloat in the Mediterranean and double-decked full length for an A/B ratio of 3.0, I have recommended—and the owner has agreed—that the boat be limited to cruising

That's the way it goes: speed/length ratio, displacement/length ratio, and so on. Figures, figures, figures. But those pesky figures are operating all the time you are out there cruising. And it behooves the careful owner to know what they are and what influence they have.

MATHEMATICAL SUPPLEMENT TO CHAPTER 6

In this supplement we will show how to make up speed-range graphs, how to calculate speed/length ratios, and how to make a couple of other applications of mathematics.

In estimating speed and range, we need two graphs to give us two factors, F_1 and F_2.

For F_1, enter Graph No. 1 (Figure 6-2) with the vessel's displacement in long tons of 2,240 pounds along the bottom line. Proceed up to the curve and read off F_1 on the edge of the graph. In the example shown, the displacement is 46 tons and F_1 is 87.

For F_2, enter Graph No. 2 (Figure 6-3) with speed/length ratios along the bottom line. For any given speed/length ratio there is an F_2 on the edge of the graph. The example shows that for S/L 1.25, F_2 is 1.65.

The horsepower required at any given S/L ratio is then $F_1 \times F_2$. In the cases of the examples drawn on the graphs, the horsepower required to drive the 46-ton vessel at a speed/length ratio of 1.25 would be $87 \times 1.65 = 143.5$ hp.

For speed/length calculations, you need a calculator with a square root function. Enter the waterline length of your vessel, converting inches to one-hundredths of a foot (46 feet 9 inches = 46.75 feet), and press the square root function. This will give you your vessel's speed in knots at an S/L of 1.0. To calculate higher S/Ls, multiply the speed at S/L 1.0 by the desired S/L. In other words, the speed corresponding to an S/L of 1.0 for a 46.75-foot waterline is 6.84 knots. To figure the speed at an S/L of 1.3, simply multiply 6.84 by 1.3 to get 8.89 knots. Making a series of such calculations allows you to make up a table, as it is better to have speed in knots keyed to your particular waterline rather than in S/L ratios.

As an example, here is a table made up to produce a speed-range curve using these rules. This table is for the Nordhavn 46.

Speed Knots	S/L	F_2	Hp $F_1 \times F_2$	Gal/Hr at 0.06 Gal/Hp/Hr	Hours Running	Range
5	0.81	0.28	12.6	0.75	1,467	7,333
6	0.97	0.57	25.6	1.54	715	4,290
7	1.13	1.02	46	2.76	398	2,786
8	1.29	2.02	91	5.46	201	1,612
9	1.45	3.20	144	8.64	127	1,146

Displacement: 26.8 tons; F_1, 45; LWL, 38.5 ft; fuel, 1,100 gal

Although horsepower figures in this table are given to two decimal places, it should not be assumed that the results can be depended on to be that accurate. But for plotting purposes, in making a smooth curve, it helps.

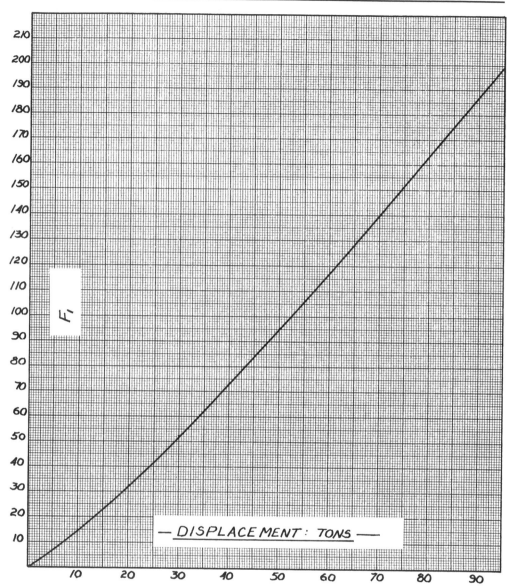

Figure 6-2. *Graph No. 1: F₁ Factor.*

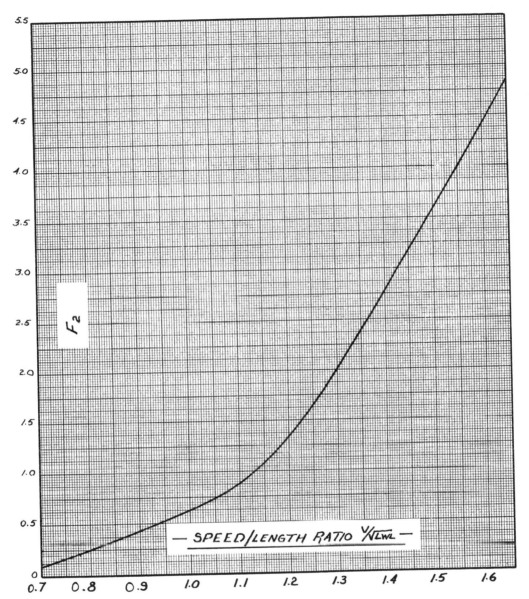

Figure 6-3. *Graph No. 2: F₂ Factor.*

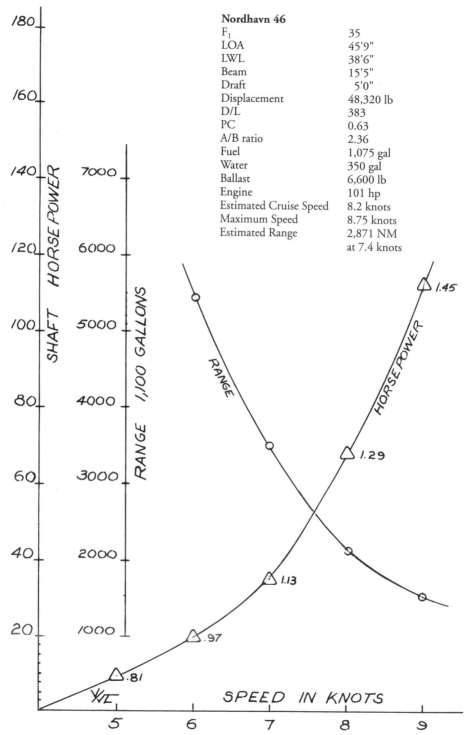

Figure 6-4. *Speed/power/range curve for Leishman's Nordhavn 46.*

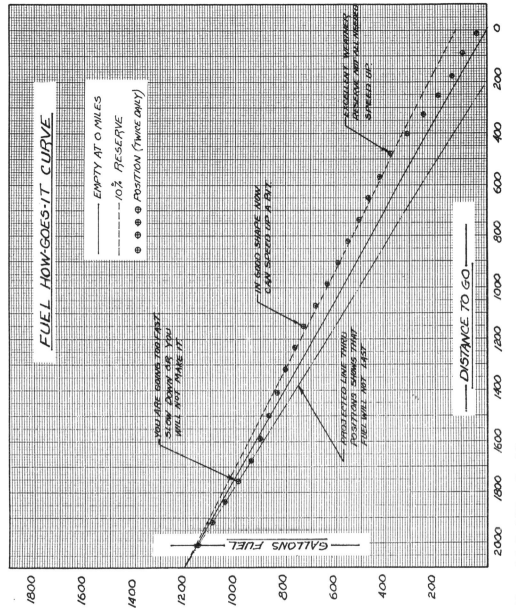

Figure 6-5. Fuel "How-Goes-It" curve.

Figure 6-4 shows the curve made from the table on page 61. The S/Ls are also indicated for reference. It will be remembered that S/L 1.0 is the limit below which the range becomes progressively more inaccurate. The ship could not possibly go more than 7,000 miles at 5 knots, for example. And the range at 6 knots is also probably somewhat overstated.

While actually operating at sea, another useful curve is the "How-Goes-It" curve. This is a graph with total gallons at the start on the left side and distance to go along the bottom. As an example, take a fuel capacity of 1,200 gallons and a 2,000-mile passage. Draw a line from the full-fuel mark to the zero-distance mark. Then draw a line from the full-fuel mark to the desired reserve-on-arrival figure, say 10 percent.

It is obvious as you plot the fuel remaining each day and the distance to go, the plotted points *must* stay *above* these lines. Ideally, you want to be above the 10 percent reserve line. But if you fall below the solid line, you *know* you are not going to reach your port unless you change what you are doing. Some fictitious plots are shown on the graph (Figure 6-5) to illustrate this.

Another useful formula is the length of waves. As waves have a constant S/L of 1.34 (which is why a vessel's hull speed is S/L 1.34), the length of the waves a boat is actually making, measured from the bow to the top of the second crest along the length of the boat, is a measure of the speed the boat is making. The formula is:

$$Length = \frac{V^2}{1.8}$$

The 1.8 in the denominator is 1.34^2. The lengths, then, for the speeds we might be interested in are as follows:

V (knots)	Length (feet)		V (knots)	Length (feet)
3	5.0		8	35.5
4	8.9		9	45.0
5	13.9		10	55.5
6	20.0		11	67.2
7	27.2		12	80.0

These lengths can be marked on deck to use as a log. Note that the difference between 6 knots and 7 knots is 7.2 feet, for instance. Surely you can judge the length to the crest more accurately than that. This system was used—to scale—finding the speeds of the model shown in Chapter 3. See if you agree with my estimate. The scale on the model is calibrated in knots, full size.

CHAPTER 7

A PASSAGEMAKER'S MACHINERY

A GREAT DEAL HAS BEEN said about the influence of hull shape on the efficiency, speed, and range of a powerboat. This chapter deals with the actual propulsion machinery, the importance of which is second only to the hull's ability to keep us afloat. While some will undoubtedly mistrust this machinery, seeing it as a potential source of irritation requiring mechanics for every aspect of service, most successful long-range cruisers take the opposite view. For them the engine is something that is deeply loved and respected. As with a yacht's attractive profile, a sweet, seakindly motion, or a comfortable layout, the engine with thousands of hours of reliable service is a source of great satisfaction. Oil changes, wipedowns, and adjustments are all enjoyable parts of the overall experience.

A SUITABLE MARINE ENGINE

In the long-range boat, the engine selected differs from one suitable for a high-speed motor yacht or a sportfisherman. For the long-range vessel, engines are always selected for their *continuous-duty use*. We are not concerned with maximum flywheel horsepower but with *continuous-duty shaft output*. This is the actual propeller-shaft horsepower (SHP) that the engine builder has determined can be drawn out of the engine for continuous use (days and days). Generally, this continuous-duty rating will be about 30 percent below the maximum horsepower the engine can develop.

Robert Beebe recommended selecting an engine that will drive the long-range cruiser at its hull speed (S/L 1.3) using about 75 percent of its rated continuous horsepower. For normal cruising this engine will be running at an easy pace, greatly enhancing reliability and engine life. A properly maintained engine can easily see well in excess of 10,000 engine hours before overhaul is necessary. Actual times between overhauls have been more than 20,000 hours in low-speed propulsion applications and well in excess of that in generator applications where rpm is reduced. If care is taken of a properly built and selected engine, it should be good for at least two circumnavigations, including many side trips. Even the nonmechanical type would have to respect this kind of service and reliability.

The recommendation of 75 percent of continuous horsepower for hull speed is a result of numerous factors. It is very important that the correct size engine be selected—too large can be worse than too small. The Nordhavn 46 requires all 101 continuous horsepower from her naturally aspirated 414-cubic-inch engine to run at an S/L of about 1.41 (8.7 knots) and will normally coastal-cruise at about 1.3 S/L (8 knots), using just under 70 percent of her continuous horsepower rating. Slowing down to 1.1 S/L (6.8 knots) for economy, or to push the range limit on a long cruise, reduces the load to about 30 hp, or 30 percent of continuous power.

While it is beneficial to run continuously at something below maximum rated continuous output, too low a speed can be equally detrimental. Injector fouling can occur and, more serious, the cylinders can be damaged by running too slowly for long periods. This is a common problem in yacht generators run for long periods with little or no load. Cylinders can glaze, leading to high oil consumption and drastically reduced service life of the engine.

An additional consideration in the selection of an engine is its efficiency at various power outputs. Most engines are designed to operate efficiently within a particular range—typically around 70 percent of rated continuous output. The fuel requirement for each horsepower can vary significantly (up to 30 percent) with the speed and output of the engine.

Both the potential for mechanical problems associated with low-speed running and the significant decrease in efficiency seem to be ignored by those marketing high-powered semidisplacement vessels as suitable for long-range cruising. The problems of semidisplacement hull efficiencies and seakeeping qualities pointed out in Chapter 6 are further complicated with the adverse effects resulting from running a high-speed, high-output, turbocharged and after-cooled engine slightly above idle speed for extended periods. This should be thoroughly discussed with a nonsalesman *engineer* employed by the manufacturer of the engine before it is tried!

Specifying suitable engines is tough and subjective. Put five promoters of two-cycle GMC power on one side of the room and a team of four-cycle Cummins advocates on the other, and you will hear enough interesting debate to fill a book.

I've always been an advocate of lots of iron, natural aspiration, wet cylinder liners, low rpm, and about 1 hp per 4 cubic inches of displacement. That generally describes the Lugger engine used in the Nordhavn 46—a 414-cubic-inch John Deere–based engine with a continuous duty rating of a little over 100 hp. However, in the high-tech world of engine manufacturing, this type of diesel is getting harder and harder to find.

The fact is, unlined (no cylinder liners) higher-speed engines may soon be the only newly manufactured propulsion plants available in the under-300-hp range. And as mechanics' labor rates approach 100 dollars per hour, overhauling an engine may cease to be economical, with a new replacement offering less down time and possibly less expense. Caterpillar, for instance, with its popular 3208 and 3116 models, has decided on unlined engines with real continuous-duty ratings

Figure 7-1. *The Lugger 668D. (Photo courtesy Lugger)*

Figure 7-2. *The Caterpillar
3116. (Photo courtesy
Caterpillar)*

of 1 hp for each 2 cubic inches of displacement—and with intermittent ratings approaching 1 hp per 1.5 cubic inches!

The Caterpillar 3116 is offered with a continuous SHP rating of about 200 hp from only 403 cubic inches. Weighing 1,540 pounds, the engine has a SHP-to-weight ratio of about 1 hp per 8 pounds. Referring back to the John Deere–based Lugger 6414, the SHP-to-displacement ratio is 1 to 4, and the SHP-to-weight ratio of this 1,665-pound engine is about 1 hp to 16.5 pounds.

The above two examples represent heavy, low-output versus light, high-output diesels. It's a safe bet that the Lugger 6414 will run more hours between overhauls than the Caterpillar 3116 and that overhauling the Lugger will be much easier due to its replaceable cylinder liners, but it's hard to ignore the current technology incorporated into the Caterpillar. The Cat's state-of-the-art design, along with turbocharging and after-cooling, produce horsepower within its most efficient range on about 7 percent less fuel than the older-design Lugger. As you will note in Chapter 9, much effort has gone into designing more efficient hull shapes, and to give up the large gains in engine efficiency of modern configurations in exchange for the perceived long life and reliability of older designs is a tough trade-off.

ENGINE ROOM

The layout of the engine room is extremely important, and the amount of space allocated for machinery must be adequate for inspection and service. A large, stand-up engine room would be ideal, but unless you are designing a very large boat or giving the engine room space priority over other accommodations, you may have to settle for less.

In the design of the Nordhavn 46, preliminary drawings showed an engine room with full headroom directly below the wheelhouse floor. This was the perfect arrangement as the watch-stander simply had to reach down from the helm and lift a floor for routine engine room inspections. The engine room ran virtually full width, and there was space for everything as the fuel tanks were located farther aft, under the floor of the main saloon. While *I* like this arrangement (see Neville design, page 136), we have found no one willing to sacrifice the stateroom accommodations it requires. We no doubt will eventually encounter someone so in love with the machinery that he will make the trade-off to create an engine room large enough to be comfortable with the diesel engine he loves. I think that's the key: an engine room with adequate space for service and inspection will do; anything more just allows you to stay longer and enjoy the wonderful equipment that serves you so well.

Beebe entreats that, "The main engine of a seagoing powerboat is the heart of the ship and must be treated with the respect it deserves." Engine spaces that require moving furniture, rugs, and floorboards just to get at the tops and outboard sides of the engines, while perhaps acceptable aboard a coastal motorboat, are certainly unacceptable on a long-range boat.

Engine access should be provided from a location outside of the mainstream of ship's activities; a hatch in the middle of the saloon or galley should not be the only access to the engine room. The Nordhavn 62 provides access into the engine room from the yacht's exterior, and interior access is through a utility room so that saloon and galley activities are not curtailed during service and inspections. Obviously this cannot be done on most 45-footers, but access from a lower passageway located beneath stairs or from within a stateroom or head compartment can be very useful.

Inspections during a passage are extremely important and absolutely must be done with regularity—at a very minimum, every two hours. There's an excellent argument for hourly inspections but I've rarely seen anyone adhere to this rule. Generally, a simple look inside the engine room will do. If there's no smoke, unusual smell, unusual noise, oil or fuel in the engine pan, or water in the bilge, things are probably okay. Such inspections conducted by the watch-standers should be adequate as long as the engineer or skipper enters the engine space *once a day* to take a thorough look at the shaft coupling, stuffing box, belts, and engine mounts and to check for problems of chafe. This complete inspection should include checking fuel quantity, engine oil, transmission fluid, etc. After three or four hundred hours on one vessel, and based upon recorded daily consumption, I became so comfortable with engine-oil consumption that we would run for four or five days straight and simply add a quart or two without shutting down. While this may sound a little reckless, it was due to the discomfort of stopping the vessel and shutting down the active fin stabilizers in a seaway (an important plus for flopper-stoppers).

Adequate space on either side of the engine is important for inspections and for service and repair. Twenty inches is about the minimum desirable space between the engine sides and outboard fuel tanks or machinery. At sea, the engine will probably be too hot to touch (particularly if it has just been shut down), and this space is needed to avoid being burned. High service items such as water pumps, fuel injection pumps, fuel lift pumps, alternators, and starter motors should have sufficient space around them for removal.

Engine space ventilation is also extremely important. A good formula is at least 1 square inch of intake ventilation for each cubic foot of engine

Figure 7-3. *Engine room of a Nordhavn 46. Note room around engine for easy service access.*

room space. Each engine and generator will have a specified ventilation requirement, but it usually isn't enough to keep the engine room sufficiently cool. A running engine's intake will usually pull enough air into the engine room to maintain a reasonable temperature (below 120 degrees with an outside ambient temperature of 90 degrees), but if the engine needs to be shut down and serviced at sea, the engine room temperature can rise. Exhaust blowers should be included to cool the space down after shutdown, but a nice addition is intake blowers. Simple DC blowers will do and, combined with running exhaust blowers, can dramatically cool the engine space, sometimes making the difference between being able to carry on with a repair or beating a retreat to wait for the cool-down. Intake blowers should be wired on a separate breaker or switch from the exhaust blowers as they can sometimes push engine room smells into the accommodations and would generally be used for a quick cool-down only when the engine space needs to be occupied.

Good engine room lighting is also essential and should provide bright illumination above and on both sides of the engine. We have found that AC lighting is a good addition to the DC lights. AC lighting is always brighter and, at dockside or with a generator running, will prove helpful to unadjusted eyes in a dark engine room.

DIESEL FUEL MANAGEMENT

Fuel management aboard the Passagemaker is of paramount concern and deserves considerable discussion. Generally speaking, it will take about 1,000 gallons to qualify the 46-footer designed within the parameters discussed in Chapter 6 as a true ocean-crosser. This should roughly give a *no reserve, reduced S/L* range of 3,000 miles—ample for Pacific and Atlantic crossings of fewer than 2,500 miles. For the size of the vessel, this required fuel load is a considerable percentage of both gross weight and interior volume. Robert Beebe best illuminates the impact on stability of a large fuel capacity:

> *The large fuel tanks required by the long-range vessel cause problems. One thing that must not be neglected is the stability of the vessel when almost all the fuel is gone. If the fuel is low in the hull as it is burned, the center of gravity will steadily move upward. This is more serious in a narrow, long, and light hull than in the heavier models with length/beam ratios of around 3.0. These heavier vessels should not put all their fuel down low, as they will undoubtedly end up with a too-stable hull that gives a bad ride at sea. Split tanks allow for adjustment of trim. It is hard to come out with level trim with all tanks full. When* Passagemaker *was fully loaded, she had a list to port and was down by the stern. It took about three days of burning fuel from port aft tanks before she would come level again. Trim could then be maintained by judicious valving of her four tanks. The real seagoer should carry some ballast. If the ballast is approximately half the weight of the fuel, she will be safe enough with empty tanks or light loads in local cruising.*

"Give that diesel engine clean fuel and she'll run forever"—that's what they say. And it's really true. Of course you have to lubricate the engine and keep it cool, but dirty fuel has probably shut down more engines than anything else. The design of the fuel tanks is a good place to start, and there are specific things that should be done here. All my experience has been with iron, aluminum, or individual (not integral) fiberglass (FRP) tanks. My preference is iron because it seems to be less susceptible to corrosion than aluminum, and in the full-displacement vessel the additional weight is no great detriment. Integral FRP sounds terrific, but until I see two experts agree on the causes and cures for fiberglass water osmosis, I'll continue to be cautious about an endorsement of fuel on one side and water on the other of a fiberglass laminate.

Whichever material is selected, inspection plates are essential. They should be large enough to allow access with a big flashlight and a scrub brush on a handle (about 10 inches in diameter) and must be located so the lowest point and the pickup lines of the tank can be seen. Baffles are a requirement on about 18-inch centers. Inspection plates between each baffle are unnecessary unless the tank is flat and lacks sufficient pitch to cause the fuel to drain quickly to the pickup point, regardless of trim. For example, an athwartship tank with three or four baffles and a flat bottom (not conforming to the hull shape) would require added inspection plates between baffles.

Inspection plates allow the periodic cleaning and inspection of the lowest point of the tank. It is worth the effort to take a look at the tanks' interiors before a long passage, particularly if the vessel has been inactive for some time. Starting off a voyage with absolutely clean tanks and fueling through a reputable source with adequate filtering on their equipment almost guarantees a trouble-free voyage. Prior to our crossing of the Atlantic aboard *Salvation II,* each fuel tank was emptied into one of the others with a transfer pump, opened up, and inspected. Some stripping of muck around the pickups was done, but the tanks were really quite clean after 22 months and 3,000 hours of running. Following this practice allowed us to cross the Atlantic with only two precautionary fuel-filter changes during two engine-oil changes.

Current regulations for gasoline-powered vessels require that pickup lines for fuel tanks must enter the top of the tank to reduce the possibility of a leak. While the U.S. Coast Guard and the American Boat and Yacht Council do not require adherence to this regulation when using diesel fuel, they do recommend it and suggest a valve be fitted where the fuel pickup enters the top of the tank. If the valve is broken, the fuel will not siphon into the vessel's bilge, and if a leak develops in the lines below the valve, it can be shut off at the tank. While a fuel pickup that enters the tank from the top does offer some safety advantages, it is a less than ideal way to supply the engine with a constant supply of fuel.

Two important keys to dealing with this type of fuel system are the positioning of the fuel-selection manifold and the addition of a boost pump. The selection manifold must be located as *low* as possible in the engine room. Ideally it should be below the lowest level of the fuel, but in a pinch can be located higher. The point to remember is that once the fuel manifold and lines are full, the selection manifold will be under pressure as long as the level of the fuel is above it. If there is a small leak, it will result in dripping, which is easily detected and dealt with. If the level of the fuel drops below the manifold, then the head of pressure disappears and a vacuum will develop. The problem here is that in lieu of an annoying drip, air can be drawn into the system, resulting in an engine shutdown. I have seen many fuel systems where the manifold is raised up very high to the most convenient location. While this may seem like a convenient thing to do, it seriously reduces the reliability of the whole works.

I believe that an in-line, appropriately rated, automatically regulated fuel pump is essential to the quick servicing of filters and the occasional necessity of bleeding the fuel system. All engines are equipped with a mechanically driven lift pump that can be manually operated, but most lift pumps are of low capacity in the manual mode. During filter changes at sea, or if the engine needs a complete bleed, the lift pump can be very difficult to deal with. I've literally worn the skin off my thumb on the hot pump handle during these exercises and would be hesitant to go to sea without the inexpensive electric backup. The pump should be located between the supply manifold and the prefilters. When activated, it will supply a gentle pressure and flow of fuel through the filter and to the engine. The pump is designed so that fuel can flow through it unrestricted when turned off. When ready to change filters, simply turn it on. It will buzz up slightly then turn off—like a pressure water pump. Turn off the supply valve on the fuel filter, then disassemble the filter to remove and replace the element. With a bucket under the water-separator bowl, drain the dirt and any water that might be present. I often crack the supply valve to allow some new fuel to flow into the filter and flush the separator bowl as clean as possible. Reassemble the filter and, with the top slightly loose or the top bleed vent open, turn on the fuel valve slightly. The pump will go to work, and in a few seconds the filter will be completely full and the system ready to go.

If you are unlucky enough to inadvertently run a tank completely dry, you'll be particularly glad the electric pump has been installed. Simply switch to the new tank and go right to the injection pump, opening the last bleed screw there. The electric pump will go to work filling the lines and filter and will blow the air right out the single bleed port that you have the wrench on. It's a one-person, one-hand job! When clear, air-free fuel is present, the engine may start. Some engines will further require an injector or two to be released, but the whole process can be done within a short time relative to trying to do it all with a thumb-actuated manual lift pump. On the Lugger 6414 the lift pump is on the starboard side of the engine and the injector pump on the port. It's almost impossible to see what's being purged out of the injector pump while operating the lift pump, and bleeding is best accomplished by two people.

Of course, good fuel filters with water separators are an absolute requirement, and these filters also should be mounted as low as practical, relative to the fuel level. It is generally not practical to locate filters as low as the selection manifold because of the need both to see the filter bowl and to get a bucket under it for draining. I recommend filters plumbed in duplex so elements can be changed without shutting the engine down.

Along with debris, water must be separated from the fuel supply. Water can be a significant problem in a long-range powerboat due to the large size of the fuel tanks. For coastal cruising, most operators will elect to run on a reduced fuel load for reasons of economy. This leaves a lot of volume within the tanks full of moist air. The cooling and warming of the tanks can condense this moisture, with the water settling to the lowest point of the tank. When changing tanks, the water-separator bowl should be closely monitored for some time after the tank change. Water will accumulate quickly, and if after about a half hour of running, the bowl has not filled with water, the tank is probably reasonably free of water. Most of the fuel-filter manufacturers offer a water probe that signals an alarm or warning light within the wheelhouse when an excessive amount of water is present in the fuel. This warning system is probably well worth the minimum expense, but it's not a total substitute for visually monitoring the separator bowl.

Offshore in rough conditions, it is advisable to keep a close watch on the separator bowls and to pay particular attention to the fuel vacuum gauges. The excessive motion can stir up debris from the bottom of the tank and cause the inevitable water pocket at the bottom of each tank to jump up and enter the pickup line If there is a lot of water on deck, it could enter a vent line. I've seen boats operated for years without a problem—then in one kind of sea, with water boarding the vessel in an unusual way, with the wind just right, a flaw in design becomes apparent. In rough conditions a check of the water-separator bowl should be done as frequently as possible. A vacuum gauge is inexpensive and can prove invaluable in monitoring the condition of the filters. The gauge will show little or no vacuum with clean filters. As the filters begin to load up, the vacuum will increase. The filter manufacturer has a maximum permissible vacuum, and when it is reached, the filters must be changed. Note that vacuum will also increase as the fuel level is drawn down. The experienced operator will learn how much working time he can generally expect from clean filters; a quicker-than-normal increase in vacuum can signal an upcoming problem, which can be dealt with prior to losing power. An important side benefit of the in-line electric fuel pump is that it can be used to add a little pressure to the fuel system, forcing more fuel through clogged filters before changing is necessary. While this may seem like a lazy man's shortcut, it could prove helpful if a condition arises where leaving the helm to change filters is not practical.

A fuel-transfer system to maintain trim and to allow the last bit of fuel to be stripped from each tank and consolidated is an all-but-essential piece of equipment on the long-range cruiser. The alternative to this is running the engine until it shuts down due to air injection when the fuel is gone. Worse yet, sludge at the bottom of the tank could foul the filters, with the possibility of water overwhelming the separator and finding its way into the injection pump and injectors.

A system we have used with great success employs a simple marine-approved, automatically regulated DC pump—identical to the boost pump between the supply manifold and the prefilters. For a moderate-size vessel with about 1,000 gallons of fuel, this pump is adequate, moving about 50 gallons of diesel fuel per hour. Of course, on larger vessels or where quick transfers are necessary, a larger, vane-type pump is specified. The benefit of the smaller transfer pump is that due to the low flow rate, the fuel can be filtered with a moderate-size filter *while it is being transferred.* The ideal configuration is a separate fuel-transfer pickup line installed within a half inch of the bottom of the tank while the engine-supply pickup is 1 inch higher. Running the transfer pump effectively strips the bottom of the tank, with water and sediment the first to go—trapped within an appropriately rated filter and separator. It's very reassuring to see this water and dirt filtered from

Figure 7-4. *Transfer pump, manifold, and filter.*

fuel being pulled up well below the level of the engine-supply pickup. The transferred fuel can be returned to the selected tank through the existing return manifold or, for ultimate flexibility, through its own return manifold.

Monitoring fuel quantity is as important as any other aspect of fuel management. An absolutely accurate method of measuring remaining fuel is necessary. If conditions change and an increase in power is required, it is essential that after 24 hours the effect of that change can be clearly calculated. As mentioned in Chapter 6, a "How-Goes-It" curve is a useful tool when operating the vessel at the limits of its capability. An increase in speed may be decided upon by the skipper if fuel permits, or a reduction may be deemed necessary to carry the desired reserves to the destination. Daily assessment is imperative.

On a vessel with 1,000 gallons of fuel, it is necessary and reasonable to be able to determine the fuel level at any time, accurate to within about 5 percent of the total volume of fuel remaining. Say, for instance, the layout of the vessel's fuel system included four 250-gallon tanks. To determine the consumption difference between 2.5 and 3 gallons per hour, a 12-gallon-per-day change in consumption must clearly be seen and entered into the log and the "How-Goes-It" curve.

While an electric fuel gauge may prove acceptable on the coastal cruiser, it is useless aboard the long-range powerboat. I personally prefer the sight gauge and feel it is the most accurate and convenient method of monitoring fuel.

With a sight gauge on the side of each tank, the actual fuel level can be noted easily. A scale on the side of the gauge should be calibrated during filling, scaled in 10-gallon increments. At sea, the fuel level will rise and fall with the vessel's motion. A good, long look is required to note both the high and low surges to pick the point of average level for the reading. Each sight gauge should have valves at the top and bottom where the gauge enters the tank, and these should be closed when not in use. Sometimes closing down the lower valve to a small opening will dampen the rise and fall during readings.

Something to watch for is the effect of athwartship trim during fuel readings. I experienced this on a transatlantic voyage, reading port-side tanks with sight gauges on their inboard sides. As the fuel level dropped, the trim changed from a slight port list to a starboard list, causing the sight-gauge reading to show low consumption. The tank was rotating under the fuel, and despite its steady consumption, the trim change

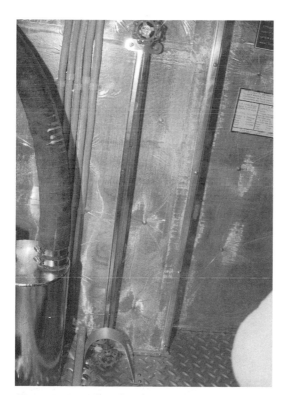

Figure 7-5. *Fuel-tank sight gauge.*

was causing a false reading. It was no big deal but caused some strange bumps in the "How-Goes-It" curve.

Sounding rods are a reasonable approach to fuel monitoring but have some drawbacks. The rods must be pulled from the top of the fuel tanks, which generally means this job is done within the living space of the vessel. It's a little messy, with fuel dripping off the ends of the rods, and there's no way to measure the average level of the tank since all you will see is the high surge. But if sight gauges are not practical to fit, sounding rods are the next-best thing.

There are numerous pneumatic monitoring gauges, which have proven to be very accurate. These sense the amount of fluid inside a tank by measuring the air pressure in a probe, which increases as the fluid level rises around it. At each reading the probe is filled with air with a small hand pump, and with careful calibration these systems can be successfully used—as long as they are cross-checked regularly with a sounding rod.

Aboard *Passagemaker* Robert Beebe used a fuel day tank, another popular method of fuel management. A day tank provides an absolutely accurate method of measuring consumption and also addresses other potential problems, but it does pose certain fuel-management responsibilities that should not be taken lightly. Properly used, a day tank will deliver an uninterrupted flow of extra-clean and water-free fuel to the engine under a light head of pressure—its greatest benefit. The problem is that the operator must be careful to make sure the fuel level within the tank is kept up. On *Passagemaker* the day tank held 32 gallons, which under cruising conditions had to be filled at least twice a day. The penalty for running out of fuel can be high, particularly in rough conditions where the vessel could assume a broadside position to the seas, causing excessive rolling and, at best, a major disruption aboard while the fuel system is being bled of air and the engine restarted.

The day tank can be filled with either a hand pump or an electric pump, and filtering the fuel of debris and water as it is being pumped into the tank virtually eliminates a sneak attack of the engine's enemies. If human error is avoided and the day tank is kept full, it can actually enhance the reliability of the system considerably. As long as you know exactly how much fuel you start with in the main tanks, and you keep an ongoing record of how much is pumped into the day tank (by reading and recording the amounts from the day-tank sight gauge), this can prove to be an excellent system. Personally, I would still sound the main tanks regularly on a passage to cross-check the running total of the day-tank fillings.

EXHAUST SYSTEMS AND ENGINE COOLING

Two types of exhaust systems are typically used aboard the long-range cruiser—wet and dry. Both offer advantages and disadvantages. Cooling the engine is greatly affected by the exhaust decision as the two systems are integral to one another.

The most popular cooling/exhaust system draws salt water into the hull with an auxiliary water pump. A strainer filters out debris, and the water is then pumped through a heat-exchanger that cools the fresh water circulated by a second pump around the engine block and exhaust manifold. The salt water is finally injected into an exhaust elbow where it mixes with and cools hot

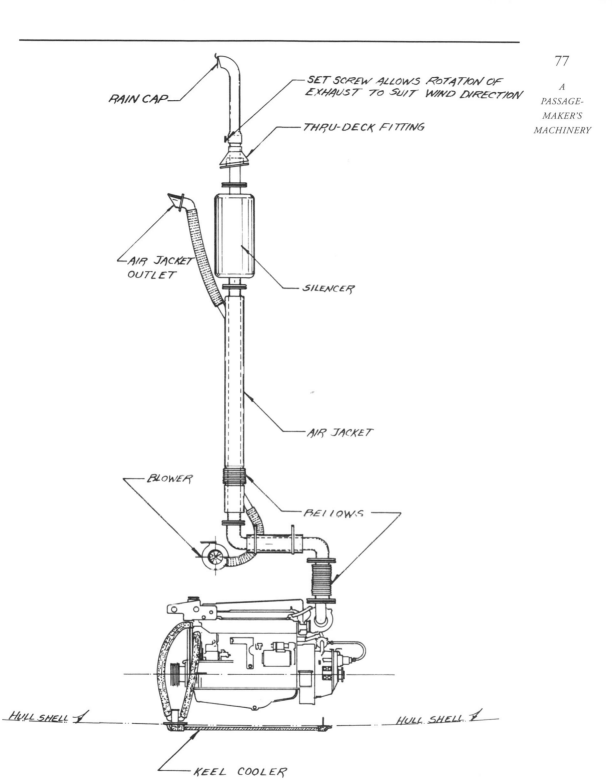

RAIN CAP

SET SCREW ALLOWS ROTATION OF
EXHAUST TO SUIT WIND DIRECTION

THRU-DECK FITTING

AIR JACKET
OUTLET

SILENCER

AIR JACKET

BLOWER

BELLOWS

KEEL COOLER

HULL SHELL

HULL SHELL

Figure 7-6. *Details of a dry exhaust system.*

exhaust gas. This rapid and drastic cooling allows the exhaust to be directed from the boat through a rubber steam hose. Generally a muffler is included in the system to silence the engine. The benefit of wet exhaust is the simplicity of dealing with the exhaust gas. The steam hose running to the vessel's stern can be routed around bulkheads and machinery with ease and minimal expense.

With dry exhaust, the cooling method generally selected uses a keel cooler to cool the fresh water circulated around the engine by the primary pump. The advantages of this type of cooling system are that it eliminates the need for an auxiliary pump, no salt water is drawn into the hull, there are no strainers to service, and problems associated with saltwater corrosion are all but eliminated. Dry exhaust generally provides greater reliability and increased efficiency. If a pool of experienced yacht owners were surveyed for problems associated with their diesel engines, fuel-related breakdowns would almost certainly rate number one—with cooling systems the number two aggravation. Most all of these cooling problems would be associated with clogged intake strainers, broken auxiliary-pump impellers, clogs or restrictions within heat-exchangers, or leaking injected-exhaust elbows. None of these problems can plague the dry exhaust system as all have been eliminated. The primary centrifugal pump simply circulates fresh water or coolant through the keel cooler, exactly the way an automobile engine circulates its water through a radiator. It's a completely closed system with no auxiliary equipment required on the engine except a water header tank and a cooled exhaust manifold. Efficiency is enhanced since the added drag of the keel cooler at low, displacement speeds is less than the power needed to run an auxiliary saltwater pump.

Dry exhaust can also increase comfort aboard while underway since the exhaust gas can be released well above the superstructure. This keeps the aft deck and accommodations free of exhaust gas and noise, regardless of wind conditions.

The problems with dry exhaust are all associated with the design, routing, and manufacture of the system. Great care must be taken with the entire assembly to deal safely with the excessive heat. Additionally, significant compromises may have to be made within the accommodations to provide for the vertical housing required to get the exhaust piping from the engine room up and out of the boat. If this takes place within the saloon (as it does in the Nordhavn), a significant amount of space must be allocated to it.

The entire exhaust housing must be lined with fireproof material, and clearances must be maintained throughout the exhaust run. A substantial increase in engine room ventilation is also needed as the exhaust housing will require a constant updraft of air to carry the residual heat. A further improvement is to incorporate shrouds around all straight runs of exhaust pipe and pump air through them to carry away the heat. Expansion bellows are also required to allow for expanding and contracting sections of pipe; a 10-foot run of stainless-steel pipe will expand almost ½ inch when fully heated by the exhaust. A large and effective muffler is required, and this too must be positioned in a very careful manner. The muffler will radiate a tremendous amount of heat due to its surface area and should be located outside of the exhaust housing in a well-ventilated, external stack.

In summary, I highly recommend dry exhaust, but for an economy-minded cruiser its cost may be prohibitive. Unless every precaution is taken, including a generous contribution to exhaust-housing space, it's safer to stick with the wet system.

Despite the high level of dependability of today's marine engines and transmissions, many feel that some source of alternate propulsion is necessary. Robert Beebe concluded that sail was not enough; some form of diesel-driven auxiliary was recommended on his designs. *Passagemaker* was fitted with a significant sailing rig, but despite a complete sail inventory, Captain Beebe felt it wasn't enough. From reviewing *Passagemaker*'s logbooks, there were times the vessel *was* sailed, but the performance proved barely acceptable. Speeds of 2 to 3 knots were noted, and a broad reach or run was the only course that could be laid.

We have found that the vast majority of buyers of our own vessels select auxiliary power, and I know of two cases where it was used with complete success. We devoted considerable research to the matter prior to selecting a system, and after three years of use, I feel the "wing engine" is ideal for a vessel in the 45- to 55-foot range.

During our research and design of auxiliary propulsion, we explored coupling the generator to the main propeller shaft, both hydraulically and through belts and chains. A generator-driven

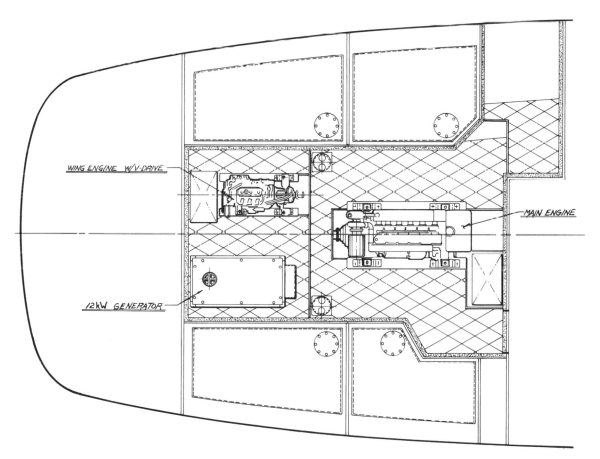

Figure 7-7. *Wing engine installation using a V-drive transmission.*

electric motor was also reviewed. One very distinct disadvantage of all these alternatives is they all drive the main propeller shaft. This only addresses a malfunction of the main engine or transmission. If the shaft coupling, propeller shaft, or propeller were damaged, or if the transmission failed and locked up, the auxiliary would be useless.

The main difficulties in adapting the generator to drive the main shaft are the lack of available horsepower and the loss of horsepower in the power transmission to the propeller. The propeller used on the average 45-foot long-range powerboat is probably in the neighborhood of 30 inches, and the propeller shaft should be about 2 inches in diameter. Testing shows that just to spin a 30-inch propeller at 400 rpm, more than 6 hp is consumed by the leading edge resistance and blade friction (this test was conducted with a special prop with no pitch). The added friction of the freewheeling transmission, stern bearing, and stuffing box also drains power prior to the development of any forward thrust.

Based upon simple calculations and experience operating our own 46-foot design, a 12.5-kW generator driving a hydraulic pump with a hydraulic drive to the main shaft would spin a propeller about 240 rpm. This duplicates the main engine's performance at the lowest throttle setting. While this would push the boat under a no wind, current, or wave condition, it would not do the job at sea. A 20-kW generator improves performance to a more acceptable level.

After further study, two additional and very discouraging problems became apparent. The equipment and labor required to install the hydraulic pump, build a PTO, modify the front of the generator sound box, include hydraulic reservoir, filters, cooling system, hydraulic motors, etc., etc., plus the added cost of a 20-kW generator (above a more suitable 8- or 12-kW) runs the price tag up to a point where it becomes unreasonable unless other hydraulic appliances are added to the system. In addition to the excessive cost, the manufacturers of the generator sets recommended against using a 20-kW generator because the light electrical demand of the boat—even if equipped with air conditioning—would cause the generator to run under such a light load that its service life would be adversely affected (a problem discussed earlier with the main propulsion engine). The concept of an electric motor using current from the generator and driving the main shaft produces similar problems.

One additional problem with all of the above systems is the requirement that the operator go into the engine room and couple the system to the shaft prior to use. This process may seem simple at dockside or during a calm-water sea trial, but just try it on a dark night in rough seas when you're tired and

Figure 7-8. *Main shaft and wing-engine shaft. Note feathering prop.*

maybe a little seasick. If your failure takes place within the entrance of a narrow harbor or close to a lee shore, you might not have time to complete the procedure.

The beauty of the wing engine fitted with a separate feathering or folding propeller is that it can be brought on-line immediately. The ultimate system includes a day tank with sufficient capacity to run for 12 hours (with a 30-hp diesel, about 10 gallons). This day tank should be kept full of filtered diesel, and even if the main engine fails due to a fuel problem, the wing engine is sitting there, warmed by the main and ready to get you out of trouble within seconds of a main propulsion failure (engine, shaft, or propeller). We have found that a 28-hp three-cylinder Yanmar engine swinging an 18-inch Martec folding prop will push our Nordhavn 46 at almost 6 knots and maintain headway into a significant head sea and wind. In addition to auxiliary propulsion, the wing engine can be fitted with high-output DC alternators and even an AC cruising generator.

On larger designs the use of hydraulic power off large generator sets is viable. On our own 62-foot Nordhavn, a 50-kW genset with a factory-installed front PTO (with electric clutch) provides up to 50 horsepower to a hydraulic pump driving a hydraulic motor coupled to a separate propeller shaft with a 20-inch MAX full-feathering propeller. The generator is completely factory designed for this type of application, and with extensive use of other hydraulics aboard the vessel, the hydraulic get-home system is a cost-effective installation.

The question of auxiliary power has to take into account the mechanical aptitude of the operator. With complete spares and with the ability to quickly replace a starter motor, injection pump, water pump, etc., the need for an auxiliary is reduced. The main components of the engine rarely fail, and it would be very unusual for the engine to be put out of commission due to an irreparable breakdown so long as the parts, skill, sea-room, and time necessary to effect the repairs are available.

CHAPTER 8

STABILIZING AGAINST ROLLING

OF HIS MANY CONTRIBUTIONS *to long-range cruising under power, Robert Beebe's work in roll reduction may be the most referred to and appreciated by today's cruisers and designers. Kolstrand Marine Supply, manufacturer of the patented stabilizing "fish," has relied upon Beebe's expertise for more than 20 years. The Seattle-based company still recommends that their customers refer to use instructions for the stabilizers that were developed through Beebe's experience.*

While designing *Passagemaker,* I was well aware of the infamous ability of small motorboats to roll viciously in any kind of a chop. Many hours spent holding on under these conditions and studying the problem convinced me that one basic requirement of a satisfactory power-only passage-maker is a method of reducing rolling as much as possible in the interests of comfort and reducing fatigue.

It was apparent in the beginning, and amply proved by our later experience, that rolling is one of the principal problems of power passage-making. We must, then, devote a good deal of thought to two problems: What causes rolling, and how to reduce it.

Briefly, the technicalities of the problem are these. Small craft do not follow the rules about rolling laid down for big ships. No combination of beam, draft, displacement, hull form, or metacentric height will reduce the roll to a satisfactory degree until you reach quite large vessels, say over 150 feet. It is important to understand this as there is still a lot of confusion on the subject, fostered by such things as a recent article on stability and rolling in a prominent boating magazine, which repeated the erroneous and obsolete idea of small and large ships rolling to the same rule.

Do not misunderstand me. The factors named above do have an effect on the amount of roll. But the effect of variations in these factors will not in itself reduce rolling to a degree that will be satisfactory to the crew. And, returning to the militant tone of Chapter 6, don't let any salesman tell you otherwise.

The reason it cannot is embodied in the concept of "forced rolling." That is, if the period of encounter with waves is greater than the natural rolling period of the ship, the ship will tend to roll in the period of the waves and not in its own period based on metacentric height. This tendency is true for small craft whenever rolling is a problem. For big ships, the reverse is true. In effect, what we call a "roll" is actually the boat trying to keep itself level with the surface of the water, as it is designed to do. But the damned sea surface keeps tilting!

In connection with "forced rolling," recent experience in this field reveals a seeming paradox: The more stable the vessel, the more it will roll when fitted with stabilizing gear comparable to that fitted on a less stable vessel. This was demonstrated when a new vessel—quite "stiff" due to hull dimensions, plus the temporary absence of appreciable amounts of topside weight—showed a roll period of 4 seconds; an older vessel of approximately the same size but with less stable lines had a period of roll of about 5.5 seconds. The geometry of their stabilizing gear, in this case the so-called flopperstoppers, was very nearly the same. Tests at sea showed the stiffer vessel rolled more than the other vessel while their flopperstoppers were in use.

This paradox is easily explained. As noted above, the "roll" in the forced-rolling situation is actually the attempt of the vessel to keep its waterline plane parallel to the water. As the boat tilts to accomplish this, the movement is opposed by the stabilizing gear, whatever it may be. With the "fish" being similar, the force available is the same. But the more stable vessel has more force generated by its shape to oppose the stabilizing force and accomplish its purpose of remaining aligned with the water's surface. Hence, it rolls to a greater degree.

While the two vessels were not tested simultaneously, persons who had sailed on both were quite aware of the difference. Estimates of the degree of difference varied from 25 to 40 percent. Four seconds is clearly too short a period for comfort. The usual range is 5 to 7 seconds in the 40- to 50-foot size. Without stabilizing gear, such vessels will roll more than a stiffer vessel, but with an easier motion. When stabilizing gear is put into use, they will roll less and still retain their easier motion.

Clearly then, period of roll is an important part of an overall evaluation and should be checked on any design you investigate. Roll is measured alongside the dock. With lines slack, one man can roll a 60-foot boat by either pushing up on the guardrail in time with the period, or by similarly stepping on the rail. When the vessel is rolling appreciably, time 10 over-and-back cycles and divide by 10 to give the period of roll. A vessel with a shorter period of roll is "stiffer" and has more initial stability.

Although the discussion above leads to the idea that increasing the period of roll by reducing initial stability would lead to even more comfort at sea while using stabilizing gear, this approach should be used with great caution as there are other factors involved. In particular, coupling an easily rolled vessel with extensive topside weights can well lead to catastrophic rolling due to the inertial forces involved. It was reported, for instance, that one yacht (a true trawler type), with extensive double- and some triple-decking, lost the use of its mechanical stabilizing gear in bad weather and rolled more than 70 degrees—with extensive internal damage. The trend in U.S. yachts toward increasing A/B ratio, which I inveighed against in Chapter 6, is an integral part of this problem.

What is needed is something external to the hull that will reduce rolling as much as possible. A good deal of work has been done on this over the years, but much more could be undertaken, particularly in the areas of reducing costs and enhancing simplicity. Devices in use fall into two classes: passive and active.

Passive devices essentially cause the roll to expend energy and reduce the roll by cutting down the energy left to roll the ship. They include bilge keels, keel plates, "flopperstoppers," or West Coast Anti-Roll Stabilizers, and steadying-rig sails.

Active devices actually produce a counterforce to the rolling force. They include *activated fins,* free-surface tanks, and U-tube or Frahm tanks. Such tanks will not work on small craft (they must be tuned to a steady period of roll) so we are left, as a practical matter, with activated fins.

To discuss passive devices first, bilge keels are so named because they are usually fitted at the turn of the bilge in large ships and have been used on these vessels for many years with good results. They project out from the side, perpendicular to it, about 1 foot wide in a 60-footer. Their length is as long as possible, and theoretically they should be lined up with the streamlines of the water passing the hull. It is obvious that such an alignment is pretty hard to accomplish under all conditions, and some drag other than surface friction of this keel can be expected.

It works out that bilge keels, while effective in large ships, do not suppress roll very much in small craft. Their bilge keels may be expected to reduce roll about 5 percent or thereabouts. To improve on this, *keel plates* have been tried. A keel plate is a horizontal plate fixed to the bottom of the keel, the plate projecting from each side about 10 inches. The idea is that the plate "turns" the water and projects it back against the motion, thereby doubling the bilge-keel effect of the ship's keel. Of course, all flat surfaces of a vessel, such as the deadwood and the rudder, have some bilge-keel effect. The evidence of keel-plate efficiency is conflicting. Some observers have reported the roll was reduced 10 percent; others have felt the plate did little good. For both bilge keels and keel plates it should be noted that their extra drag is present at all times, even when roll reduction is not required. The obvious reason these two devices do not do much good is that their lever arm times the antiroll force produced is not great as they are too close to the center of the vessel.

It is the big advantage of flopperstoppers that they greatly increase the lever arm, allowing a smaller surface to do the job. The way they work is shown in Figure 8-1. The stabilizer, which is shaped like a delta-winged jet plane, is towed from the end of a boom projecting from the vessel's side. The stabilizer is so shaped and rigged that it will dive down with little or no resistance when the boom rolls down toward it. But when the boom attempts to pull it up, it goes flat and resists the pull very effectively. My research has convinced me that the stabilizer can generate resisting forces up to 10 pounds per square inch of surface. This is no mean item in a 300-square-inch stabilizer; until we realized what a tiger we had by the tail and beefed up our gear to handle it, we had problems aboard *Passagemaker* with our F/S rig.

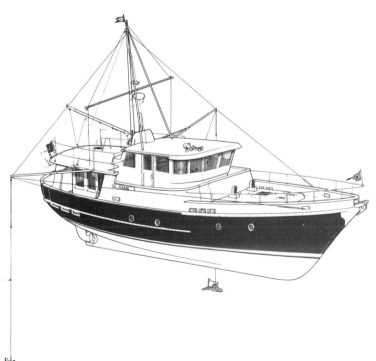

Figure 8-1. *Flopperstopper rig deployed on Nordhavn 46.*

Figure 8-2. *Activated fins installed on* Salvation II.

Steadying sails do a fair job when the wind is right and can even function in a dead calm when cut flat and strapped down hard amidships. But unless the rig is quite large, its effect will not match flopperstoppers. As we had both on *Passagemaker*, we could make the comparison. The practical result was we never used sails for steadying; the F/S gear was so much better. If there was a strong beam wind, we would use the sails to steady the roll to windward and a single flopperstopper on the windward side to steady the opposite roll. This produced good results and a slight increase in speed.

Turning now to the active devices, activated fins at present comprise the only system that is tested and available. It consists of one or more fins projecting from the side of the vessel. These are controlled by a gyro unit that commands a mechanism to turn the fins to oppose the roll. In effect, the fins work like the ailerons of an airplane. When conditions favor their use, they are the champions in roll-reduction, consistently turning in records of 5 degrees or less under conditions where the craft might roll up to 30 degrees without them.

In summary, there are two devices that lead the field: the passive flopperstopper and the active fin. In our case, the flopperstoppers reduced rolling by two-thirds, and our cruising showed this to be highly satisfactory. Fins can do better, of course, under certain conditions. But as a specification to apply to any device, I think our experience has established that reduction of rolling by two-thirds *on all courses and at all speeds* is a satisfactory *minimum requirement*.

This two-thirds reduction brought down our rolling to less than 15 degrees most of the time, and days with only 5 to 10 degrees were common. We had hoped for this and we got it. What we had not realized was the significant manner in which this would change the whole aspect of the way we cruised. And this is what I want to talk about now.

There were two significant by-products of roll-reduction. It made going to sea in *Passagemaker* a pleasure even for persons who had never been to sea before. And it reduced the fatigue factor from motion to just about zero.

Roll reduction made cruising with inexperienced persons possible as the environment produced by our stabilizing gear proved to be extremely comfortable. People cruising with us would come to the end of a long voyage and say they had never felt more fit. I finally figured out what was happening. The ship would always roll some, but the roll was not to a degree where you had to hang on, or use bunkboards, or brace yourself in a seat, or anything like that. Ordinarily one could stand without bracing if one wished, though a hand on something was more usual. At the beginning of a voyage, people would be a bit tired at the end of the day, but they soon lost this feeling. What actually happened was, there was just enough roll to give everyone a gentle isometric exercise of continuously tensing one muscle after another. This was tiring until you got used to it, then it induced a sense of fitness such as I personally have never gained in any other way. The essential thing was, there was never enough roll to cause increasing fatigue. Not for us the yearning to arrive at the next port so we could get some rest. In fact, on one passage from Panama to San Diego, the crew caucused and voted to ask the skipper to pass up Acapulco and keep going! I've never heard of such a thing happening in any other vessel. And, en route, it was seldom the crew was not entirely satisfied to leave any port in three days. This again is in contrast with sailing voyages where days—even weeks—may be spent resting and refitting.

It is apparent that there is a dividing line in average degree of roll that produces these contrasting results. It would be interesting to try to determine this limit and apply it to sailing voyages as well as power. Eric Hiscock mentioned this in his *Voyaging Under Sail* when he compared his fatigue to that of the crew of another boat that apparently rolled less than his did. It is too bad he did not examine this matter in depth.

As we have seen, there are only two practical methods of roll reduction good enough to meet our criterion of a two-thirds reduction. Let me give the advantages and disadvantages of each method. In doing this, I have nothing to sell. And I would be glad to hear the ideas of anyone who could contribute to revising these judgments. This is mentioned because a couple of articles in the yachting press that praised fins and glossed over their faults while disparaging flopperstoppers turned out to have been written by fin salesmen. This is dirty pool, to say the least.

Figure 8-3. *Anchoring stabilizers, top and bottom views. As the boat rolls one way, the stabilizer moves downward in the water and triangles of rubber allow the water to flow upward freely. Then, as the boat rolls the other way, the triangles form an unbroken surface and resist the upward movement, damping the boat's rolling.*

Advantages of Flopperstoppers

1. The rig is thousands of dollars more economical than fins.

2. They are not mechanical, so there can be no mechanical breakdowns.

3. They work on all courses and at all speeds. They are particularly efficient in running off before a gale at low speed, when they allow a course farther off downwind than is possible without them.

4. Using a special anchoring stabilizer, a simple device, they work when stopped or at anchor (see Figure 8-3).

5. The gear is out of the water when not needed, offering no resistance or damage potential.

Disadvantages of Flopperstoppers

1. Their rigging has special requirements that must be part of the boat's design and may interfere with the desired layout. The rig must be handled when put into use, a maneuver that could be difficult in heavy weather.

2. They cause drag, which reduces range. *Passagemaker* lost about 0.7 knot. Other ships, larger and smaller, have reported less. This means a continuous small fuel cost.

3. The "fish" are hard to launch and retrieve without special equipment, and may damage the sides of the vessel in the process.

4. In spite of continuing attempts to improve them in this respect, the fish are noisy in operation, transmitting a weird whine through the tow wire. Substituting the wire with appropriate-size chain can reduce this noise significantly as it is the harmonic vibration of the cable transmitted through the pole to the structure of the vessel that causes the noise.

Advantages of Activated Fins

1. They supply antiroll at the touch of a switch, which is very convenient.
2. They stabilize better than flopperstoppers at cruising speeds in ordinary seas.
3. They require no rigging that may interfere with the rest of the vessel's layout.

Disadvantages of Activated Fins

1. The vessel must be moving at a certain velocity to make them work. The minimum speed at which they are reliable is in dispute. Fin salesmen say 5 or 6 knots. More disinterested observers have said as high as 8 knots. The significance of this for running off before a gale is obvious.

Figure 8-4. *Close-up of activated fin with kelp cutter mounted forward.*

2. There are reports they do not work well running directly downwind; one user felt compelled to "tack" downwind.

3. They will not work at anchor or stopped.

4. Being mechanical, they are bound to break down sometime.

5. They are expensive. While progress in reducing costs has been made lately, if *Passagemaker* had been originally equipped with them, it would have increased her cost by some 20 percent. In considering their cost, don't forget to include the spares required and the installation charges.

6. Once fins are installed, they will forever induce added drag even when not in use.

7. Added care must be taken when gunkholing in shallow water or operating in areas where excessive debris may be encountered (such as the Pacific Northwest).

CONCLUSIONS

My conclusion is that, if your budget will permit, the well-equipped craft should have both roll reducers: fins for ordinary stabilizing at the touch of a switch and flopperstoppers for the hard chance, for use at anchor, and when the fins break down. Looking back on my own cruising, the courses we followed in strong winds and gales, and the speeds used, I cannot in good conscience recommend that an ocean-crossing motorboat be equipped with fins alone, equipment that would have been useless in a majority of our hard chances due to reduced speed and the courses followed.

The plain fact is that fins, no matter how convenient, cannot fill the specification our experience dictated; that reduction of rolling by two-thirds *on all courses and at all speeds* would be a satisfactory minimum requirement. This failure is due to their dependence on speed to make them work. Hence the recommendation to have flopperstoppers for the special situations.

Of course, if your budget will not cover fins, your only alternative at present is flopperstoppers. Make no mistake about it: *Stabilizing is an essential element of satisfactory passage-making.* I have had "rough and tough" sailors kid me about my concern for roll reduction. What they forget is that the motion of an unstabilized motorboat at sea is very much worse than that of a sailing vessel. A wind-powered vessel must set its sails to have the wind impinge on them. This has a great stabilizing effect, and the sailing cruiser is usually quite steady even if she does have a large angle of heel. The exception to this is running downwind, where a sort of synchronous rolling sets in. Reports of fatigue on long runs in the trades give this as the main factor. It would be easy to break up this rolling with a small, single stabilizer in the high-speed setting, under both sail and power, as the forces rolling the ship are not large but tend to build up.

As far as I know, *Passagemaker* was the first *yacht* designed to use flopperstoppers. We had to make quite a few changes in the rig before we got it to its present state, where it has been trouble free for years. Our experience produced certain rules that must be followed to achieve equivalent results:

1. The F/S rig should receive high priority in the design stage and not be tacked-on as an afterthought. Remembering that the stabilizing force is the pull of the stabilizer times the length of the pole plus one-half beam, poles should be made as long as they conveniently can be within strength limits in this highly stressed column.

2. The proper position for the ends of the poles in the working position is 28 percent of LWL forward of the stern. In all locations appreciably forward of this point, performance grows progressively worse. If located too far forward, when the vessel pitches up, both fish will resist, causing double drag, to no purpose.

3. Strength of rigging must be carefully worked out. A satisfactory result ensues if the breaking strength of the tow wire is used as the load and the rig strengths are made equal or better than this by graphical static analysis in the athwartships plane alone. (See Figure 8-5.)

4. The tow wire should be as short as possible while still keeping the fish underwater. Our rig, on a 15-foot beam with 20-foot poles at 30 degrees up angle, put the fish 14 feet underwater at rest. As we skipped one only once in a gale in the Aegean, that was about right. For those who wonder what happens if a stabilizer is pulled out of the water, ours soared straight through the air like a porpoise, dove back in, and went back to work.

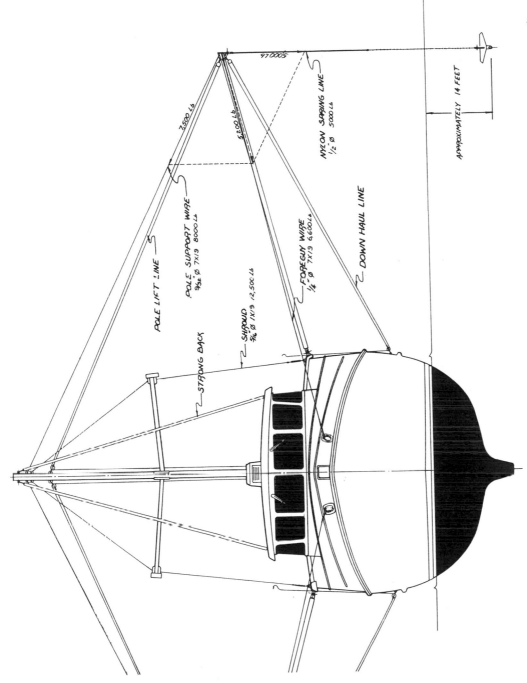

Figure 8-5. *F/S rig designed by Jeff Leishman for Nordhavn 46. Note the chain, shown here in lieu of
a tow cable—¼-inch High Tex with a breaking load of 7,750 pounds has been successfully used.*

5. A nylon spring of about 7 feet should be used in the tow wire to ease the strains on the rig from jerking.

6. The forward guy should be led as far forward as possible. The wire should be one size larger than the tow wire.

7. No rigging to the stabilizer other than the tow wire is required. It is absolute nonsense to have lines "to keep the stabilizer from going aft too far," or other lines suggested by some users.

8. The stabilizer sizes given in the Kolstrand Company bulletin on the subject work out well in practice. This company is the licensee for the patented most popular type. (Address: 4739 Ballard Ave. NW, Seattle, WA 98107.) We used the No. 300 size on *PM*. For tradewind running, where the rolling force is not great but the speed may become excessive running down the long swells, we wished we had some No. 192s. All stabilizers should be ordered with the high-speed arm (see Figure 8-6). The hole used for towing should be as far forward as possible while still keeping the tow wire taut when diving. The setting is very sensitive to speed.

9. Shackles located at either end of the tow wire and spring must have their pins inserted from *starboard to port!* If you don't do this, you will lose the whole assembly. The rhythmic pulling motion on each shackle causes the pin to rotate clockwise when viewed from the starboard side of the shackle. Don't learn this the hard way, as we did.

10. There is a great deal of wear at the towing lug on the pole. Parts should be well oversize. *PM*'s lugs are now ⅝-inch steel, 2 inches wide, using shackles with ¾-inch pins. When the hole wears egg-shaped at 7,000 miles, it can be built up with chrome-moly weldment and will then be good indefinitely. Towing shackles last about 15,000 miles. Dab them with waterproof grease when you get the chance.

11. A hold-down strut should be fitted to prevent the poles from flipping up if they are left out when there is no fish towing.

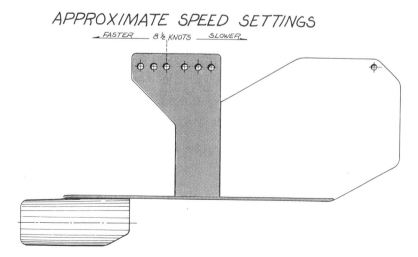

APPROXIMATE SPEED SETTINGS

FASTER   8½ KNOTS   SLOWER

Figure 8-6. *Stabilizer configured with a high-speed "arm." Speed settings for the shackle are approximate.*

12. Trouble with commercially produced stabilizer-towing nylon springs has occurred often and has been reported by several users. Apparently professional riggers do not appreciate how great and continuous the strains are on this spring. To my knowledge, at least four vessels have had eye splices pull out. So make your own. A satisfactory splice must have *at least five full tucks with three half-tucks!* The whole should then be tightly wrapped with plastic electrician's tape (which will stretch with the nylon). A marlin serving may be added, but this is mostly for appearance as the continual stretching of the splice will soon separate it—and the tape does the job.

HANDLING THE RIG

Passagemaker's rig used a pole that was held in place by forward and aft guys, the foreguy taking the strain when operating. It was a two-man job to put the poles out, as the aft guy had to have a tackle in it to adjust for the fact that the guys and the pole hinge were not in line with each other. The tackle's blocks would separate about 8 feet when the pole was lowered.

That one man could not lower the pole alone was a nuisance, particularly in some of my single-handed short trips. To fix this, the "singlehanded pole" was invented. As Figure 8-7 shows, the pole is equipped with a fixed aft guy and a strut to the pole that keeps it under control during the raising or lowering process. The foreguy is arranged to be taut in the down position and goes slack when the pole is raised. It can then either be cast loose and coiled up at the pole or held down by shock cords that take up the slack. It is important that the rig be adjusted so the strut does not put a bend in the pole when in use, as any such stress could lead to rapid failure of this highly stressed compression member. Strut end connections that have considerable play would be useful in avoiding this problem.

Picking up the fish can be done in two ways: When poles are out, Kolstrand's small, smooth grapnel can be thrown out to hook the wire, which can then be drawn in until the crew can grab it and hoist the fish the rest of the way. Or the pole can be raised, which puts the wire right in hand.

Figure 8-7. *A single-handed pole for an F/S rig.*

Figure 8-8. *Cable grab being fitted to a tow wire to pick up a stabilizer.*

Figure 8-9. *Cable grab supporting stabilizer's full weight.*

The singlehanded rig provides the easiest way to raise the pole and get the wire. This in-and-out drill is simple compared to the machinations we had to go through on *PM*. In the four vessels that now have the singlehanded F/S rig, retrieving the fish is accomplished routinely.

To further simplify matters, a "cable grab" (Figures 8-8 and 8-9) has been invented. The fish is not particularly heavy, about 40 pounds, but pulling it up by hand while grasping the slick wire requires four hands (two people) to do it easily. The new cable grab is made so it can be attached at the cable's middle, locked, and slid down until it hits the stabilizer; then any upward pull will grab the wire. Attached to the grab is a piece of manila rope, the rough surface giving an excellent grip and making lifting easy for one person. To make things even easier on vessels that can use it (like *Mona Mona,* described in Chapter 13), a small crane with a snatch block can project out from the overhead to allow the fish to be pulled in with a downward pull. The cable grab was greatly appreciated on its first test cruise, the only problem being that it was horribly expensive. Modifications to make it cheaper are in hand.

LATER DEVELOPMENTS

Robert Beebe certainly proved the value of the flopperstopper rig, not only on *Passagemaker* but on numerous other designs. My own experience has confirmed Beebe's conclusions, except that the

Figure 8-10. *A stab-
ilizer rig on a Garden-
designed 36-foot Vega
trawler model.*

Figure 8-11. *Carleton
Mitchell's 62-foot*
Land's End, *showing
her F/S rig. Note strut
that prevents A-frame
pole from kicking up.
She also carries
activated fins.*

F/S rig may actually work even better than he claimed when comparing it to active fin systems. I
have had the opportunity to make repeated open-ocean passages on different Nordhavn 46s—
identical boats except for the type of stabilizing gear selected—and encountered Force 8 conditions
during two of these voyages. One vessel was equipped with Koopnautic active fins with 5-square-
foot blades and the other with a flopperstopper rig using 300-square-inch Kolstrand fish on 18-foot
poles. I must say that the flopperstopper rig out-performed the active fins not only in the rough-
est seas but in moderate conditions as well.

An interesting observation of the active fin systems is their inability to deal with a "sneaker" sea
or one that is completely out of rhythm with the rest. The sneaker can cause the vessel to lurch,
oftentimes dislodging carelessly stowed gear or throwing a beverage can from a countertop. There's

no way of anticipating the sneaker, but as soon as the gyro senses the roll, the fins are deflected and things are brought back on an even keel. On the other hand, the deployed flopperstoppers fight the sneaker the very instant it hits and deeply dampen the disturbance. I've often been amazed at how rough it can be before things start falling off countertops when the flopperstoppers are in use.

Criticizing the active fin system is not to say I wouldn't recommend it. To the contrary, fins are a better choice for a good many owners. The handling requirements of the flopperstopper rig should not be underestimated, the effort required being somewhat comparable to dealing with sail aboard a sailing yacht. After thousands of miles in the Pacific and across the Atlantic with active fins, I think they work well, and I believe they are adequate for worldwide cruising.

It is true that I've never had to run downwind during a severe gale with an active fin system, and it is under these conditions they may not perform well; however, my opinion differs slightly from Beebe's in that my experience with *Salvation II* (which now has over 30,000 miles under her keel) and her Koopnautic fins indicates that nothing more is needed. I do agree though that once active fins are selected, the only negative aspect of adding flopperstopper gear is the added cost. By contrast, if you can deal with the physical requirements of the flopperstopper gear, it would be a shame to add fins, as the added drag and vulnerability to damage will forever accompany the vessel (see Figure 8-4).

The difficulties Beebe experienced with the flopperstopper gear revolved around deployment and retrieval, and with the noise created by the towing cables. Our own experience with the system has brought us to similar conclusions regarding the negative aspects of the gear. We have come up with a few alterations to procedures and design that address some of these issues.

The humming problem has been more severe on the Nordhavns than we anticipated, and I'm sure the problem is our use of extruded aluminum poles rather than the wooden poles used aboard *Passagemaker.* As a sailboat manufacturer it was natural for us to use our existing sparmaker, so our mast and poles have been custom fabricated to sailing-yacht standards. The lighter weight and design of the gear have dramatically reduced the effort required to raise and lower the poles, but the extruded aluminum transfers the humming and vibration of the cable right into the fiberglass hull structure. Additionally, the retrieval of the 300-square-inch fish has proved to be a significant chore, particularly in rough weather. The problem is that with the fish in its flying position, each time the vessel rolls or heaves, the 40-pound weight of the fish is dramatically increased, making retrieval without a block and tackle and cable grab, as described above, very difficult. After trying numerous variations, we have come up with a procedure that works quite well.

Figure 8-12. Eden II, *a 50-foot Krogen design, has an excellent F/S rig. Note that poles secure to the cabin side.*

Below the spring line we use chain—in lieu of cable—with a breaking strength below that of the spring line. Quarter-inch or ⁵⁄₁₆-inch chain has worked well on our Nordhavn 46s and has com-

pletely eliminated the bothersome humming. We haven't been able to measure the drag of the chain relative to cable, but it doesn't appear to be much greater. The harmonic vibration of the cable may, in itself, offer drag comparable to the nonvibrating chain.

Addressing the second problem, that of retrieval, the use of the cable grab is not possible with chain, but handling chain is far easier than handling small-diameter cable. A system that works well requires a retrieval line of about ⅜-inch diameter with a carabiner hook attached to the chain at a point slightly below the static waterline. When the vessel is running, the chain and fish stream aft, and this attachment point rises above the water. When retrieving the fish, the vessel is slowed and the retrieval line is pulled downward from a fairlead block attached to the overhead of the aft deck, bringing the tow chain alongside the gunnel. A block and tackle is then lowered from the tender boom, which remains on the centerline position above and is attached to the chain with another carabiner—as far below the retrieval-line attachment as possible. A three-purchase block and tackle fitted with a cam cleat makes easy work of raising the fish clear of the water and stowing it in its transom-mounted brackets.

Typically the F/S poles are lowered at the beginning of a passage, and the fish go in and out of the water as conditions warrant. On a recent voyage from Dana Point to Panama, the poles were raised only once—while docked in Acapulco. It is important to have a good method of retrieval without raising the pole, and using a grapnel doesn't work all that well. The problem is that the vessel has to be moving forward, and the hook is thrown in front of the advancing cable to catch it as it passes. Once the cable is caught, the boat must be stopped or the resistance of the wings will be so great it can't be pulled up. The process has to happen once on the port side and again on the starboard—slowing, then stopping, moving ahead, then stopping again. With the retrieval line the vessel simply has to be slowed once. The process of retrieving the fish in rough water is similar to raising or lowering a headsail on a sailing yacht. When the wind is blowing, there is a point when the sail can flog. The goal is to get through this precarious period as fast as possible; the longer the process takes, the greater the potential that someone will get hit by a flogging sheet or clew. With retrieval lines, the fish can be brought in very quickly.

CHAPTER 9

BEEBE'S PASSAGE-MAKERS—AND BEYOND

Turning now from PASSAGEMAKER and what was learned from her, and from the general requirements of designing and stabilizing, we will discuss how this experience and these rules have been applied to a new generation of Passagemakers. This chapter shows my own ideas on design. Later chapters have examples of work by other designers.

We have already shown the plans of *Passagemaker* and some of her smaller predecessors that were essentially sailing models with extended range under power—the type of vessel envisaged in my 1946 *Rudder* article on cruising in the postwar Pacific.

In recent years, responding to the requests of clients, I have found myself concentrating on Passagemaker types that will provide a real home afloat for owner and wife. This makes sense to me—for the truth is, as already mentioned, such vessels are becoming so expensive they don't make much sense unless they are used practically full time. Ideally, they should be used as homes afloat; then their cost can be viewed as the cost of any comparable home. Granted this premise, we can see a design will not fill the need unless it provides nearly all the amenities of shoreside quarters.

We are thus faced with a demand for superior accommodations. How to supply this need? One way was mentioned in Chapter 4, the use of double-decking. This can be seen at its practical limits in Bob Sutton's *Mona Mona* in Chapter 13. She is a real home afloat for living in the Mediterranean and, with her 1,200 gallons of fuel, can cross the Atlantic and return.

But she does have a high A/B ratio of 3.0, with lots of glass. And she cannot use the French canals (see Chapter 16). Would it be possible to develop a model that would be seaworthy enough to have no area restrictions, fit the French canals, and be a real home afloat, too? This was the problem posed by a client in Texas. What evolved is a yet-unnamed vessel, Design 96 (Figure 9-1).

This configuration comes so close to filling the specifications, I don't see how she can be improved. Not only does she gain room by double-decking the pilothouse, but is greatly improved in the galley/saloon area by having the midships cabin extend out to the sides of the vessel. As a result she has almost as much galley/saloon area as *Mona Mona*, a larger owner's cabin, a larger engine room (though with less headroom), and guest cabins just slightly smaller.

Besides the extra room, she scores with the pilothouse aft—much the best position for sea work.

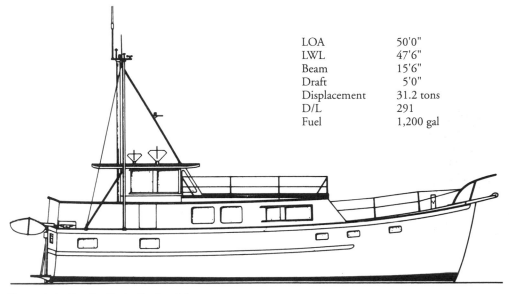

LOA	50'0"
LWL	47'6"
Beam	15'6"
Draft	5'0"
Displacement	31.2 tons
D/L	291
Fuel	1,200 gal

Figure 9-1. *Profile, Beebe Design 96.*

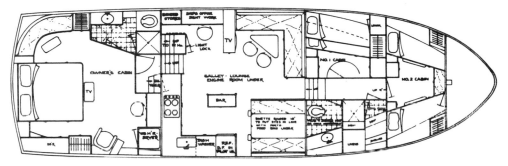

Figure 9-2. *Accommodation plan, Design 96.*

And she is planned to fit the French canals to the limits given in Chapter 16 if the pilothouse is broken down at the lower edge of the ports. Her comparatively low A/B ratio of 2.6, together with smaller areas of glass that are amenable to shutters, allow her to operate with no area restriction other than the usual one of voyaging in each area's best season. The penalties for all this, if you can call them that, are that one must go up and over the cabin to go forward, and her appearance is a bit unusual. As to the first, I have owned vessels built like this and found it no problem, especially in a motorboat where there should be no necessity for going forward in bad weather—there is nothing up there. As to appearance, it is interesting to note that five other designers recently have gone to the same configuration as it is the last remaining way to gain space. So I think we will see more of this design, and its appearance will be accepted.

The layout appeals to me so much I have repeated it in sizes from 42 to 50 feet. And the quest for more usable space has been carried to the logical conclusion of putting the steering gear

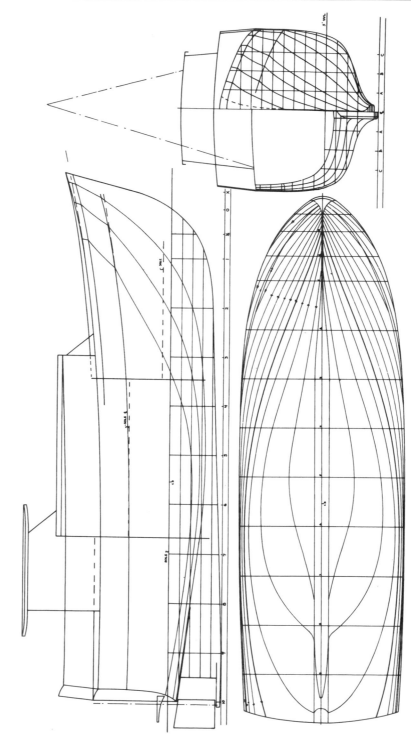

Figure 9-3. Lines, Design 96. In the final version the knuckle in the bow was removed. The unique double-waterline plan was to facilitate interior accommodation planning.

outside on the stern where it does not intrude on the aft cabin arrangement nor require the use of a lazarette for the rudder head. This also has the advantage of eliminating the rudderpost hole in the hull and makes the rudder accessible for repair.

As a matter of fact, the requirements of the client forced a review of the whole layout problem before the final features of Design 96 were settled. Here are the various factors affecting decisions that must be made about accommodations:

The problems of the motorboat are different from those of the sailing cruiser. Not only does the motorboat have larger engines but their maintenance demands more elbow room, workbenches, and the like. Then, too, fuel tanks become a major problem. If flopperstoppers are a part of the stabilizing gear, their positioning (to the rules given in Chapter 8) is of vital importance.

A sheltered steering station is essential, with an open-air station also desired by many owners. These must be capable of being completely blacked out to protect the watch-stander's night vision. The galley and dining area will generally be larger than in the sailing cruiser. The comfort of the cook is a cardinal principle. Large saloons with no convenient handholds must be viewed as dangerous at sea. With the motorboat's ability to drive hard into a head sea, an arrangement must be available for the crew berthed forward to come aft to sleep. As I learned aboard *Passagemaker,* while standing at the forward end of her fore cabin, such a vessel is quite capable of throwing you up against the overhead.

The possibilities offered by motorboat layouts for increased glass areas, compared to sailing vessels, must be approached cautiously, with consideration for location and suitability of storm shutters.

The designer must balance all of these factors, and more besides. Complicating his task immensely is one bane of his work—that human bodies do not change in size along with a change in boat length. Hence a layout that might work well at, say, 50 to 55 feet LOA, may not be practical or desirable in a smaller version.

Looking at what has been done in this field, several distinct patterns emerge. It is thus possible to classify many yachts by type of accommodations. Figure 9-4 shows my own classifications.

Type A is the most common arrangement, found in many sizes, from 50 feet down, among what are called trawler yachts. The first boats of this type appeared in the Pacific Northwest and were sometimes called "tri-cabins," an apt description. The Type A sketch shows how the boats are divided into three distinct sections: the bow with guest cabins and head; the amidships area comprising a central cabin at or a bit below the sheerline, with the engine room beneath; and the owner's cabin aft with its own head and shower. There is usually a lazarette aft of this, but as it is by no means necessary; it must be charged as part of the aft cabin in figuring space. The proportions of each section can be varied somewhat to suit individual owners. In the well-known Grand Banks 42, for instance, the breakdown from forward to aft is 13 feet, 14 feet, 15 feet.

The advantages of this layout are: it is simple and economical to construct, it concentrates the saloon and galley amidships, it provides a large engine room—though with rather restricted headroom—and it has a reasonable A/B ratio.

The main disadvantage of this layout, and one that in my opinion inhibits its use for really long-range passage-making, is the inability to black out the piloting area unless all other activities in the living area cease. This is hard to manage when someone has to wash the supper dishes or work up the evening stars, or if the off-watch crew wants to play cribbage. Banishing the watch-stander to the topside steering station during this period is unsatisfactory. The lights from the cabin

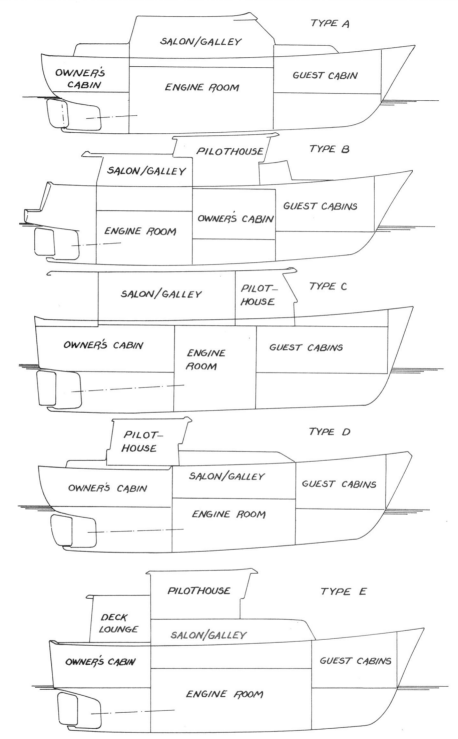

Figure 9-4. *These are the classification letters assigned to the various types of motorboat layouts discussed throughout this book.*

may bother him anyway, the weather may be inclement, or a radar watch may be desirable at the set, which is normally located below.

101

*BEEBE'S
PASSAGE-
MAKERS—
AND
BEYOND*

This layout has no double-decking and is about as simple as possible. Whether it is satisfactory is up to the individual skipper and his crew.

Probably the next most popular configuration is shown as *Type B*. This arrangement was brought to perfection by William Garden. His *Kaprice* and *Blue Heron* are great beauties. Unfortunately, this usually does not work out to best advantage unless the boat is 60 feet or so. Some attempts to use it in shorter models do not work out so well.

What has been done is to sink the saloon-galley down into the hull, aft as much as possible, and still put the engine under it. In smaller craft this results in the engine being what I call "sole buried." That is, the only access to the engine is through large hatches in the sole. While there are thousands of motorboats built this way, tucking the engine away inaccessibly in a seagoing vessel does not seem to me a sensible thing to do, inhibiting the regular inspection of machinery while underway.

The pilothouse is forward of the saloon and raised to give double-decking in its area, with a stateroom under it and other cabins forward. The result is all the cabins are jammed into the bow, certainly not the best place in a blow.

This model, nevertheless, provides a superb saloon-galley area and usually an excellent pilot house with enough room to be a social center—it is as large as the stateroom under it. In fact, for in-port living and entertaining it is hard to beat.

Clearly, for the greatest amount of interior room in a given length, double-decking must be used as much as possible. This arrangement we call *Type C*. The sketch shows how much room there is. The Grand Banks 50 shows this design feature taken about as far as it can go. And it should certainly be arranged to take advantage of the superb expanse of top deck, with regular stairways instead of vertical ladders.

Type C, however, is expensive, difficult to make handsome in sizes under 50 feet, has a poor A/B ratio, and other drawbacks. Nevertheless, it has a lot of appeal as a real home afloat. How one of them, *Mona Mona*, worked out at sea is the subject of Chapter 13.

To take care of the objections to the common Type A layout, the configuration shown as *Type D* was evolved. The revisions are: make the aft cabin full width without a trunk, as has recently been done in the Grand Banks 48, then place the pilothouse over it and aft of the center living cabin. The living cabin may be full width (as in Design 96) or trunked. The division of the three areas (again measured from forward in feet) can be quite variable. In Design 96, it is 19.5, 15, 15.5. In the 42-foot size my favorite is 14, 14, 14, with only two bunks forward. In 48 feet—considered to be the minimum length for fitting two good-size double cabins forward with separate head and shower—a consensus of several skippers came up with 16.5, 15.5, 16. And it does appear that 16.5 feet is about the minimum for this arrangement of two doubles. But, during our cruise in *Mona Mona*, my wife and I sketched out our own ideas of a 48-footer and came up with 20, 14, 14.

As this configuration is double-decked in the pilothouse, it has a clear gain in interior room of the length of the pilothouse over a similar boat not double-decked. For instance, a 42-foot boat in Type D would have the equivalent room of a 48-footer in Type A. This is an appreciable increase with no added length.

As for the size of the pilothouse, you have a deck area as long as the aft cabin to be divided between inside and outside spaces. The proportion to be allotted to each is an individual choice.

One might say that a yacht expected to spend the majority of its time in warm waters could well have the outside space larger. *Passagemaker*'s pilothouse was 5 feet from aft bulkhead to the steering wheel bulkhead. It was about perfect for the watch-stander's convenience, but when the rest of the crew showed up for happy hour, it got a bit crowded. Six feet would have been better and 7 luxurious. For outside eating on deck around a table, 7 feet is about the minimum.

Would it be possible to design a configuration with as much room as a Type C, yet with a more seaworthy shape and a lower A/B ratio? Some preliminary work for a client, who eventually turned to another designer for a Type C, convinced me that the answer could be yes. The sketch shown as *Type E* shows this. It consists of the essentials of Type D as a base: a midships full-width saloon/galley, and the cabin on the aft deck over the owner's cabin. But instead of this cabin being the pilothouse, it is an on-deck saloon connected with the outside area. It could be a bar, library, or TV room. The pilothouse is placed forward of it, on top of the midships cabin.

It may not look it, but Type E has as much room inside as the double-decked full-length Type C. In addition, it has several other features that recommend it: The A/B ratio is smaller; the pilothouse is aft of amidships—much the best place, in my opinion—and there is enough area aft so she probably will not sail around her anchor, as Type C does mightily. If there were full headroom in the engine room, she would have a bit of triple-decking, so we must be concerned about her inertial rolling as discussed in Chapter 8. But the aft and high position of the pilothouse allows it to be made much lighter, with thinner glass than is safe when the pilothouse is far forward. Visibility for all types of maneuvering would be superb, and the seating forward of the pilothouse is a highly desirable outside lounging area in good weather.

Unfortunately, we run into trouble with our incompressible people again. It appears that the layout must be at least 55 feet long unless the draft is much increased over the usual 10 percent of the length. But Type E has a lot of appeal and I intend to keep working at it.

There are other possible layouts, of course. Included among these would be those based on unconventional engine placement. Figure 9-5 shows Bill Lapworth's *Feng Shui,* which gains room by having the engine in the bow. The exhaust actually goes up the foremast. She is also interesting for the manner in which her topside cabin is kept small, with very large outside deck space. The *Mona Mona,* Chapter 13, goes the other way and places the engine in the stern with a V-drive. This was done to place the point where full 6-foot 4-inch headroom was required (that is, in the owner's cabin aft) farther forward where it is possible to lower the sole because the hull is deeper. There is not full headroom in the engine room, but it is quite adequate. This allows the top of the main cabin to be lower, and in fact, she has a lower silhouette than the GB 50 (which has a conventional amidships engine location) although the amount of double-decking is about the same. Both *Feng Shui* and *Mona Mona* have their fuel

Figure 9-5. *William Lapworth's 50-foot* Feng Shui. *The engine is located in the bow and the exhaust runs up through the foremast.*

tanks amidships with a short passageway between them. This allows the tanks to be so large in the athwartships dimension that 1,200 gallons uses only 30 inches of length, a very definite contribution to living space.

All of these arrangements must be fitted into the hull itself, which is the responsibility of the naval architect. And it was to help the reader to judge the architect's work that Chapter 6 was written. In addition to the factors discussed there, several others affect the hull and can be varied within limits to make the best overall solution to your needs. These include such matters as freeboard, flare of bow, beam, draft, and deck plan.

There are no particular rules for freeboard other than to be aware of its influence on the A/B ratio. But some general remarks about the effect of variations will be useful. It is usually judged at the bow, at the stern, and at its lowest point. I have already mentioned in Chapter 4 how we wished *Passagemaker*'s bow had been higher to increase the speed in seas from ahead without taking water over the bow. This problem actually has two parts—the height and the flare. That is, if *Passagemaker*'s bow had remained the same height but the flare of the sections had been increased, she would have been able to increase speed to some extent. But I am not at all sure I would want to do that.

Some years ago, in the 1950s as I recall, the matter of bow flare in fishing boats was a widely debated subject. The proponents of what might be called a "soft bow" claimed that such a shape would throw less spray in rough seas, and while the flared bow would admittedly keep solid water off the deck longer, it would also produce more spray that would be blown aboard in greater quantity. The debate was primarily concerned with the danger of icing up in freezing weather. While we do not expect yachts to encounter such conditions, the contrast between the two types of bow remains. At that time, I was inclined toward the "soft bow" school, and the lines of *Passagemaker* show this.

Since then, the debate, as far as motor yachts are concerned, has been won by the advocates of flare. The advent of molded fiberglass has allowed the pro-flare forces to flare bows to their heart's content, unhindered by the shape limitations of wood planking or metal plating. It does *look* good and, in fact, this is the main reason it is done. Naval architect Philip Bolger, when he was working in Spain, suggested to me that I use more flare "*para la vista*," as his clients said. Flare is recommended for "high-speed launches" in *Naval Architecture of Small Craft,* but for vessels proceeding under hull speed I remain unconvinced. The problem is this: When the flared bow goes over the top of one wave and down into the trough of the next one, the flare not only reverses this "down" motion to a new "up" motion more rapidly but also causes more deceleration in the forward motion due to the much greater relative increase in resistance as the broad part of the flare is immersed. I know from experience that flared bows can cause screams from the galley due to deceleration alone. I once went out San Francisco's Golden Gate, tide against wind, in a vessel with such extreme bow flare that it slammed very badly, throwing sheets of spray not only to the sides but forward. It seemed to me the owner was fooling himself. It's true we took no water on deck over the bow, but every time she bunted a wave we came practically to a dead stop. None of the crew appreciated it, and I don't think it was doing the vessel any good either. So my personal preference remains that I would rather slow down slightly, so the water does not come over the bow, and have an easier motion.

Freeboard amidships and at the stern is largely determined by desired accommodation. There seems to be no particular disadvantage to higher sterns. In fact, the high sterns of the dhow and the

103

BEEBE'S
PASSAGE-
MAKERS—
AND
BEYOND

Chinese junk have a great deal to be said for them. Not only does the stern provide superb accommodations, but because of increased windage aft, the hull shape heaves-to very well and lies quietly at anchor, while the higher-bow types sail around their anchors to a sometimes terrifying degree—terrifying to their neighbors, that is.

Low freeboard aft is largely a legacy from fishing vessels, where it is necessary to ease the work of getting the catch aboard. This is something that does not concern the yacht. What is important is getting the crew aboard, not only from the dock but from the water. It is vital, for instance, that there be some way for a man overboard to regain the deck unassisted. There are too many tales of crewmen, lulled by the safety of harbor, and working alone, who have fallen overboard and been unable to reach the deck of a high-sided motorboat. The minimum requirement is a series of combination handholds/steps. The ideal is the stern platform, originated on the Pacific Coast, which not only performs this function but provides a "sheltered harbor" that has to be experienced just once to be appreciated by someone climbing out of a dinghy in a blow.

Beam and draft combine to be determinants of hull volume and displacement; that is, beam at the waterline. There is no reason beam at the sheer cannot be increased separately if desired. It increases stability when a boat rolls deeply, and in this day of high dockage fees, provides space that is "free" if fees are based on overall length.

Draft is another matter that can stand variation. Shoal draft is not useful if the vessel does not go into shoal waters. But excessive draft can be troublesome in harbors. In a cruiser suitable for East Coast passage-making and crossing the Atlantic to enter French canals, my limit is 5 feet. Even so, in the Intracoastal Waterway and French canals you will bounce off the bottom occasionally. But these bottoms are soft—no trouble. In the Bahamas, less draft is preferable much of the time, though not strictly necessary. My observation of many boats reveals that draft usually runs about 10 percent of the length—a good general rule.

The deck plan (a view of the vessel from above) of many seagoing motorboats shows what appears to be a vestigial tendency to follow the form of sailing vessels: pointed at the bow, which is necessary, and curved in at the stern, which is not. A narrow stern does give better steering in a vessel that heels under sail or rolls deeply, but stabilized motorboats don't do this, so a narrow stern becomes a case of aesthetics versus practicality. In a vessel with living cabins aft, the urge to broaden the stern is almost overwhelming and certainly shows in my designs. When the engine is in the stern, one can have more inward curve to the topsides aft. But in the case of *Mona Mona* with her large deckhouse, the owner wanted the cabin straight-sided for building economy, so I did not pinch in the side appreciably even though the engine room is all the way aft.

Another consideration that affects the deck plan is the placement of the stabilizing gear. When flopperstoppers are fitted using the singlehanded pole recommended in Chapter 8, especially if the pole is stowed in the up position at the spreader of a mast also used for sail, then the line between the two hinges (pole and strut) must be horizontal and parallel to the centerline of the hull to seat the pole in the spreader notch when hoisted. Masts used for this purpose cannot have any rake. If the pole is secured to some other point, such as the overhang of the cabintop, the hinges can be out of line to some extent but placed to ensure that the end of the pole is exactly in line with the fastening of the topping lift to the mast in the working position. This is to ensure that no fore-and-aft strains are put on the rig and can be seen on the profile of Design 96.

NEW DEVELOPMENTS

105

*BEEBE'S
PASSAGE-
MAKERS–
AND
BEYOND*

Captain Beebe's experiences and ideas with his cruising concept continued to develop for more than 20 years after the launching of *Passagemaker*. His research was never ending, and a vast record of his correspondence with other designers, yachtsmen, and manufacturers of equipment exists, illustrating his unquenchable thirst for any knowledge that might help advance his work.

From a technical standpoint, Beebe's Passagemakers were all ahead of their time, and all would prove as useful and capable today as when originally designed. The fact of the matter is that—with the exception of electronics and construction techniques, along with some styling trends—not a great deal has changed. Beebe's forward thinking and the nearly inflexible rules of hydrodynamics collectively ensure that the majority of his work will be useful for decades to come.

Seakeeping and efficiency are the most difficult areas in which to effect improvements in the general performance of a vessel. The finest minds in naval architecture have pursued gains in these areas for hundreds of years, and it was long ago established that a vessel of a certain weight and shape generates a specific amount of resistance at given speeds and behaves in a predictable manner relative to the ocean upon which it rides. Of course, we now have more efficient machinery for propulsion and improved materials that allow greater flexibility in hull shape, but today's computer-assisted study of the relationship between these hull shapes and how they run through the water has yielded only moderate improvement, testimony to the skills of history's "slide rule" naval architects.

Bulbous Bows

During the development of a new 62-foot ocean-crosser, we decided to put strong emphasis on efficiency and seakeeping qualities. We were after a hull form with fine lines for minimal resistance and moderate initial stability for stabilizing ease. Our desire for efficiency was not only for the long range and cost-effective operation it would afford but also to reduce engine size for quieter and vibration-free operation.

We were aware that some progress had been made in the effect of modified bulbous bow shapes on the water resistance of vessels under 100 feet. Numerous commercial vessels in the Pacific Northwest were fitted with bulbs, and reductions in operating costs had been documented. While these moderate reductions in resistance seemed very appealing, it wasn't until we heard of the reported dramatic reduction in pitch motion that we really became interested.

There are very effective methods of dealing with roll, as detailed in Chapter 8, but pitch, a sometimes miserable motion when running into head seas, can only be controlled by a course change or reduction in speed. Decisions in the design process about bow shape will have an effect on pitch motion. As described by Robert Beebe, trying too hard to reduce pitch can create a bow that buries too easily. Conversely, designing a bow that will never bury can accelerate pitch in moderate conditions. When we heard that it might be possible to reduce pitch while not compromising the vessel's ability to run hard into head seas without burying her bow, we decided to pursue the matter in depth.

As our new vessel would be tooled up for fiberglass construction, large, expensive molds would have to be produced. The cost of an error in any aspect of the hull design could be financially disastrous. A decision was made to model-test the design for resistance and seakeeping qualities, and this proved to be a perfect opportunity to check the effect of various bulbous bows relative to a standard entry configuration. We contracted with the British Columbia Research Facility outside Vancouver and began construction of a 9-foot exact scale model of our proposed design.

BC Research conducted extensive testing for the fishing fleets of southeast Alaska and accurately predicted the effect of modified bows in model testing as proven by the sea trials of completed vessels. BC Research engineer Gerald N. Stensgaard was very helpful in suggesting the types of bulbs that might best suit our design.

It is difficult to predict the effect of a bulb. Jerry Stensgaard points out that the influence of the bulb on vessels they have tested has varied from being detrimental to showing an improvement of 15 percent at cruising speed, all on the same hull, with slight changes in the placement, depth, length, size, and shape of the protuberance. Model testing has proved to be an invaluable tool in adapting the correct size and shape bulb to a given hull.

With more and more testing, guidelines are beginning to emerge for shapes and sizes of the most effective bulbs. We tested two bulbs, both with a sectional volume equal to 20 percent of the volume of the largest midsection of our hull design. One was cylindrical and the other parabolic, with the largest section of the parabola just forward of the stem line. We understood that longer bulbs perform best, but anchor-handling restrictions limited the length on our boat to 1.5 times the diameter. We located the top of the bulb 30 percent of its diameter below the full-load waterline. The longitudinal alignment of the tube ran parallel with the waterlines, and the aft sections of the tube faired into the hull.

The finished model was first tested for resistance in a 270-foot-long test tank in a standard configuration (with a conventional fine-entry bow) on nine computer-monitored runs at speeds between 6 and 11 knots. The computer accurately converts the resistance measurements into effective shaft horsepower, which at all speeds tested correlated closely with the mathematical predic-

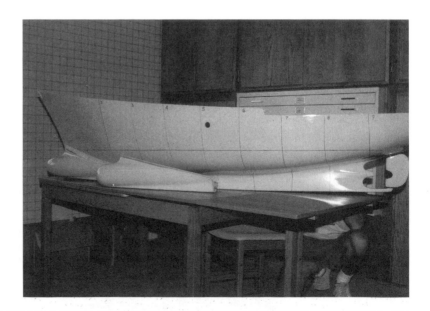

Figure 9-6. *Scale model of the Nordhavn 62 with the bulb at the bow and the second bulb that was tested on the same model.*

107

*BEEBE'S
PASSAGE-
MAKERS—
AND
BEYOND*

tions developed using methods reviewed in Chapter 6. We then ran the model at the exact previous nine speeds with the two different-style bulbous bows. The results were very satisfying, showing a reduction in effective shaft horsepower of up to 12 percent at the upper ranges of cruising speed. Based on the resistance test results, we selected the parabolic shape and began seakeeping tests to analyze the motion of the vessel at different boat speeds into head seas of varying frequencies. Again, we ran the model in a standard configuration (with conventional fine-entry bow) and measured for pitch amplitude, pitch acceleration, heave (at the center of buoyancy), and resistance. Eight runs were made using constant-height seas at four varying frequencies, with the model running at two different speeds. This data was stored in the computer, and we repeated the test using the parabolic-style bulbous bow.

We were again pleased with the results, which indicated a tremendous improvement in seakindliness, with a 20 percent reduction in pitch amplitude, an 18 percent reduction in pitch acceleration, and a 5 percent reduction in heave. The reduction in motion is primarily a result of the resistance of the horizontal surfaces of the bulb resisting vertical movement. This resistance is clearly demonstrated by the almost identical effective horsepower requirements of the standard bow and the bulbous bow while running into the worst of the head seas.

While the reasoning for the reduction in pitch seems easy to comprehend, the reduction in resistance is more difficult to understand. Frankly, I don't think anyone knows for sure what happens, but the most widely accepted explanation is that the bulb has an effect on the bow wave. It's been said that wavemaking (residual resistance) accounts for about 75 percent of all resistance with a vessel running at an S/L of 1.34, and it increases as the S/L climbs. At an S/L of something around 0.9 and below (depending upon hull shape and type), frictional resistance actually climbs above residual resistance. The tests clearly showed that the bulb began to help around an S/L 0.95, with 7.7 percent reduction at an S/L of 1.09, 8.3 percent reduction at S/L 1.22, 10.9 percent reduction at S/L 1.36, and finally, at an S/L of 1.49, the reduction in resistance was 12.4 percent. At an S/L of 0.82 (6.3 knots), the frictional drag caused by the bulb's added wetted surface actually required 12.9 percent more horsepower than the same vessel without the bulb.

The above test results seems to support the theory that the bulb affects the bow wave. The explanation I've heard is that the perfect bulbous bow creates a pressure wave that is equal in amplitude but opposite in shape to the normal bow wave. This welling of water from below tends to

Figure 9-7. *Model without the bulb running at S/L 1.48. Note formation of bow wave, trough, and stern wave.*

Figure 9-8. *Model with bulb running at S/L 1.48. Note trough and stern-wave reduction.*

reduce the bow wave and the divergent waves that follow. Don't worry if this doesn't make sense to you; the foremost experts in the field can't all agree. And some new bulb types on ships are showing up to 15 percent improvement in resistance operating at S/Ls below 0.6, where there is supposed to be almost no residual resistance at all. This certainly seems to suggest that there might be something more to the bulbous bow than its effect on wavemaking.

BC Research Tank Test Predictions—Nordhavn 62

Knots	S/L	Hp Required	*Gal/Hr	**Gal/Hr
6	0.8	22	1.32	
7	0.9	35	2.10	
8.0	1.1	58	3.48	
8.5	1.15	75	4.50	
9	1.20	95	5.70	
9.5	1.28	127	7.62	6.23
10	1.35	178	10.68	8.74
10.5	1.40	244	14.64	11.98

*Figured using 0.060 gallons per horsepower per hour

**Figured using Caterpillar 3306 DITA—best fuel burn of 0.350 pounds of fuel per horsepower per hour

Comparing the above tank test results with actual performance data collected during sea trials and a passage to Hong Kong requires consideration of the active fins stabilizers (12 square feet), an 18-inch feathering propeller for auxiliary propulsion, a 12-inch bow-thruster tube, and two large pods that housed side-scanning sonar transducers. Based upon experience, the fin blades alone should slow the vessel by ½ knot at higher cruising speeds.

At 1,850 rpm the boat ran 10 knots and burned 10 gallons of fuel per hour. Based on a fully advanced throttle and higher than normal pyrometer readings (exhaust gas temperature), we concluded that the vessel was overpropped, as the engine is rated to run at 2,000 rpm, where it will produce 228 SHP and burn 11.8 gallons of fuel per hour. As tested, we concluded that the 3306 Caterpillar was developing about 200 hp, or about 22 hp (or 11 percent) above the tank test predictions.

Considering fin and appendage drag, and that the vessel was tested at a weight considerably

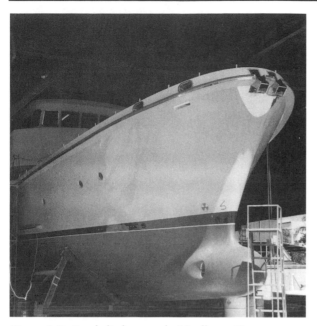

Figure 9-9. *Parabolic bow on the Nordhavn 62.*

109

*BEEBE'S
PASSAGE-
MAKERS–
AND
BEYOND*

above her designed half-load (tank testing was for a vessel in a half-loaded condition), we felt that the actual performance of the vessel was very close to or slightly better than what was predicted by BC Research during the tank test program. It was recommended that 1 inch of pitch be removed from the propeller at first haulout to allow the engine to develop its full rated horsepower and increase top speed slightly.

During our tank testing, David Hamilton, an experienced owner of one of our 46-foot Nordhavns, was as impressed as we were with the test results. Our discussions soon revolved around what the effect of a bulbous bow would be on the 46, and we reasoned that for less than the cost of actually model testing the 46-foot design, we could install a bulb designed around the same relative dimensions as the tested 62 bulb. If the result was unacceptable, the bulb could be removed with the total cost still below that of model testing. The availability of reasonably priced fiberglass tubes (of all diameters) meant the cost of a cylindrical tube would be far less than the parabolic shape for the retrofit, and since

Figure 9-10. *Actual performance of the Nordhavn 62 closely matched tank test predictions of BC Research.*

Figure 9-11. *Cylindrical bulb retrofitted to the bow of 46-footer.*

the noted difference between the two shapes during the 62 testing was negligible, we decided on a cylindrical bulb.

A few months later the job was completed, and after careful testing through a measured mile and in offshore conditions, the bulb proved to be a complete success in the area of pitch dampening, which was the owner's main goal. We were somewhat disappointed that the addition yielded only a 4 percent reduction in resistance at an S/L of 1.34. We concluded that with the fuller lines of the 46-footer and greater beam/length ratio, the bulb did not reduce resistance to the degree it did on the 62-foot design. Jerry Stensgaard (of BC Research) felt the smaller boat *could* benefit more from the bulb and that we might not have gotten the best shape and size combination for the boat. It's all a very imperfect science and, at this point, the sea is not giving up all her secrets. Tank testing seems to be the only reliable way to predict the bulbous-bow outcome.

Although I'm satisfied that the benefits to efficiency and seakeeping far outweigh any disadvantages, a well-rounded discussion of the bulbous bow would not be complete without touching on the points of criticism.

The bulb does have the ability to catch floating debris, nets, and line (which may be better than driving everything down to the running gear). In the event of a collision with a heavy object, the energy of the impact might not be absorbed by the vessel riding up and driving the object under the way a standard stem might. On the other hand, if the bulb is foam-filled and includes a collision bulkhead where it intersects with the normal stem line it could act as a great sacrificial bumper, crushing and absorbing tremendous impact while preserving the integrity of the hull.

The bulb can cause some pounding under very specific sea conditions, and this was noted during tank testing. As the bow drops into a trough, water displaced by the bulb breaks away from the bulb's upper surface and rushes inward—horizontally—slapping the sides of the advancing ship only a couple of feet above the waterline. Subsequent experience aboard bulb-equipped vessels has confirmed the slapping, but it has been mild and occurs only in very specific conditions. A slight course change will generally minimize this phenomenon.

Ducted Propeller Systems

Another interesting subject with potential for yacht use is the ducted propeller, or *Kort nozzle*. After years of definitive testing and actual use, variations of a shroud or tunnel around a modified propeller have proved to increase bollard pull (static pull) and the towing capability of a vessel over that of a similar ship with an open conventional screw. Having devoted significant effort to reducing resistance in our design by incorporating the bulbous bow, we were interested in the further potential increase in performance the ducted propeller seemed to offer.

I have always found it discouraging to see the efficiency ratings of various propellers. For example, our Nordhavn 46 fitted with a 30 x 22 four-bladed prop and a three-to-one reduction gear has a propeller efficiency of only about 60 percent. That means for every 100 shaft horsepower consumed, only 60 horsepower is effectively converted into thrust; the rest is lost to propeller slip, cavitation, friction, etc. The concept of improving efficiency has great appeal, and there is evidence to suggest a ducted propeller can reduce loss of this precious horsepower.

One of our 46s was recently retrofitted with a nozzle built by Harrington Metal Fabricating and Machining in Fennville, Michigan. According to the engineer at Harrington, the predicted result of the nozzle is an increase in bollard pull from about 2,200 pounds to almost 3,500 pounds, but the benefit decreases as the vessel begins to move forward toward its cruising speed.

Unfortunately, at the time of this writing, preliminary testing has yielded disappointing results. Nozzle designer Nils Lucander is confident that when the proper propeller is fitted, the vessel will be able to maintain the same cruising speed with about 20 percent less shaft horsepower. As speed increases, the benefit of a nozzle is ultimately negated by the nozzle's added drag, but this point is generally expected to occur significantly over displacement speed.

For towing applications the nozzle's benefit is well documented, and nozzles are gaining popularity in ice-breaking vessels, which closely relates to towing. In ice-breaking applications, many find the nozzle offers the additional benefit of protecting propeller tips from ice damage. I can think of situations where the shroud around the propeller could be either beneficial or detrimental, depending on the type of collision or grounding, but generally it probably offers greater protection.

In a conventional centerline propeller arrangement with a single rudder, the installation of a nozzle will result in an increase in the turning radius of up to 30 percent if the rudder is not modified. If significant benefit is derived from the nozzle, this would not deter me from considering the change since low-speed maneuvering using propeller blast against the rudder would not be as adversely affected, although propeller-blast maneuvering with a conventional rudder would be compromised somewhat by the turning resistance of the added vertical surface area of the nozzle sides. Conversely, directional stability might be enhanced by the nozzle, particularly off the wind in rough conditions. Commercial vessels designed with nozzles generally have multiple rudders installed within the back of the nozzle that actually enhance propeller-blast maneuvering over a conventional open-screw arrangement, and this could be adapted to the motor yacht.

Two additional and very important reported benefits of the

Figure 9-12. *Propeller nozzle designed by Nils Lucander. (Photo courtesy Nils Lucander)*

ducted propeller are a reduction of cavitation and of propeller noise. The nozzle controls and directs the water out the stern, whereas the tips of an open screw throw water off at high speed that collides with the hull above, creating rumble and vibration. A standard part of any noise-control program on a new yacht is the incorporation of sound and vibration dampening into the propeller aperture and surrounding area. This construction effort illustrates the significance of the noise problem.

Cavitation is likely to occur at higher propeller loads, where the vessel is being pushed to higher S/Ls. Low pressure developing on various areas of the propeller causes a breakdown in the boundary layer of water flowing over the propeller blades. An absolute vacuum develops within which the water actually turns to low-temperature steam. As these pockets of steam collapse back against the propeller, a snapping, high-pitch screeching sound can be heard. Ducted propellers seem to work best under heavy loads, as evidenced by the dramatic effect on bollard pull, and the nozzle's effect of reducing cavitation may be partially responsible.

I've had a difficult time collecting definitive data that would support the nozzle's benefit for a yacht running free at normal cruising speed in open-ocean conditions. One study suggested that the ducted propeller offered efficiency improvement in calm conditions, but when running into head seas more horsepower was required to maintain a given speed than was necessary for the same test model with an open screw. One would expect the opposite to be true as bucking a head sea might simulate a towing situation, but speculation was that the irregular flow of water into the intake of the nozzle caused by the pitching motion had an adverse effect.

There do appear to be benefits to be gained with variations of the Kort nozzle on the long-range motorboat, but further testing is required.

Bow Thrusters

A good many of today's single-engine, long-range cruisers are fitted with bow thrusters. Despite the fact that a deep and heavy Passagemaker will have a good grip on the water and, with relatively low windage, should be quite manageable in tight quarters, some maneuvers can be difficult without control of the bow—their success depending upon quick and decisive control inputs by a skilled operator. Directional control forces are conventionally exerted by the rudder at the stern of the vessel, and in tough conditions the stern can be under control but the bow is responding to wind and current. This same problem can be faced by the twin-screw operator, but to a lesser degree.

The addition of a bow thruster allows complete control of both the bow and the stern and allows a captain of only moderate experience to virtually scoff at the toughest of docking requirements. Mediterranean-style moorings can be handled with a calm and ease never before possible.

Twelve-volt electric thrusters, while limited in power, are popular on smaller boats (under 45 feet), offering the most economical means of controlling the bow. For a more serious application or a larger vessel, a hydraulic system must be considered.

Figure 9-13. *Bow thruster.*

A 5-hp 12-volt thruster works well in moderate conditions, but when the wind on the beam gets above 12 to 14 knots, this low-power unit can only be relied upon to hold the bow of a 45-footer in position and not much more. A more powerful 12- to 15-hp hydraulic unit is more useful, but the expense runs almost *three times* that of the electric system. Operating off of a main-engine hydraulic pump, the thrust at idle is about comparable to the 5-hp electric unit, and for added thrust engine rpm must be advanced. This requires bringing the transmission into the neutral position, then advancing the throttle (single-lever controls are out) to generate the horsepower required to spin the thruster up to its rated power. This calls for fast hands as the throttle will quickly have to be brought back to idle, the engine must spool down, and then the transmission can be engaged; and don't forget the need to spin a sizable steering wheel back and forth to maintain control of the stern.

I view a bow thruster as a valuable aid for docking and maneuvering in light to moderate conditions only—probably 90 percent of time. I know from experience that in a really tough scrape, where there's a lot of wind, an experienced captain will be so busy spinning the helm and managing the main engine and transmission that he may not even reach for the thruster control—except for slight adjustments after the docking is essentially made.

113

*BEEBE'S
PASSAGE-
MAKERS–
AND
BEYOND*

CHAPTER 10

THE ECONOMY PASSAGE-MAKER

IN ALL THE DISCUSSION OF passage-makers in the previous chapters, the emphasis has been on taking our fund of experience and evolving the perfect next boat, if such a thing is possible! Here we must face the fact that a vessel with all the desirable design features plus comfort and convenience equipment to make her a true home afloat becomes quite expensive—well beyond the reach of all but a fortunate few. Can we lick this? Can we develop an economy model that will lengthen the list of owners?

Well, we can at least try, and a discussion of the factors involved may provide useful ideas. First, size. Regardless of whether a boat is commercially built or home-built, it appears that cost-per-pound tends to remain more or less steady as weight is varied. Thus we see a pressure for smaller, shorter, lighter boats as a route to economy.

But this approach immediately conflicts with several other factors: accommodation, cruising speed, and storage capacity, all of which would be better if the boat were larger. From a naval architecture point of view, for instance, waterline length is a critical factor in the speed/length ratio. That is, two boats of the same weight could attain the same S/L ratio with the same horsepower, but the longer one would make a greater speed in knots, apparently adding speed at no extra cost. But in this imperfect world, such things don't happen. Greater length means never-ending higher costs for berthing and haulouts. In fact, the extraordinary rise in berthing costs in certain areas is starting a trend toward vertical stems and sterns, together with increasing beam, as exemplified by my 42-footer, Design 101. Length also has a virtue at sea in that it delays the onset of pitching by "bridging" waves in higher wind speeds longer than the shorter vessel can. Of course, the pitching time eventually comes for every vessel, even 1,000-footers. I was aboard one once when it pitched so hard in heavy weather its bow was torn up.

In ordinary coastal winds of 15 to 20 knots—wind speeds often encountered at sea—there is a marked difference of motion between vessels of 28- to 32-foot WL and those around 46-foot WL when steaming into the waves. The shorter-WL vessels will need to slow down when the wind reaches about 15 knots while the larger ones will forge ahead well until the sea is liberally covered with whitecaps at, say, 20 knots. As will be discussed in Chapter 15 "Voyage Planning," seagoing motorboats try to avoid these courses. But such steaming conditions are experienced by all boats, and on the West Coast they are a major fact of life. Based on the area to be cruised, a prospective owner must decide how important a longer WL would be to both motion and speed, and select these design elements accordingly. Unquestionably, this discussion tends to show the superiority of the longer waterline for those owners who will not often be subject to the tyranny of docking fees: the retired, long-range cruising folk and the like.

But if a boat is made longer, with weight remaining the same, it follows that she must have decreased beam or draft, or both. As her D/L decreases she becomes more prone to the ills of relative lightness. This leads to an increasing A/B ratio and lack of stability to carry topside weights. In fact, such a procedure soon prohibits double-decking. Can such a boat be satisfactory?

Certainly it can, if you feel you can settle for a hull without any double-decking. The amount of room required to keep the crew happy is a personal thing and can be largely the result of prior experience. We found, for example, that the people who bought *Passagemaker* thought her accommodations were huge because their former boat was a 45-foot yawl. I've met people living quite happily full time on a Grand Banks 42, yet she seemed much too small to my wife and me after five years aboard *Passagemaker*. And so it goes. I really cannot give definitive advice on this subject; each decision is personal.

Below I have summarized some pertinent points that bear on this problem:

1. The influence of D/L on available space. I have noted that a 44-foot boat with 37-foot LWL, weighing 16.5 tons for a D/L of 325, has actually made voyages of 17 days underway with a crew of five and had almost 400 miles of fuel left on arrival.

2. The length for "bridging" waves calls for as long a boat as you can afford and militates against the ultra-small vessel for open-sea work.

3. The lighter a boat is, the more lively its motion and the greater the need for good stabilizing gear.

4. With more dependency on stabilizing gear, it is also more important to make careful provision for easy handling of the gear to keep it set properly for speed.

5. With the livelier motion, particularly pitching motion, it is critical to ensure crew comfort. Ideally the pilothouse, galley, dinette, and sleeping accommodations should all be concentrated amidships or a bit aft. As this is impossible, be careful how you make your compromises. Consult the cook!

To further explore the question of length, we must remember that a well-designed passagemaker will do its long passages at speed/length ratios between 1.1 and 1.2, and will be able to run locally at hull speed or a bit better. So here is a table that shows these speed values:

| | Knots | | | Days to Make 1,000 Miles | |
LWL	S/L 1.1	S/L 1.2	S/L 1.34	S/L 1.1	S/L 1.2
25	5.50	6.00	6.70	7.60	6.90
30	6.03	6.58	7.35	6.90	6.33
35	6.51	7.10	7.93	6.40	5.87
40	6.95	7.59	8.48	6.00	5.49
45	7.38	8.05	9.00	5.65	5.16
50	7.78	8.48	9.48	5.36	4.91

On *Passagemaker* we did our preliminary planning on the basis of 1,000 miles a week, and always did better. *Passagemaker's* best run was 210 miles in a day with a strong beam wind and all sail set. Her worst run was 90, going up the West Coast into the teeth of the summer northwester, averaging this speed for three days until we rounded Cape Mendocino. My personal preference in balancing all the above factors would be not to go below 40 feet LWL, but I've been spoiled by longer waterlines.

THE HUSBAND-AND-WIFE BOAT

The early long-voyage sailors who followed in the wake of Joshua Slocum were often eccentric loners, what we today frequently call "dropouts." While there are still such types sailing the Seven Seas, the tremendous proliferation of "world voyagers" in the last few decades has been primarily in husband-and-wife teams. Without doubt, foremost among ocean voyagers was Eric Hiscock and his wife, Susan, who in their *Wanderers* circumnavigated the world so many times that most of us lost count. Hiscock's *Voyaging Under Sail* (International Marine, 1981, incorporated in *Cruising Under Sail)* is still the bible of the long-range voyager.

This group is also exemplified by the Seven Seas Cruising Association. Chapter 15 urges prospective voyagers under power to read both Hiscock and the bulletins of the SSCA. Here, we will only give their comments on the matter of size for the husband-and-wife boat.

Hiscock bluntly says, "The bigger the better, provided the crew can handle her," and cites couples who have handled sailing vessels up to 46 feet in voyages around the world. The SSCA did a poll of its members and arrived at an "average recommended size" of 38 to 42 feet for a husband-and-wife sailing vessel.

These experts are primarily concerned with shorthanded sail handling, which is not a motor-boat problem. It is notable that this advice does set a low limit of 38 feet as suitable for full-time living and cruising for a crew of two. I agree with this because I reached the same conclusion some years ago by a different line of reasoning. There are husband-and-wife teams cruising the world in smaller boats, but I wonder if they are entirely satisfied with their space.

Beebe's Concept

Throwing all this into the pot and sticking to my preference for a minimum LWL of 40 feet, a first try at an economical Passagemaker might look like Figure 10-1.

Design 105 shows certain basics I would like in any boat. No overhang aft and very little forward seems indicated by conditions previously mentioned—economy, slip rentals, etc. The vertical stern offers two advantages: It is best for a stern platform, an item I would not do without, and it makes possible an outboard-mounted rudder so there is no hole in the hull and easy access for repairs. An anchor-handling bowsprit is also required. The heavy guardrail is needed not only for rough overseas docking but to protect the stabilizing-gear hinge.

She is 42 feet overall. The enclosed pilothouse is from amidships forward. It is long enough to permit a high bunk in line with the ports, as recommended for singlehanding in Chapter 3. When not used for this, it could be lowered and used as a settee, though there is also a permanent seat for the watch-stander. The engine will be under the pilothouse with nearly full headroom. Aft, right on the center of gravity, is the galley and dinette for four, and abaft that, the owner's quarters with head and shower. The mast, primarily for the stabilizing gear, rests on the bulkhead

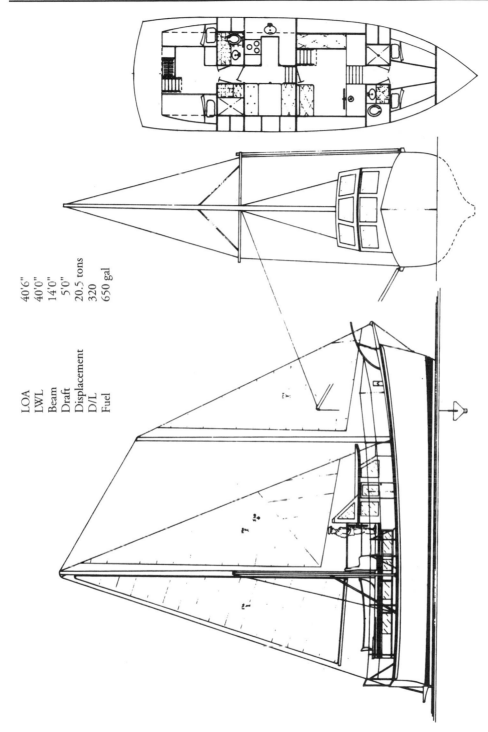

LOA   40'6"
LWL   40'0"
Beam   14'0"
Draft   5'0"
Displacement   20.5 tons
D/L   320
Fuel   650 gal

Figure 10-1. *Profile and accommodation, Beebe 42-foot Design 105.*

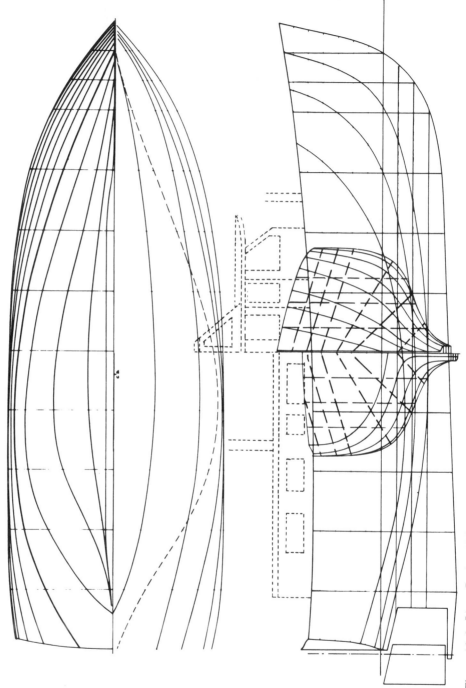

Figure 10-2. *Lines, Design 105.*

between cabin and galley. It is located forward of the ideal position but not excessively so. The mast can carry some sails to play with, but if sails are the emergency power it would be well to have more area. We must remember that a motorboat's sailing rig is a touchy question. If large, ballast must approach sailboat amounts to prevent the vessel taking a knockdown from rig windage alone.

I prefer this layout to one having the pilothouse farther aft and the galley forward, as we have found it easier to put up with motion away from the center of gravity in the pilothouse, where everyone is or can be seated most of the time, than in the galley, where the cook has a stand-up job. It is also easier to provide a truly dark pilothouse for the watch-stander with this arrangement. The engine room is under the pilothouse with headroom of 5 feet 6 inches.

With a displacement of 20.5 tons, she would have a D/L of 320 and need 650 gallons of fuel to go 2,400 miles at an S/L of 1.1. She could easily be made "French-canal capable" (see Chapter 16). She is well suited to the type of cruising discussed in Chapter 18 ("Round the World Passage-Making") and broadens the field of husband-and-wife long-range cruising for those without the experience, strength, or inclination to consider a purely sailing voyage.

A Later Approach

Almost adhering to the preferred waterline length minimum, one newer vessel that appears capable enough and could truly fall into the economy category—for a new build—is a design by George Buehler. *Diesel Duck* was designed for a West Coast couple coming from sail and wanting a powerboat capable of some long-range cruising, including use within the Pacific Northwest. Maximum accommodation and capability within a minimum length were prerequisites for this design, and Buehler and his clients have come up with something worth looking into.

It is interesting to note that the waterline length of *Diesel Duck* is an inch longer than her on-deck measurement and 20 inches longer than the hull waterline. This, of course, is a result of the large outboard rudder, and it's debatable whether this extended waterline length should be used for S/L ratios when calculating performance. The outboard rudder certainly does contribute to directional stability, is virtually foolproof, and can benefit engine placement and shaft angle due to the extreme aft position of the propeller.

Economy abounds in this design. Substantial beam and a long waterline make economical use of expensive slip space, and its construction material is well suited for the small custom yard or backyard builder. With ¼-inch steel plating, *Diesel Duck* is built to last. Many steel vessels of this size use plating half that thick, but Buehler points out that the stout scantlings were requested by his clients, and he was happy to oblige. Throughout the design process emphasis was placed on strength, reliability, and simplicity, and despite the heavy scantlings one would be hard-pressed to find a capable cruiser that could be built more economically.

Figure 10-3. *Buehler-designed* Diesel Duck. *(Photo courtesy George Buehler)*

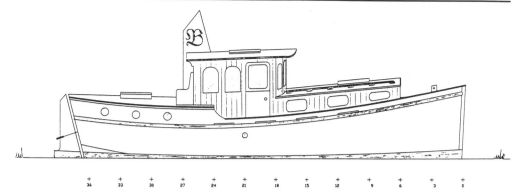

Figure 10-4. *Outboard profile,* Diesel Duck.

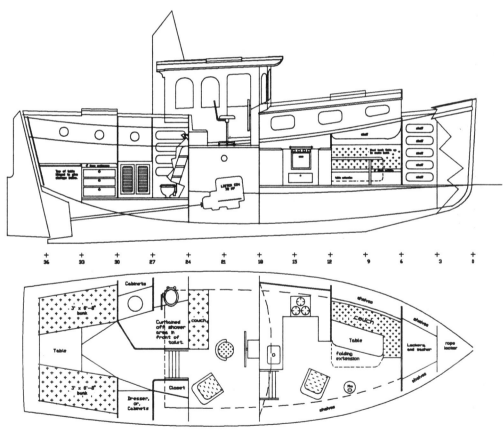

Figure 10-5. *Interior layout,* Diesel Duck.

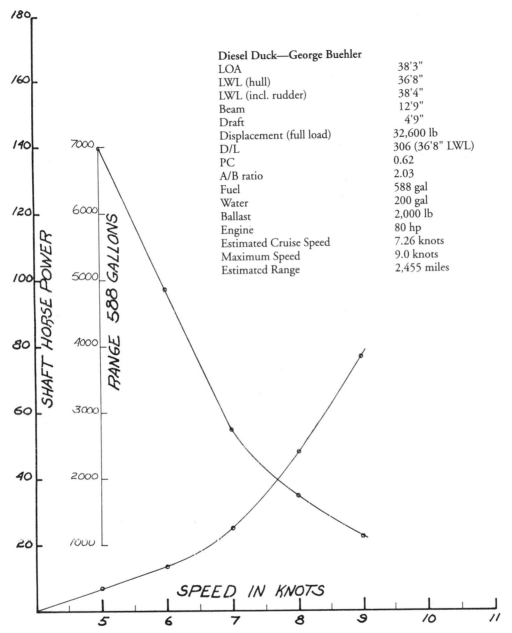

Diesel Duck—George Buehler

LOA	38'3"
LWL (hull)	36'8"
LWL (incl. rudder)	38'4"
Beam	12'9"
Draft	4'9"
Displacement (full load)	32,600 lb
D/L	306 (36'8" LWL)
PC	0.62
A/B ratio	2.03
Fuel	588 gal
Water	200 gal
Ballast	2,000 lb
Engine	80 hp
Estimated Cruise Speed	7.26 knots
Maximum Speed	9.0 knots
Estimated Range	2,455 miles

Figure 10-6. *Range graph for* Diesel Duck.

Interior accommodations are completely dedicated to maximum comfort and space for only two people. This approach provides true liveaboard space, even within the confines of 38 feet. In a pinch the forward settee could serve as a double berth for guests or, as an alternative, pipe berths could be rigged above each of the two single berths aft. For a couple wishing to cruise primarily without guests, this makes sense. During longer passages when help might be needed, four good sea berths would be available in the aft cabin. After the passage the upper pipe berths could be stowed until needed again.

A full-standing engine room is provided under the wheelhouse, and a diesel engine of about 80 hp is specified. Fuel capacity is 588 gallons, split between two tanks located outboard of the engine, with the top of the starboard tank serving as a tool bench and storage shelves located above the port tank.

It should be quite easy to adapt a flopperstopper rig to this design with the addition of a mast just aft of the wheelhouse. The centerline bulkhead of the head compartment could be adapted to handle the compression loads, and the poles could mount on the outboard edge of the deck—just far enough inboard to be protected when docking. With the addition of sturdy rails, *Diesel Duck* should be well suited for long-range cruising.

Using the formulas from Chapter 6, *Diesel Duck* could run at an S/L of 1.1, or 6.6 knots, for 2,610 miles and still have a 10 percent reserve. Crossing the Atlantic, the 1,800-nautical-mile leg from Bermuda to the Azores could be made at an S/L as high as 1.2, or 7.26 knots. With an all-out range at this speed of 2,113 miles, this would provide a reserve of more than 15 percent. These figures do not reflect the added drag of stabilizing gear, which can decrease range up to 10 percent.

George Buehler quickly points out that in lieu of *Diesel Duck* he has larger designs offering multiple staterooms, aft lounging decks, and more conventional arrangements; and there's always the option of working a few more years to accumulate the funds necessary for a larger vessel. However, at the front of the Buehler design catalog a quote by Sterling Hayden offers a word of caution: "The years thunder by. The dreams of youth grow dim where they lie caked in dust on the shelves of Patience. Before we know it, the tomb is sealed. . . . "

COSTS

Robert Beebe built *Passagemaker* in 1962 for about $43,000. As mentioned in Chapter 4, *Passagemaker* left Singapore with only the most basic equipment, and by today's standards she was extremely simple. Her interior was not complete, she lacked refrigeration, had no generator, and was void of any electronics except an autopilot and depth indicator. She was not even equipped with a radio transceiver. Despite this simple configuration, she was cruised successfully and enjoyed immensely.

As Beebe stated, "Whatever the costs are, they are sure to go up—that's about the only certain thing you can say." While this is certainly true, the good news is that it is probably less expensive to go voyaging under power today than in the 60s. This may sound ridiculous, but remember that to acquire a powerboat suitable for passage-making more than 30 years ago was almost impossible—so much so that Beebe had to design his own and then travel halfway around the world to have it built, investing a year of his own time supervising construction. *Passagemaker* was a simple vessel, built in an extremely economical location with Beebe dealing directly with a small and cooperative builder. Think of the home that could have been purchased in 1962 with $43,000 and then compare it to the cost of a *new* but comparable home today.

Of course, building a custom vessel nowadays is extremely expensive but fortunately not a necessity as it was for Beebe. There are suitable new semiproduction yachts available and a wide range of brokerage vessels that, with a little modification and upgrading, can be fine ocean-crossers. A good argument could probably be made that the same $43,000 (with an assigned value for Beebe's design and supervision) adjusted for 30-plus years of inflation could buy a new semiproduction vessel comparable to *Passagemaker* today.

With regard to construction materials, Beebe notes that wood, steel, fiberglass, and other materials all have something good to be said about them, and something bad, too. He also notes:

Chapter 13 tells the story of an owner-built boat—a large, one-off fiberglass vessel of my design. I have also seen an owner-built, Airex foam-core fiberglass vessel, 62 feet long, on which a gang of five laid down her lines, set up the mold, and applied the outer skin in 10 working days. The ingenuity and tenacity of the better amateur builders are something to behold. I heard of a charter boat operator out of the West Indies who needed a new boat, went to the Puget Sound area, hired a Hertz truck, filled it with red-cedar planks, and drove it to Florida. He found a building spot, set it up, built a triple-planked hull, and was ready to charter again in six months! (And then someone came along and made him an offer he couldn't refuse. So now he is a boatbuilder again.)

So we can be sure, no matter what the problems and the escalation in costs, there will always be individuals ready to tackle the difficulties and overcome them to get their dream vessels. They are a dedicated bunch and have minds of their own. If the ideas in this chapter can help them a bit, it will have served its purpose. Good luck!

CHAPTER II

FROM SAIL TO POWER—THE NORDHAVN SERIES

*V*OYAGING HAS LONG BEEN THE domain of the sailor, but as Bob Beebe so eloquently stated about offshore sailing:

> *It is an activity of youth, or for those older men and selected women to whom it has become a way of life over a period of years. I know whereof I speak: I have done my time on the end of a bowsprit muzzling a jib on a black night in the middle of a squall, and enjoyed every minute of it. But even the experienced sailor arrives at a time when that sort of thing loses its appeal. And for many, the long passage under sail is effectively barred, because they have come to their love of the sea late in life or they have wives and families who do not share their enthusiasm.*

While my own company's 46-foot design can't claim exclusivity to the term "a sailor's power-boat," that is certainly what we intended her to be. After 10 years of delivering more than 200 sizable cruising sailboats, the idea of an alternative for the type of use our sailboats were getting became more and more a topic of my own thoughts.

We had produced a 63-foot ketch designed by Al Mason that, despite excellent sailing characteristics, was referred to as a motorsailer. Based on earlier designs by Philip Rhodes and John Alden, these beautiful sailboats featured a raised deckhouse and a wonderful cockpit. Equipped with dodgers and generally with soft enclosures, the six we produced were all fitted with Detroit diesels of sufficient horsepower to maintain 8 knots, even into weather, and carried enough fuel to run in excess of 2,500 miles.

I had the pleasure of making numerous passages aboard these vessels during deliveries between boat shows. We were shorthanded and had to maintain a strict schedule, making show dates from Newport, Rhode Island, to Houston, Texas. These passages were all offshore, and due to limited crew and tight schedules, we ran the engine much of the time. The experience of consistent 200-mile days, an enclosed cockpit entered through a door, a proper helmsman's chair, a quiet, smooth-running engine, and a raised deckhouse with windows one could really see out of all had a profound effect on me. This was a more comfortable and capable vessel than any sailboat I had operated in the

Figure 11-1. *Mason 63 motorsailer.*

Figure 11-2. *Jeff Leishman.*

125

*FROM SAIL
TO POWER—
THE
NORDHAVN
SERIES*

past, and I was most impressed by how easy and pleasurable it was to motor wherever we wanted. We arrived rested and on time, and the fuel we burned each 24 hours was less expensive than a businessman's hotel room.

As time went by, I found myself dreaming of cruising not on a sailboat but aboard a rugged, cruising powerboat. I began to research some of the few long-range cruisers and fell in love with some of the Romsdal, Garden, and Seaton designs. It wasn't long before I discovered Robert Beebe and *Voyaging Under Power.* Jim Gilbert's preface to the second edition caught my complete attention when he stated: "We want the pleasure of voyaging without undue hardship. We want to be tested, but not tortured. We want to experience what is basic and elemental in voyaging and at the same time take full advantage of the wonderful technological innovations that are the birthright of the 20th-century man."

I had found the beginning of a solution to a problem—an alternative to sail that could offer a higher degree of success to some of the many people I knew who wished to cruise the world's oceans.

THE NORDHAVN 46

Our long-range motorboat evolved conceptually over a period of years, but it wasn't until 1987 that the design was completed. So convincing were Robert Beebe's recommendations that we tried to stay within the parameters outlined in the original *Voyaging Under Power.*

An interesting point about this design is that its development was virtually free of marketing and business influence. In fact, the preliminary design work was done as part of the final requirements for Jeff Leishman's degree in naval architecture through the Yacht Design Institute in Blue Hill, Maine.

Making the conversion from a professional draftsman and practical yacht designer to a *naval architect,* Jeff was required to submit an academic powerboat project, which presented me with an opportunity to develop my own thoughts and to make use of Jeff's exceptional drafting ability, all on company time. Pacific Asian Enterprises (PAE) had been exclusively involved with sail, but funding higher education within the design room, and encouraging it on company time, gave professional justification

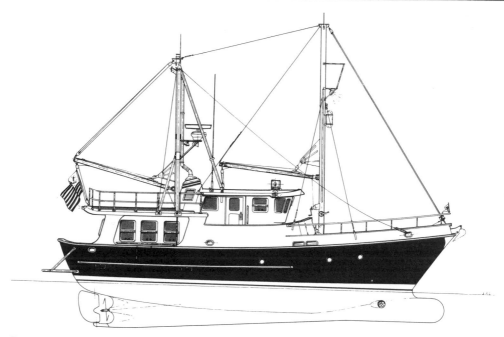

Figure 11-3. *Outboard profile, Nordhavn 46.*

to this departure from the company specialty. I like to think of this as a very successful design and believe it does lend credibility to Beebe's assertion that an amateur, without professional restraints, can go where his interest and passion take him—which often results in exceptional work.

As we say, "The Nordhavn 46 was designed on a completely clean sheet of paper." This was not a larger or smaller version of a previous vessel, and we were not influenced by any competitor's design. We were able to develop completely every aspect of the design, applying our own standards to aesthetic details and including accommodations and features that we felt necessary for seakindliness and seaworthiness, all from a sailor's perspective.

Being so familiar with the living space in our own 44-foot and 54-foot Masons, Jeff and I used these vessels rather than other powerboats as a measure of what was acceptable for the live-aboard cruiser. We developed numerous profiles and layouts, ultimately settling on a design 45 feet 9 inches overall, with a waterline length of 38 feet 4 inches. Our association with Al Mason and the evolving Mason series of sailboats had given us an appreciation for classic styling. We felt overhangs would enhance the appearance of our powerboat design, hence the significant spread between LOA and LWL.

With a beam of 15 feet 5 inches, a draft of 5 feet, and displacement approaching 50,000 pounds, the available interior volume seemed enormous. It quickly became obvious that the living space available in our 46-foot powerboat design was significantly greater than in our 54-foot sailboat. This design seemed to offer our target customer the best combination of ample accommodations with a size reasonably managed shorthanded.

127

*FROM SAIL
TO POWER—
THE
NORDHAVN
SERIES*

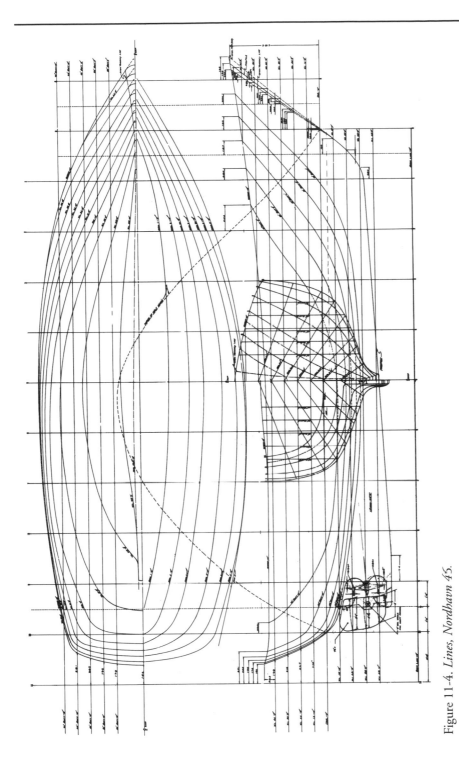

Figure 11-4. *Lines, Nordhavn 45.*

Our undertaking was unique: we were designing a semiproduction boat to be promoted as a go-anywhere offshore cruiser suitable for shorthanded passages normally possible only under sail. An honest design approach was essential to ensure the boat would be adequate for its intended use. After delivering 40 of these vessels, I still feel our size selection was appropriate but don't disagree that smaller or larger can better suit specific requirements. Chapter 12 provides examples of other long-range vessels—ranging from 39 to 70 feet.

The Hull

The hull design of the Nordhavn 46 is quite conventional other than its relatively high displacement/length ratio. The high D/L is primarily due to heavy scantlings but partially to the shorter waterline length. With the same displacement and an increase in waterline length to 40 feet, the D/L changes from 383 to a more moderate 337. While I would still retain the heavy scantlings, in retrospect I think the vessel could have benefited, at a minimal compromise to appearance, with slightly more length on the waterline.

In actual use the hull form has proven to work well, providing wonderful steering qualities, a period of roll only slightly too fast, and a pitch motion that is a good compromise when you consider that the vessel can proceed into extreme head-sea conditions without burying her bow. As detailed earlier (Chapter 5), I've seen our 46-footer outpace a 100-foot-plus motor yacht against head seas exceeding 15 feet. I attribute this exceptional windward ability to the reserve buoyancy in the bow, due in part to flare but more to ample overhang. In moderate head seas the ride is really quite comfortable, with the bulk of reserve buoyancy high enough that it doesn't come into play until conditions get rougher. Then pitch acceleration becomes greater as the bow rises quickly enough to prevent water from coming aboard. The high D/L of this design minimizes deceleration when passing through such head seas.

For a fully loaded vessel with a moderate amount of weight on the boat deck (dinghy and outboard), the period of roll is under 5 seconds. It had been our goal to keep the initial stability at the upper end to reduce the amplitude of rolling when the vessel was not fitted with or using stabilizing gear. While the stiffer hull does reduce roll, the acceleration and deceleration of the roll is a little snappier than ideal. I actually never noticed this until we started fitting a flybridge to the design as an option. The added weight of the bridge caused a softer, more comfortable motion than in the standard version. We noticed this phenomenon when we added a foremast to some of the boats; the moment arm of the mast slowed things down just enough to make a difference. We now encourage our owners to carry a sizable dinghy and deck boxes on the boat deck.

This mild critique of our own design is only intended to illustrate the importance of getting exactly the right amount of stiffness in a hull. I'm always amazed at the way people make assump-

Figure 11-5. *The Nordhavn 46 powering into head seas.*

129

*FROM SAIL
TO POWER—
THE
NORDHAVN
SERIES*

tions about hull forms. It's almost standard practice for individuals—even experienced enthusiasts—to make the blanket statement that "round-bottomed boats roll too much," which fosters the misconception that by simply increasing initial stability with harder chines, the whole rolling problem can be eliminated. I've spent thousands of offshore hours aboard our 46, and my conclusion, in a nitpicking way, is that our unstabilized motion could have been improved had we *reduced initial stability* slightly more through reduced midships sections.

The specifications for the Nordhavn 46 are as follows:

LOA	45'9"
LWL	38'4"
Beam	15'5"
Beam at WL	13'9"
Draft	5'0"
Displacement (pounds)	48,320
Displacement (long tons)	21.57
Displacement (cubic feet of seawater)	755
Longitudinal Center of Buoyancy Aft Sta 0	53.75%
D/L	383
PC	0.63
A/B ratio	2.3
Fuel	1,075 gal
Water	300 gal
Ballast	6,600 lb cast iron
Engine	Lugger 101 hp @ 2,200 rpm— continuous rating
Estimated Ocean-Crossing Speed	7.4 knots (S/L 1.2)
Maximum Cruising Speed	8.7 knots (max. continuous hp)
Estimated Range	2,871 NM (S/L 1.2)

The range graph for the Nordhavn (Figure 6-4) was developed using the formulas in Chapter 6 and has been confirmed by the vessel's actual performance. The graph does not take into account any stabilizing gear and is calculated at half-load. My experience is that an active fin system with a pair of 5-square-foot fins will decrease speed by a little less than ½ knot. With a flopperstopper system, expect each deployed fish to reduce speed about ³⁄₁₀ knot—for a total reduction of just over ½ knot.

Deck Layout

The general deck layout with the wheelhouse in a midships position has proved superb. Visibility through about 270 degrees is excellent, but a view directly aft does require a trip out to the Portuguese bridge (a substantial fixed coaming surrounding the front and sides of the wheelhouse) or, if the boat deck is not too cluttered, the small aft-facing windows provide some view of what's coming up astern. The location of the wheelhouse offers numerous benefits. For docking maneuvers the helmsman is in the middle of the vessel—the best position for knowing where the surrounding boat is relative to the dock. Two steps to port or starboard allow a confirming glance down or aft. With a little experience one's perception becomes very keen and, despite many clients' initial concerns, docking becomes second nature from this location. Another benefit is that walking from the helm out onto the starboard side deck and aft for line handling takes but 2 or 3 seconds and allows the helmsman to play an active role in mooring the ship. As an option we have installed an upper station for those who felt docking required this elevated position, but the convenience and ease of the wheelhouse controls generally preclude upper-station use.

Another benefit of the midships wheelhouse is that the pitching motion is much better tolerated here than farther forward. All navigational and operational decisions are made here, so it's imperative that this be as comfortable a location as possible. Additionally, the *relatively* aft position of the wheelhouse combined with the forward angle of the front windows, partially protected behind the strong wheelhouse coaming, reduce the possibility of storm damage to the wheelhouse glass.

The Portuguese bridge has proved to be an invaluable feature as it allows the watch-stander to leave the wheelhouse at any time, with the high coaming providing exceptional protection and all but eliminating the concern of being thrown or falling overboard. Often it is necessary to go outside with binoculars during a watch to visually confirm a radar target or to study lights and details in the distance, and without such protection this can be risky, particularly in rough weather.

All external doors slide, which is an interesting discussion in itself. Sliding doors offer significant benefits, primarily relating to convenience. The problem with conventional exterior doors aboard yachts is that to provide desirable ventilation, they have to be able to swing through the opening arch and conveniently stow in the open position, a requirement that would have necessitated significant alterations in size and position of both the port-side door to the wheelhouse and the saloon door on the Nordhavn. In general the sliding doors have worked very well, but they cannot be sealed quite as tightly as the swinging type and are expensive to build. Additionally, they do require care during rough conditions as they can slam shut easily, endangering the fingers of a careless user. We chose conventional doors for our larger, 62-foot design, primarily due to ease of construction.

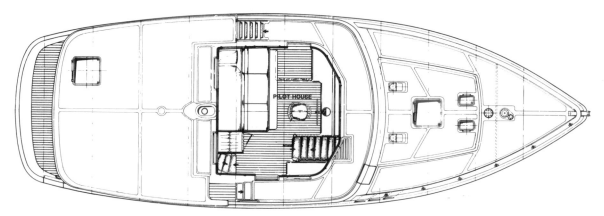

Figure 11-6. *Deck layout, Nordhavn 46.*

131

*FROM SAIL
TO POWER—
THE
NORDHAVN
SERIES*

Appropriate threshold heights for exterior doors depend upon the ability of the area outside the door to hold water. At the port-side wheelhouse door, water coming aboard can be temporarily trapped within the Portuguese bridge, but only on the port side. To starboard the water simply cascades aft, down the steps and onto the side deck, but to port it is backed up against the steps leading up to the boat deck. We raised the port-side threshold to about 10 inches above the outside deck level, and I've been grateful for this forethought on the numerous occasions a wave top has popped up and collapsed over the front side of the wheelhouse, temporarily pooling until it could drain off through the sizable freeing ports.

Accommodations

Our original concept for the interior was based upon my own ideas, which put greater emphasis on engine room space and the desirability of simply lifting a hatch near the helm in the wheelhouse to look into the engine room. I also wanted full standing headroom and a workbench. Jeff drew it up this way, but when it became apparent that we would actually build and market this dream ship, my two business partners of 20 years, Dan Streech and Joe Meglen, tactfully pointed out to Jeff and me that this interior would not be well received by the general market. I agreed, and a more conventional layout was adopted. I recently pulled out the original drawing, and it still appeals to me for the original reasons. In the final design the engine room was moved aft and more space was devoted to saloon and staterooms.

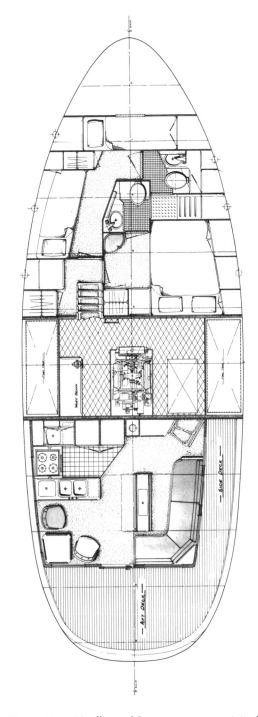

Figure 11-7. *Nordhavn 46 arrangement as originally drawn with wheelhouse access to the engine room.*

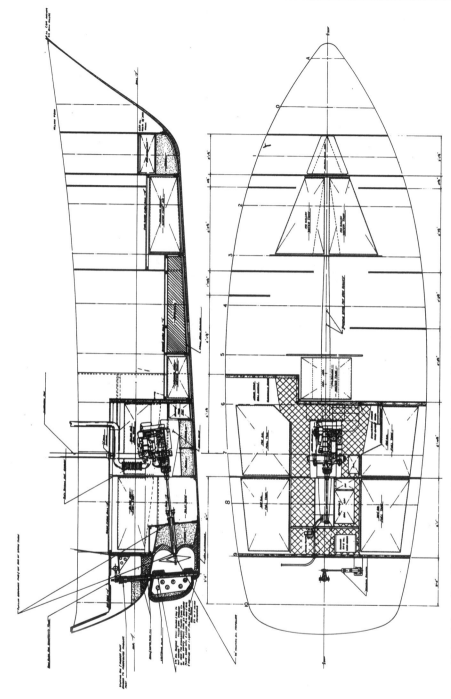

Figure 11-8. *Inboard profile showing machinery installation, Nordhavn 46.*

133

*FROM SAIL
TO POWER—
THE
NORDHAVN
SERIES*

Experienced offshore sailors are more understanding of the need for real sleeping accommodations while underway and more willing to accept compromises to the vessel's interior to ensure proper bunk placement. In contrast, it's commonplace to lay out a powerboat's interior for maximum appeal at dockside or, worse yet, securely nestled in a boat-show cradle. On a proper ocean-cruising sailing yacht, the owner always sleeps aft, with guests and crew forward. The same rules should apply on a voyaging powerboat. We plugged the owner's stateroom right into the middle of our design, and I've yet to encounter conditions where a decent night's sleep wasn't possible.

The fact is that during passages, any sleeping cabin in the forward third of the vessel will not be a full-time stateroom; the saloon settees and sometimes the floor will provide alternative sleeping accommodations. Any time moderate seas are forward of the ship's beam, the vertical accelerations and decelerations can cause even the toughest of seamen to scurry aft for relief.

We placed the bunk in the owner's stateroom in an athwartships position, a feature some have questioned. Sailors want berths parallel with the centerline of the vessel because of the port and starboard heel of the ship. But heel, or roll, is the axis of motion we can control on a long-range motorboat; roll is almost eliminated by our stabilizing gear. Yaw is not much of a problem, but pitch is uncontrollable except with a speed reduction or course change. If sailors have concluded that the best sleeping position is aligned with the axis of greatest variation, then an athwartship bunk in a stabilized powerboat makes perfect sense.

As for the guest cabin in the Nordhavn, it is forward—and as the guest of numerous owners, I've been run out of there on many occasions by head seas. Crossing the Atlantic aboard *Salvation II,* I spent six nights either bent up behind the dinette table or laid out on the floor. Many later Nordhavns are fitted with a sleeping-length settee on the starboard side of the saloon. With a backrest that folds up to become an additional berth, this arrangement offers two decent berths that would have been greatly appreciated by the crew of *Salvation II.*

The after section is a bit unusual: the main saloon and galley are offset to the port side, and a passageway on the starboard side of the saloon allows external access to the Portuguese bridge. This increases the size of the saloon/galley area, which is condensed a bit farther aft than normal due to the midships location of the wheelhouse. It has been a trend lately to eliminate all side deck,

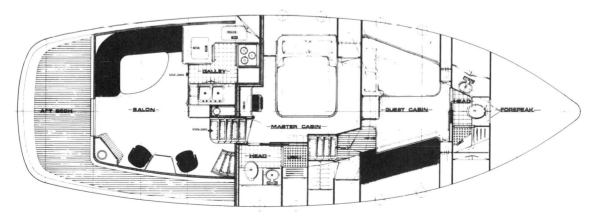

Figure 11-9. *Interior layout, Nordhaven 46.*

but feeling that would be too big a hindrance to docking and mooring, we compromised by eliminating the passageway on the port side only. This arrangement has worked out extremely well, the only criticism being aesthetic. Personally, I don't mind it and wouldn't hesitate to include this feature in any vessel where added interior space is desired.

An interesting point about the offset of the saloon is its origin. While we were incorporating this offset into our design, Jim Krogen was simultaneously including this feature in a 54-foot design of his. I think it was pure coincidence that both designs included this unusual arrangement, but I'll admit that we got our idea from a 40-foot William Garden design called *Porpoise*—built 30 years ago. As my father always says, "There's not as much new in this world as you might think, but there are a lot of new people doing old things." With regard to functional hull- and deck-shape development, this wisdom may apply.

In this chapter I've tried to assess accurately some of the features of our own design. The next chapter examines other offshore vessels and varying approaches to the issues taken by their designers.

CHAPTER 12

THE WORK
OF OTHER
DESIGNERS

It HAS OFTEN BEEN SAID THAT a yacht is comprised of a series of compromises that are influenced by its intended use. The word *compromise* seems to carry a negative connotation, but when we speak of seagoing motorboats, the compromise creates the kind of features that appeal to me. The concept of "form follows function" dictates that the real seagoer carry a lower and, to my eye, more attractive profile than the coastal cruiser. Her construction must be far more rugged with heavier, better hardware and more shiplike features—features that will lend to a longer useful service life and better resale value and that create a very solid and satisfying feel and look to the vessel.

Designing a proper motor yacht to be safely taken to sea requires an honest approach meeting solid, well-defined performance criteria. Clients are generally experienced, demanding quality and attention to detail. Specified machinery must be the best, rated for commercial, continuous-duty operation, and all systems must be able to stand up to liveaboard use. The designers who have become renowned within this category have proven over and over their expertise in meeting the rigorous requirements of these heavy-duty and specialized vessels; these are the experts we asked to submit examples of their work.

Robert Beebe's original introduction to this chapter still applies:

> *We owe a debt of gratitude to all the designers who*
> *contributed the results of their knowledge and experience to make up this chapter. The*
> *remarkable diversity of solutions to the problem of the seagoing motorboat shows how much*
> *scope there is for different approaches to achieving what essentially is a single specification—*
> *that the product be a seaworthy motorboat with a range of x miles.*

Featured here are examples of proper seagoing motorboats with, at a minimum, suitability for a summertime Atlantic crossing using the route between Bermuda and the Azores (1,850 nautical miles).

CHARLES NEVILLE AND ASSOCIATES, INC.

Of all the designers contacted, none showed more enthusiasm for long-range cruising than Chuck Neville. He was quick to provide an extensive package of published magazine articles and dozens of excellent examples of his work, clearly illustrating the wide scope of his expertise in this area.

Figure 12-1. *Chuck Neville.*

Neville 39

I couldn't help but fall in love with one of his smallest designs, a 39-foot motor yacht designed for a client in Texas. Neville's Design 9005 features a well-balanced and extremely pleasing profile with nice yacht features spiced with the slightly commercial look of utility. I'm admittedly biased, but I love this style and haven't seen a Neville design that wasn't pleasing to my eye.

The arrangement of this design is a bit unusual and doesn't correspond to any of the five types shown in Chapter 9. This layout offers the accommodation and features of a vessel 7 or 8 feet longer and would well serve an experienced couple wanting a smaller vessel for cruising and willing to sacrifice plush accommodations for occasional guests. The reduced cost and additional features gained by making this concession have great appeal.

Forward is a very nice stateroom with adequate hanging-locker space and with excellent ventilation through Dorade vents, an overhead hatch, and opening ports in the side of a raised house. There's plenty of floor space and, presumably, a set of deep drawers beneath the berth. A large head compartment with an excellent stall shower is provided. The downside to this stateroom is its location relative to the motion of the vessel: running off the wind it will be quiet and very nice, but with a significant sea forward of the beam, sleeping there will be difficult at times. All things considered, it is a workable compromise. Sleeping in the saloon may occasionally be necessary, but the vast majority of the time the forward stateroom will be just fine, and no other layout will work as well in this relatively small vessel.

Moving aft to the steering station, we find things starting to get interesting. The wheelhouse is far enough aft that motion in a seaway should prove acceptable. An excellent settee in the wheelhouse—long enough to sleep on—could fold up into an upper and lower berth to provide ample accommodations for occasional weekend guests. Underway the settee is used by the helmsman while the autopilot perpetually steers. Excellent separation between the wheelhouse and the saloon means lights and activity in the saloon will not disturb the operation of the ship. The forward-sloping windows are a wonderful feature for night vision because they eliminate bothersome reflection from engine gauges and lighted instruments mounted below eye level on the panel; any light reflecting into your eyes must come from above. As far aft as the wheelhouse is, and with its forward-sloping windows and the small house forward, it should be capable of withstanding a lot of green water without sustaining window or structural damage.

Beneath the wheelhouse is an engine room with partial standing headroom in front of the engine. This ideal arrangement allows the watch-stander to conduct frequent engine room

(continued on page 139)

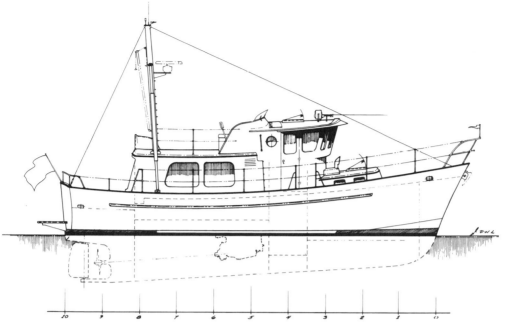

Figure 12-2. *Outboard profile, Neville 39.*

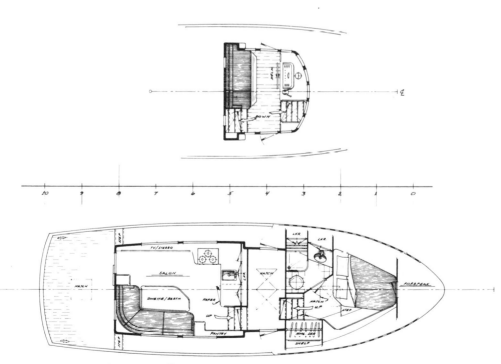

Figure 12-3. *Interior layout, Neville 39.*

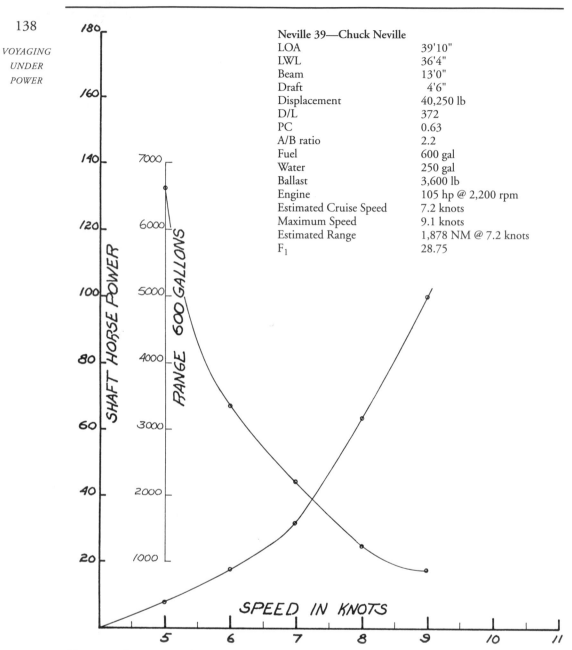

Neville 39—Chuck Neville

LOA	39'10"
LWL	36'4"
Beam	13'0"
Draft	4'6"
Displacement	40,250 lb
D/L	372
PC	0.63
A/B ratio	2.2
Fuel	600 gal
Water	250 gal
Ballast	3,600 lb
Engine	105 hp @ 2,200 rpm
Estimated Cruise Speed	7.2 knots
Maximum Speed	9.1 knots
Estimated Range	1,878 NM @ 7.2 knots
F_1	28.75

Figure 12-4. *Range graph, Neville 39.*

inspections with absolute ease. It also allows for engine room space normally seen only on larger vessels.

The saloon is conventional, with the galley on the port side and a dinette to starboard. The aft deck is very large for the size of the vessel, and its relationship to the saloon is an important feature that has great appeal.

The profile shows a mast and flopperstopper rig that appear to be a little farther aft than ideal (about 25 percent of LWL from the stern) but should still be effective. The aft bulkhead of the saloon (and a boxed section) handles the compression loads of the stabilizing gear; moving the mast forward would require a compression post in the middle of the saloon, adversely affecting the layout. Chuck Neville has incorporated a flybridge into this design while still keeping the A/B ratio down to a very respectable 2.2.

This capable small passage-maker should serve a cruising couple well. Her concept and layout provide maximum comfort and features, with reduced guest accommodations her only significant compromise. Her moderate size will provide economy in construction, use, and maintenance. It also means easier handling and minimal crew requirements, allowing greater independence while voyaging—an important consideration to some.

Neville 48

The second Neville design is a classic example of a Type A layout (Chapter 9). While I personally have problems with this arrangement, I must admit that it is probably the most popular configuration for vessels in the 36- to 48-foot range. There's little question that this layout offers maximum interior accommodations without double-decking, and it gives the vessel a

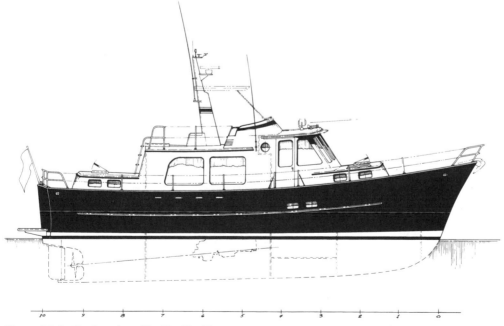

Figure 12-5. *Outboard profile, Neville 48.*

very low A/B ratio. This design should be a capable and seaworthy passage-maker.

A huge owner's cabin is located aft, with an almost equal guest cabin forward. Both state-rooms will be wonderful dockside, but each has potential drawbacks at sea. Motion will present the usual problems forward, and propeller cavitation and shaft rumble could cause disturbance aft. A large reduction gear, a carefully faired propeller aperture, and the best running and steering gear should minimize noise. Added hull dampening around the propeller aperture and beneath the floors will also help. There's little doubt that Charles Neville, an authority on the subject of noise and vibration control, has addressed this issue.

Among the nicest features of this design are a gigantic engine room and a fantastic utility room/workshop. There are always jobs to be done aboard, and the workshop—with tool and spare-parts storage—will be greatly appreciated. The easy entrance from the workshop to the engine room is ideal, and with 6 feet of headroom around the engine, maintenance will be a joy.

Within the saloon, galley, and wheelhouse, less space as been provided, probably at the owner's request. The wheelhouse is well separated from the saloon and slightly higher, accommodating only one or two watch-standers.

My main objection to the Type A layout is the lack of aft deck space. This a is subjective issue, but being able to walk from the saloon to the aft deck is a valuable feature, allowing the two areas to be used simultaneously and creating a most pleasant atmosphere. Of course, a full-width

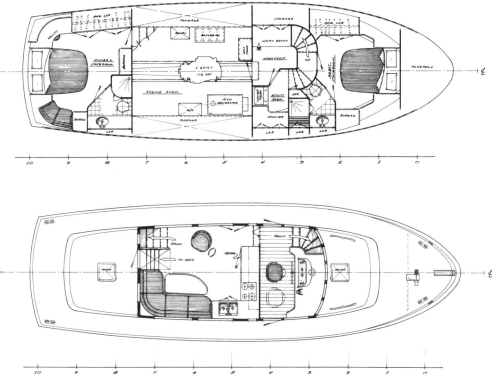

Figure 12-6. *Interior layout, Neville 48.*

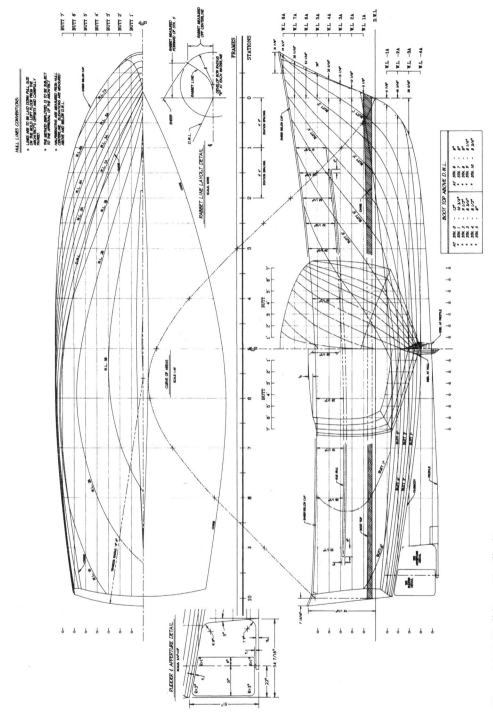

Figure 12-7. *Hull lines, Neville 48.*

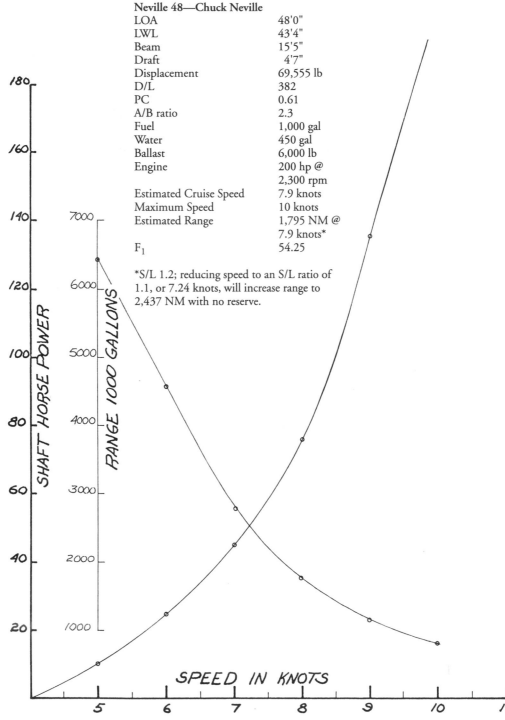

Neville 48—Chuck Neville

LOA	48'0"
LWL	43'4"
Beam	15'5"
Draft	4'7"
Displacement	69,555 lb
D/L	382
PC	0.61
A/B ratio	2.3
Fuel	1,000 gal
Water	450 gal
Ballast	6,000 lb
Engine	200 hp @ 2,300 rpm
Estimated Cruise Speed	7.9 knots
Maximum Speed	10 knots
Estimated Range	1,795 NM @ 7.9 knots*
F_1	54.25

*S/L 1.2; reducing speed to an S/L ratio of 1.1, or 7.24 knots, will increase range to 2,437 NM with no reserve.

Figure 12-8. *Range graph, Neville 48.*

aft stateroom is a significant trade-off, and for some, the saloon/aft deck relationship is not worth the sacrifice.

My only other comments on this design are about the wheelhouse. Its forward position and the conventional slope of the glass make its forward windows vulnerable to storm damage. Very heavy safety glass (about 12 millimeters) and easily installed acrylic storm plates would be important if an ocean crossing is contemplated. An additional concern is the absence of high bulwarks, which would expose a watch-stander leaving the protection of the wheelhouse to considerable risk, particularly at night. This requires strict rules about staying inside the wheelhouse. I would even require a safety gate across the wheelhouse door when the vessel is running with these doors open.

JAY R. BENFORD—BENFORD DESIGN GROUP

Jay Benford has shown his design talents in a wide variety of vessels, both sail and power, and for both pleasure and commercial use. Anyone interested enough in voyaging under power to read this book would be well advised to contact the Benford Design Group and order the available catalogs showcasing their work. I enjoyed reviewing the dozens of small freighter, ferry, and unique "small ship" designs for which Jay Benford has earned an enviable reputation. About these capable vessels Benford writes, "I find this type to have a refreshing frankness about them, with an absence of tricky styling and glitter and glitz. While too many of the production boats are busy selling sizzle, we've been delivering steak—to those astute enough to recognize the difference."

Figure 12-9. *Jay Benford. (Photo by Donna Benford)*

Little Sindbad

Benford's 45-foot 6-inch design *Little Sindbad* caught our eye as having the proper ingredients of a passage-maker while including some interesting design features worth looking into. A more rugged-looking vessel would be hard to find, and in this case looks do not deceive. The only thing *little* about *Little Sindbad* is her name. Built with ¼-inch steel hull plating and an aluminum superstructure, this ocean-crosser has a robust D/L of 406.

Benford selected the Gardner 6LXB diesel, a 638-cubic-inch, naturally aspirated British diesel with a legendary reputation for reliability and efficiency. Documented times between overhaul in commercial applications have routinely exceeded 50,000 hours. These heavy-duty engines are available through Detroit Diesel.

Little Sindbad is fitted with a dry exhaust system, which I'm partial to. Many seem to have had an aversion to dry exhaust, telling stories of excessive heat buildup and soot-covered decks. My company has had a lot of experience with dry exhaust, and I'm certain that any operational problems experienced by others are a result of an improperly designed or built system. In actual use, dry exhausts have been a delight and are well worth their high initial cost and added space requirements. In the case of *Little Sindbad,* the exhaust stack serves as a mast and compression post to

(continued on page 146)

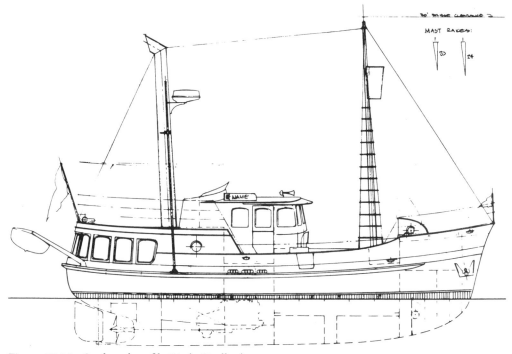

Figure 12-10. *Outboard profile,* Little Sindbad.

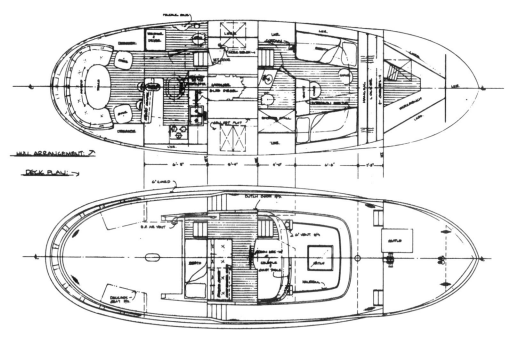

Figure 12-11. *Interior layout and deck plan,* Little Sindbad.

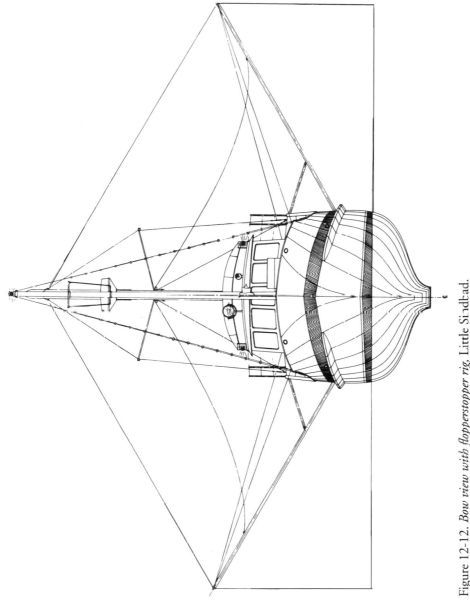

Figure 12-12. *Bow view with flopperstopper rig,* Little Sindbad.

support the flopperstopper rig. This is an excellent method of installing a dry exhaust as the actual steel or stainless steel exhaust pipe can run up the interior of an extruded aluminum sailboat spar section. The spar provides an excellent heat shroud, and as long as plenty of air is allowed to enter the bottom of the spar section from the engine room, there will be a natural draft upward, carrying off the heat from the exhaust.

With her heavy D/L, fine lines, double-ender stern, and moderate beam, *Little Sindbad* should have a very seakindly motion. Despite her heft, efficiency will be good. With a full load of fuel, this vessel should be able to make the longest ocean passages at high speed. Calculations show that even at 8 knots she can make a 3,000-mile passage. Slowing down to a very reasonable 7 knots will allow for more than 5,000 nautical miles of running.

The midships location of the wheelhouse is ideal from a motion standpoint, and with 10-millimeter glass the small wheelhouse windows should be secure. While not reverse-sloped, the windows are nearly vertical, and the whale-back foredeck, the turtle hatch, and the distance of the wheelhouse aft of the bow all combine to ensure a good, seaworthy structure.

A considerable amount of space has been allotted to the wheelhouse, which includes a large settee and berth. The chart table is to starboard of the helm, and there is plenty of room for chart storage under the settee. Like the Neville-designed 39-footer, *Little Sindbad's* wheelhouse sits above the engine; hourly checks will be a snap by simply lifting the floor hatch. A nice feature of the wheelhouse is Dutch doors on both sides. Low bulwarks are shown with a single rail on top. Adding a second rail would increase height to provide greater security when exiting to the side decks.

Going down and forward into the owner's cabin further confirms that Benford designed this ship to go to sea, for here lies a seagoing stateroom that has few rivals. Full width with two single berths and ideally located from a motion standpoint, this will be a comfortable and quiet cabin. The head in its aft location is large and insulates the stateroom from what little sound the slow-turning Gardner produces—any that finds its way through the insulated, watertight bulkhead. The cabin is perfect, with abundant hanging lockers, shelves, and drawer space, but this does not come without cost. As you can see, this wonderful cabin is only possible when it has priority over a second stateroom with internal access. I think it's fantastic, but this kind of specialized layout is generally seen only in a custom boat—where the customer knows exactly what type of use the vessel will get. A production yacht of this size would almost have to have two staterooms, even though the result is two that are compromised rather than one that's perfect. Actually, the workroom forward, with its deck access, is large enough to accommodate upper and lower berths and a hide-away head, which probably is all the second stateroom needs on a 45-foot vessel.

Moving aft, things become a little less conventional. The engine room is no less fantastic then the owner's stateroom, with full standing headroom and a sizable workbench. After paying the price of the Gardner diesel (approximately twice the cost of a Caterpillar or Lugger of comparable horsepower), this is a requirement. It's not that you need the space to work on the engine; you just have to have adequate room to stand and admire it. This 150-hp workhorse is referred to as "bomb-proof," and 50,000 hours between overhauls is 5.7 years of continuous running, which would allow *Little Sindbad* to circle the earth almost 14 times. A Hundested controllable-pitch propeller has been included for ultimate efficiency.

The saloon and galley are particularly interesting in that they collectively run to the absolute stern of the vessel. While this approach is certainly controversial, it does maximize interior space. My initial reaction to this was negative, but as I gave further consideration to the total design,

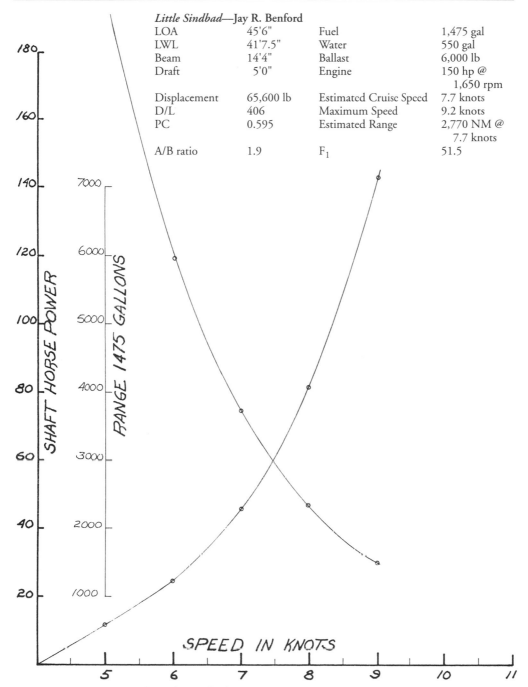

Little Sindbad—Jay R. Benford

LOA	45'6"	Fuel	1,475 gal
LWL	41'7.5"	Water	550 gal
Beam	14'4"	Ballast	6,000 lb
Draft	5'0"	Engine	150 hp @ 1,650 rpm
Displacement	65,600 lb	Estimated Cruise Speed	7.7 knots
D/L	406	Maximum Speed	9.2 knots
PC	0.595	Estimated Range	2,770 NM @ 7.7 knots
A/B ratio	1.9	F_1	51.5

Figure 12-13. *Range graph,* Little Sindbad.

I found this unconventional arrangement quite appealing. The spaciousness of the saloon and galley, along with an "on-deck" head and a washer and dryer for laundry, are nice. My only problem is giving up the traditional aft lounging deck. Of course there is the upper deck, but it probably would feel a little uncomfortable perched up there—outside the protection of the flybridge—particularly underway. Looking further, I suspect that the open deck space aft of the whale-back could be a great alternative area for lounging, with adequate room for chairs and the raised foredeck giving some protection from the breeze. In fair weather the wheelhouse, with its wide side decks, and the space forward of the low trunk cabin would be the gathering space, providing the same interface between inside and outside activities as the saloon/aft deck in a conventional layout.

Handling dock lines from the upper aft deck should not create any insurmountable problems and probably is preferable to having a traditional aft deck with the popular full-width saloon and no side decks. There is quick access from the flybridge to the aft deck, and it's only four steps up from the wheelhouse helm. Boarding requires a little different approach, using the midships port and starboard doors. A ladder is required when using a tender.

All in all, *Little Sindbad* is pure Passagemaker. She's equipped with flopperstoppers, a foremast with crow's nest, and an interesting davit system that hinges upward with the tender to provide greater clearance underway from wave action.

WILLARD MARINE—BUILDERS AND DESIGNERS

Anyone growing up in the Newport Beach, California, area knows of Willard Marine, but not through their advertising or their daily presence. Just when we began to realize we hadn't seen much of them, another giant yacht would appear, closing off local streets and frightening city officials as the boat was hauled from the builder's landlocked plant across the aging Arches Bridge and on to the old Lido Shipyard for launching and commissioning.

Willard 40

The Willard 40 has been built since the early '70s but in limited quantities. At the time of this writing only about 25 had been produced. Willard Marine keeps busy with government boatbuilding contracts and has been content to build the 40 when time permits and as the occasional orders come in. The original design was by Hale Field, with a hull form that closely resembled the William Garden–designed Vega 36 (see Figure 8-10), but with fuller lines amidships.

Over the years numerous deck designs have evolved. I recently had the opportunity to view a new, nearly complete pilothouse version, which was soon to be delivered to Ralph Poole, the publisher of *Western Boatman*. Ralph has been cruising the West Coast from Alaska to Acapulco for years, and this new 40 will be just the ticket for his increased cruising schedule.

Longtime Willard designer Rod Swift has done much of the pleasure-boat design work for the company and was responsible for the pilothouse version of the 40. I looked this particular vessel over very carefully and was impressed with this capable little cruiser. Willard's years of catering to the demands of the Navy, Coast Guard, and American Bureau of Shipping surveyors are evident throughout. While these vessels are simple and lack exotic joinerwork and fancy hardware, the machinery, tankage, and electric and plumbing work are superb. I got the feeling

Figure 12-14. *Willard 40.*

Figure 12-15. *Ralph Poole's pilothouse version.*

that this vessel could leave the builder's yard, be fueled, and put to sea—with very few problems to be solved.

The Willard 40 is an excellent coastal cruiser as she's offered in her standard configuration, but with minor modifications she'd be ready to go anywhere. The general construction, in terms of laminate schedules and scantlings, is just fine. My only recommendation is either to increase the strength of the windows with thicker tempered or safety glass or to provide removable storm plates. The standard windows are ¼-inch tempered glass in plastic frames, and while the framework is okay, I don't think I'd want to take green water against these windows due to their thinness. Really, regardless of what glass is used, storm plates are a good idea on any windows that are considered vulnerable. I would recommend plates for the saloon windows and for the front wheelhouse windows. The placement of the wheelhouse near amidships is excellent, but the back-sloped windows might still have to stand the brunt of some heavy and fast-moving water unbroken by any other structure (such as a Portuguese bridge).

For passage-making, some form of stabilizing will be important. Flopperstoppers could easily be installed.

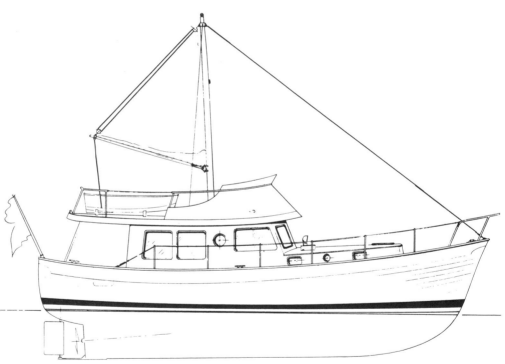

Figure 12-16. *Outboard profile, Willard 40.*

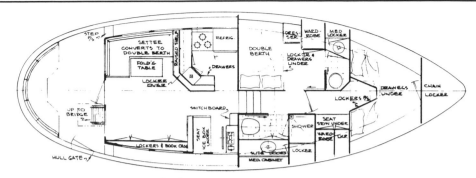

Figure 12-17. *Interior layout, Willard 40.*

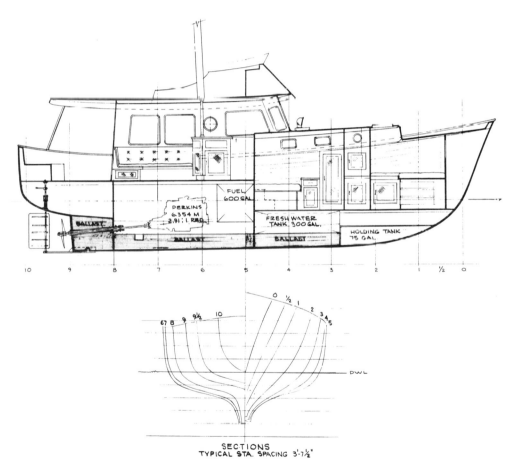

Figure 12-18. *Body plan, Willard 40.*

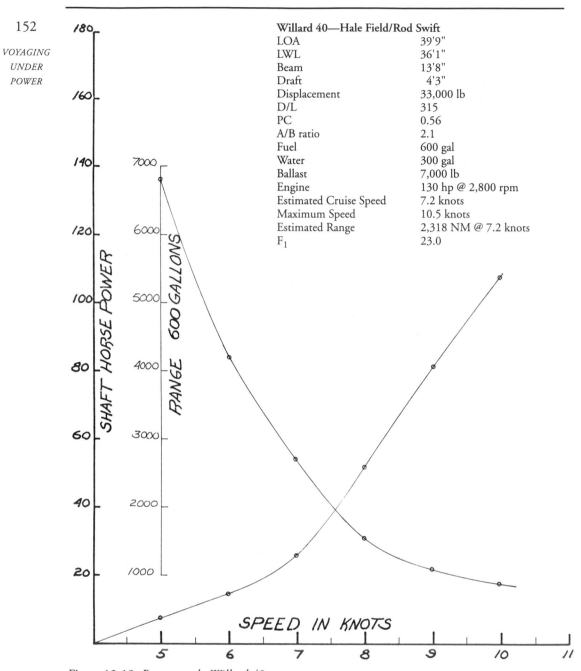

Willard 40—Hale Field/Rod Swift

LOA	39'9"
LWL	36'1"
Beam	13'8"
Draft	4'3"
Displacement	33,000 lb
D/L	315
PC	0.56
A/B ratio	2.1
Fuel	600 gal
Water	300 gal
Ballast	7,000 lb
Engine	130 hp @ 2,800 rpm
Estimated Cruise Speed	7.2 knots
Maximum Speed	10.5 knots
Estimated Range	2,318 NM @ 7.2 knots
F_1	23.0

Figure 12-19. *Range graph, Willard 40.*

JAMES S. KROGEN AND COMPANY

Few designers have enjoyed more success with their long-range powerboat designs than has James Krogen of Miami, Florida. The Krogen-designed 42-footer has survived 20 years of production. To date, more than 177 of these stout vessels have been built.

Krogen 42

My complaints about the Krogen 42 are the standard ones: the forward position of the wheelhouse, the owner's cabin forward, and the lack of protection when leaving the wheelhouse. But when we realize that ocean passage-making was not the first priority with this design, there are valid reasons for the configuration. The 42 is intended for serious coastal cruising, but she certainly has the ability to cross oceans, with the principal required modification being storm plates for windows and doors. For serious offshore use, stabilizing is desirable. Krogen 42s have been successfully fitted with both flopperstoppers and active fin systems.

By virtue of the long production run and the widespread distribution of the Krogen 42s, there are probably boats available within one's price and condition range—from the 20-year-old "fixer-upper" to a new version with all the latest features. In proper condition, and with slight modification, this popular 42 will do the job.

Figure 12-20. *James S. Krogen.*

Figure 12-21. *Krogen 42 (Photo courtesy Kadey-Krogen Yachts)*

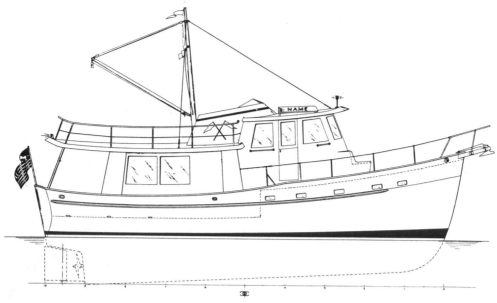

Figure 12-22. *Outboard profile, Krogen 42.*

A notable characteristic of Krogen designs is the attention to weight. James Krogen writes about the 42:

> *For most displacement vessels, the most economical speed is around the speed/length ratio of 1.0. But most yachtsmen really don't want to run that slowly (6.2 knots for the 42). When cruising locally, we aim for a cruising speed between 1.3 and 1.34, which can be accomplished without much penalty if the displacement/length ratio is kept in the 270–290 range. This is certainly possible with today's construction materials and methods—and still be able to carry good cruising gear and ballast besides. With this range of displacement/length ratios and prismatic coefficients around 0.60, good speed and low wakes result. I do not see the necessity of designing more weight into boats of this type as they can carry the extra weight without a fuss and can be loaded well below normal with extra gear for those special passage-making voyages.*

To save weight, the Krogen 42 is built using a foam core that separates two hull laminates, which also adds rigidity. Ballast is minimal at only 2,800 pounds (still more than half the weight of the fuel load). A combination of a low D/L of 293 and a PC of 0.594 creates an exceptionally efficient hull.

It is interesting to note that our Nordhavn 46 has a waterline length within 6 inches of the Krogen but, with a much heavier D/L of 383 (light load) and a PC of 0.63, requires considerably more horsepower to drive her at cruising speed. For the Krogen, our standard formula shows a fuel consumption rate of approximately 3 gph at 8 knots. On the Nordhavn the fuel consumption is 4.2 gph at the same speed. The graphs predict that when slowing to 7 knots, the Krogen will burn 1.63 gph; the heavier Nordhavn will burn 2.10 gph. After 20 years, the performance of the

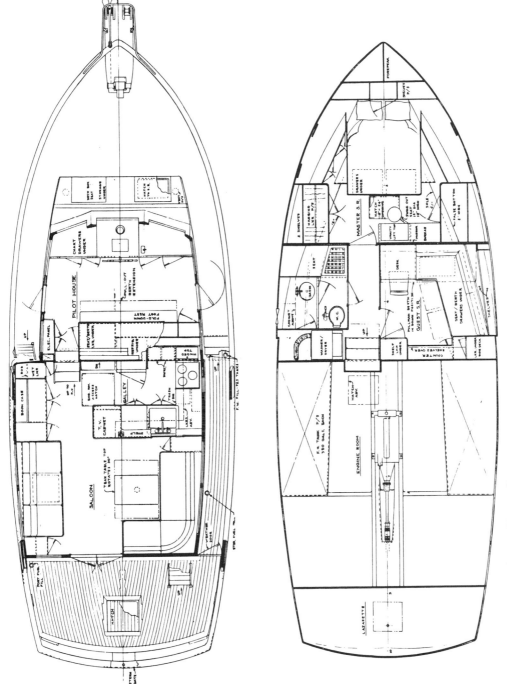

Figure 12-23. *Interior layout, Krogen 42.*

Krogen should be well known to her designers, and James Krogen indicates that the vessels are running at 8 knots and burning only 2½ gph (15 percent better than our graph predicts). This certainly illustrates the difference that D/L makes, and if Krogen's claims are correct the lower PC of .059 (Nordhavn 0.63) comes into play.

It has been the practice of most designers to incorporate heavy scantlings into their ocean-going vessels as the hull can still be relatively efficient and the weight is not generally viewed as being detrimental. In fact, weight is often considered to enhance the seakeeping qualities of the offshore vessel. Yet we should remember that for years extremely strong and seaworthy ocean-racing sailboats have been built using cored hulls and lightweight construction. With the illustrated effect of D/L and PC, Krogen's philosophy must be carefully considered.

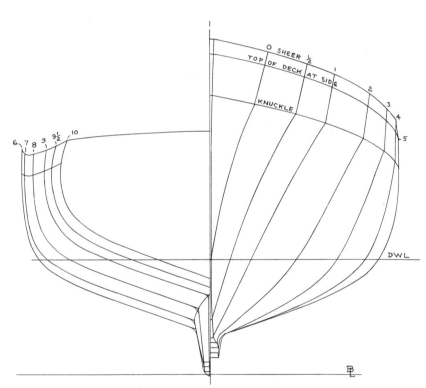

Figure 12-24. *Body plan, Krogen 42.*

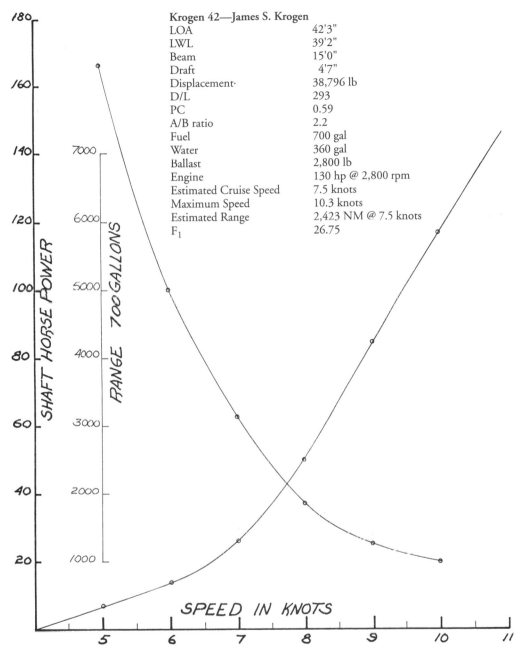

Krogen 42—James S. Krogen

LOA	42'3"
LWL	39'2"
Beam	15'0"
Draft	4'7"
Displacement·	38,796 lb
D/L	293
PC	0.59
A/B ratio	2.2
Fuel	700 gal
Water	360 gal
Ballast	2,800 lb
Engine	130 hp @ 2,800 rpm
Estimated Cruise Speed	7.5 knots
Maximum Speed	10.3 knots
Estimated Range	2,423 NM @ 7.5 knots
F_1	26.75

Figure 12-25. *Range graph, Krogen 42.*

NILS LUCANDER

Finnish designer Nils Lucander prides himself on his philosophy of forward thinking. He pointed out in a recent conversation that 150 years ago the simple communication that we were enjoying now, between Washington and California, would have required pen and paper and mail service via horse courier or wooden sailing ship, and the exchange would have taken weeks, not the minutes necessary to converse over the telephone. This is a modern age, and Nils suggests that our adherence to and belief in rules of hull speed developed in the last century are absurd. Rather, through advances in hull shape that allow a reduction in wave making, today's displacement vessels can efficiently run at higher speed/length ratios than what was previously thought possible.

Bob Beebe expressed some skepticism about Lucander's claims, but at the same time he realized that hull speed is not really an absolute limit of speed but a point beyond which it becomes impractical for various reasons, mostly economic, to push the vessel any faster. With this in mind, the limit on speed becomes subjective, and there is reason to believe that changes in hull shape (such as the bulbous bow) may allow this maxi-

Figure 12-26. *Nils Lucander.*

Figure 12-27. *Stern underbody of 3-Point 49 showing twin keels and ducted propellers. (Photo courtesy Nils Lucander)*

mum speed to increase slightly; however, large increases in speed are still hindered by the same wave-making resistance that held back steamships built a hundred years ago. It's interesting to note that today's surface ships with diesel and even nuclear power are being held to speeds only slightly higher than what was possible at the end of the last century by the steam-turbine vessels of that era. These marginal gains are more a result of powerful propulsion and lighter construction (usually through the use of alloy superstructures) than changes in hull design.

Figure 12-28. *Outboard profile, 3-Point 49.*

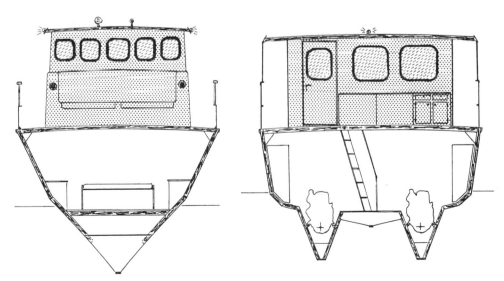

Figure 12-29. *Forward and aft sectional views, 3-Point 49.*

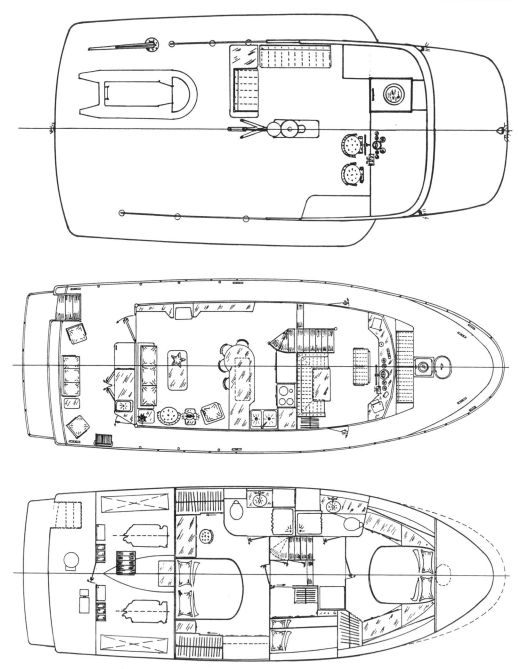

Figure 12-30. *Interior layout, 3-Point 49.*

3-Point 49—Nils Lucander

LOA	48'6"	D/L	488	Engine	2 x 100 hp	
LWL	40'0"	A/B ratio	2.6	Estimated Cruise Speed	7.6 knots	
Beam	17'4"	Fuel	2,200 gal	Maximum Speed	9.6 knots	
Draft	5'0"	Water	450 gal	Estimated Range	3,823 NM @ 7.6 knots	
Displacement	70,000 lb	Ballast	0	F_1	54.5	

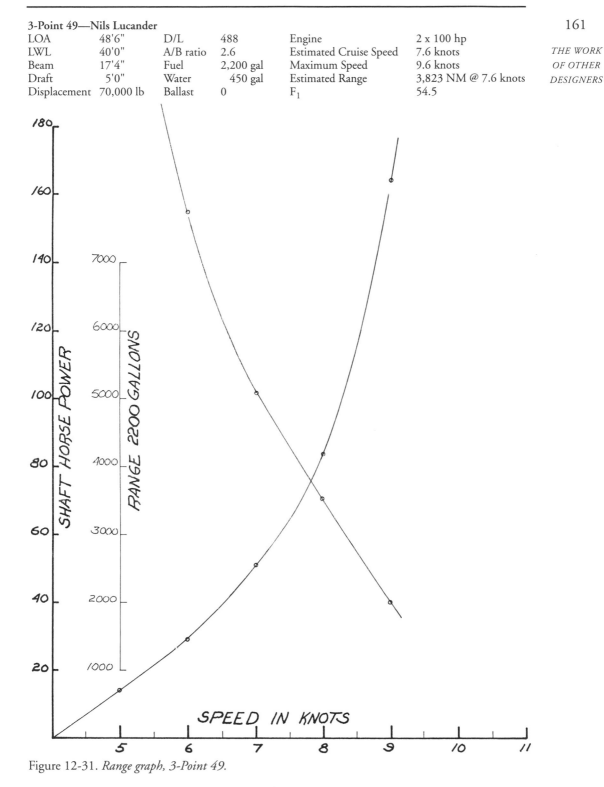

Figure 12-31. *Range graph, 3-Point 49.*

3-Point 49

An interesting example of the Lucander philosophy is the 3-Point 49. According to her designer, this vessel will run economically at S/Ls in excess of 20 percent above formula hull speed, which is more than 10 knots. Using the graphs in Chapter 6 that are applicable to conventional hulls, this would be possible using about 240 shaft horsepower, which could easily be available between two diesel engines and (presuming normal engine efficiency) would require a about 13.5 gallons of fuel per hour—for a fuel consumption rate of about 0.75 nautical mile per gallon. This could hardly be considered economical performance, but Nils Lucander claims that by increasing the volume of the hull sections aft and keeping forward sections finer with some hollow near the waterline slightly aft of the bow, he can reduce the transverse bow wave and subsequent midships trough and stern wave, creating a hull that will operate at these high S/Ls with greater efficiency than our above calculations would indicate.

In this unusual design, twin keels aft and outboard of the centerline are large enough to accommodate the twin engines. The benefit here is that shaft angles are reduced or eliminated, generally possible only in a conventional single-engine arrangement with the engine nestled within the keel cavity. Nils suggests that the twin keels further reduce wave making and aid in damping the roll of the vessel. Ducted propellers within Lucander-designed nozzles are also fitted.

The 3-Point design does offer some interesting benefits such as isolated bilges below the engines, stability during beaching or haulout, and the ability to mount the engines so far aft, allowing for greater interior flexibility. The prop protection provided by the keels/skegs along with efficiency increases due to shaft angles make this twin-engine arrangement a reasonable alternative to a conventional single-engine configuration, especially when discussions of in-harbor maneuverability and mechanical failure—get-home capability—come up.

I must admit that I am skeptical about some of the performance predictions for the 3-Point 49, but even if the performance only matches that of a conventional long-range hull, it is still interesting for some of the appealing features the hull configuration offers.

STEPHEN R. SEATON

I'm sure if Bob Beebe could visit Steve Seaton's busy design office in Seattle today, he would praise their current work as he did 20 years ago. Steve has recently received recognition for his work on large, full-displacement vessels—designed and built with an appealing commercial flavor. Of the four designs Steve submitted, three were full-displacement. The fourth was a very interesting semidisplacement model—not appropriate for this book but a good example of Steve's versatility.

Sluggo

This 53-foot Seaton boat is actually a 10-year-old design built in 1984. It is a variation of both the Type A and Type C arrangements (as described in Chapter 9), and some of the perceived weaknesses

Figure 12-32. Steve Seaton.

Figure 12-33. Sluggo.

of each configuration have been effectively addressed. As pointed out earlier, the saloon/aft deck relationship possible in a Type B layout is quite appealing, and its loss with the Type A layout is a compromise some owners are unwilling to make. In Seaton's design the owner's cabin is aft and full width, yet there is still reasonable access from the saloon to the flush aft lounging deck: the indoor/outdoor interface, although more separated by a difference in height, still exists.

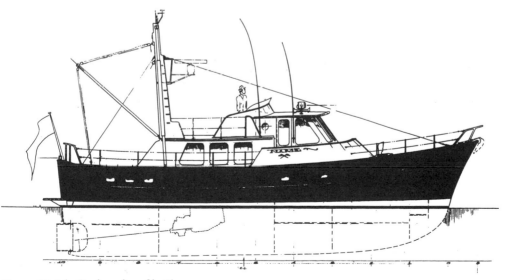

Figure 12-34. *Outboard profile,* Sluggo.

Unlike the normal Type C arrangement, *Sluggo* features a reasonable A/B ratio. A Portuguese bridge deck provides complete side-deck security for watch-standers and also offers the usual protection for the wheelhouse structure from boarding seas. There's little doubt that this is a capable offshore design.

Superb stateroom accommodations are one of *Sluggo*'s strong points. The saloon and galley are small for a boat this size, but this is difficult to overcome in this arrangement. Most Type As gain expanse by not partitioning the wheelhouse, but that's not a practical option in a serious offshore design.

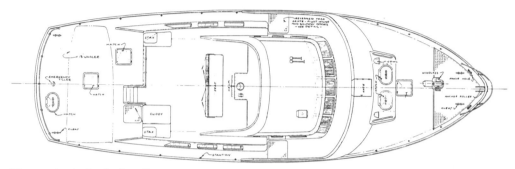

Figure 12-35. *Deck plan,* Sluggo.

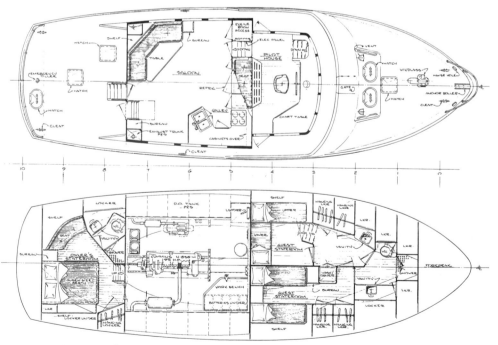

Figure 12-36. *Interior layout,* Sluggo.

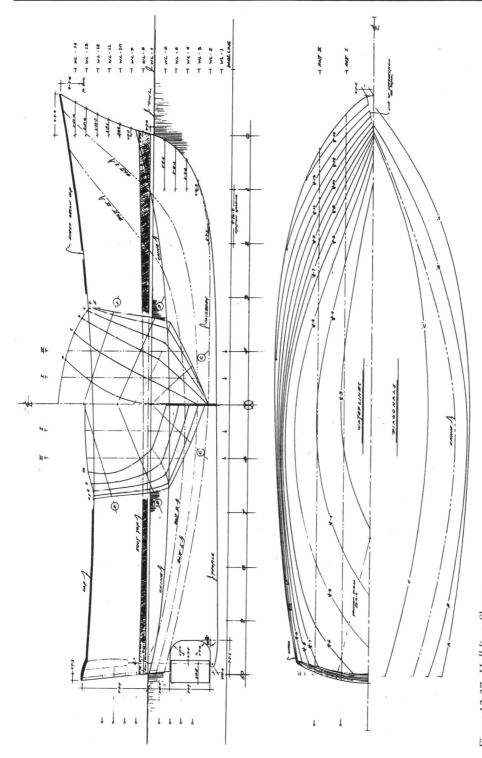

Figure 12-37. *Hull lines*, Sluggo.

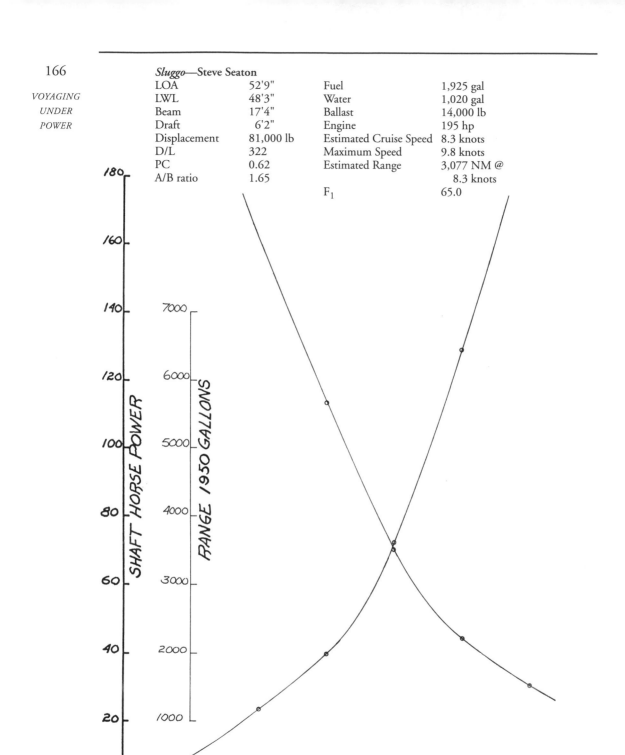

Sluggo—Steve Seaton

LOA	52'9"	Fuel	1,925 gal
LWL	48'3"	Water	1,020 gal
Beam	17'4"	Ballast	14,000 lb
Draft	6'2"	Engine	195 hp
Displacement	81,000 lb	Estimated Cruise Speed	8.3 knots
D/L	322	Maximum Speed	9.8 knots
PC	0.62	Estimated Range	3,077 NM @
A/B ratio	1.65		8.3 knots
		F_1	65.0

Figure 12-38. *Range graph,* Sluggo.

Seaton has incorporated the flopperstopper rig into the main-engine and generator dry-exhaust stack housings, which rise up on both sides of the vessel. The entire hull and superstructure are a steel construction so there were few problems in designing and building these stacks with a cross-connecting assembly capable of the load demands imposed by the stabilizing gear.

From the graphs in Chapter 6, *Sluggo* requires 87 hp to drive her at an S/L of 1.25, or 8.68 knots. The fuel burn will be about 5.25 gph, and with her generous diesel supply of 1,925 gallons, this ocean-crosser should be able run in excess of 3,000 miles at this speed.

Seaton Design 256

While just 6 feet longer than *Sluggo,* this 58-foot motor vessel is more than double the size of the 53-footer if measured by weight. At a nominal displacement of 226,000 pounds, this heavyweight is the type of vessel Steve Seaton has become known for in recent years.

With a staggering D/L of 658, this is the bulldozer of yachts. She has much to offer in terms of accommodations and capability, but even with more than 4,000 gallons of fuel aboard, she'll have to run at low S/Ls to cross oceans. Our standard formula shows that a cruise at S/L 1.25 (9.14 knots) requires 305 shaft horsepower and about 18 gallons of fuel per hour. Slowing to an S/L of 1.1, or about 8 knots, brings the fuel burn down to a more reasonable 10 gallons per hour. Trying to push this big guy at formula hull speed of S/L 1.34 would barely be possible with the 403-hp Caterpillar—flat-out and guzzling about 24 gallons of fuel per hour.

Economical operation is clearly not the emphasis of this design, but getting past this aspect we can see the benefits afforded by size. Interior volume is enormous compared to the standard

Figure 12-39. *Outboard profile, Seaton 58.*

set by a more conventional 58-footer. The key to this is extensive double- and triple-decking, and with a 9-foot draft the boat's A/B ratio remains a respectable 2.4. Of course, the excessive draft will limit access to many beautiful cruising areas, but for some this is an acceptable trade-off.

We could devote a lot more ink to a walk-through of this boat, but the drawings speak for themselves. Suffice to say that accommodations are luxurious yet practical. An interesting point is Steve's decision to incorporate an asymmetric saloon and eliminate the starboard walkway; with all the space already available in this design, this compromise illustrates the demand for maximum interior volume.

The Seaton design office has been busy with vessels of this type—some in excess of 100 feet. The efficiency of these designs seems poor, but one could reason that compared to the purchase cost of these vessels, a 500-dollar-per-day fuel bill is not that excessive and might even be considered reasonable.

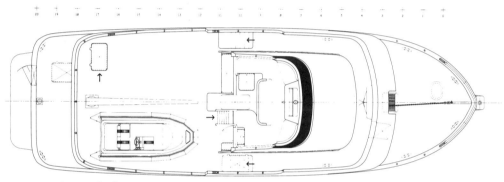

Figure 12-40. *Deck plan, Seaton 58.*

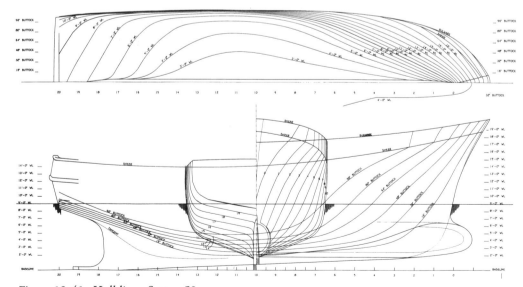

Figure 12-41. *Hull lines, Seaton 58.*

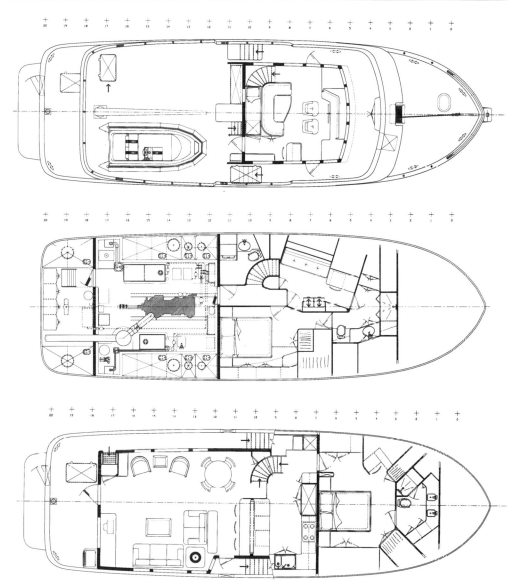

Figure 12-42. *Interior layout, Seaton 58.*

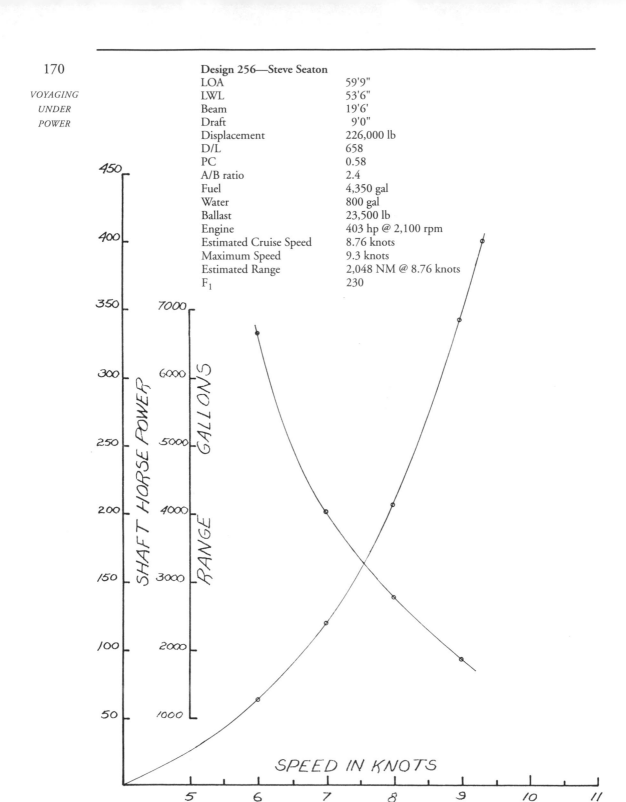

Design 256—Steve Seaton

LOA	59'9"
LWL	53'6"
Beam	19'6'
Draft	9'0"
Displacement	226,000 lb
D/L	658
PC	0.58
A/B ratio	2.4
Fuel	4,350 gal
Water	800 gal
Ballast	23,500 lb
Engine	403 hp @ 2,100 rpm
Estimated Cruise Speed	8.76 knots
Maximum Speed	9.3 knots
Estimated Range	2,048 NM @ 8.76 knots
F_1	230

Figure 12-43. *Range graph, Seaton 58.*

No.	Designer	Boat	LWL	D/L
1	Jeff Leishman	Nordhavn 46	38'4"	383
2	Jeff Leishman	Nordhavn 62	55'0"	294
3	Robert Beebe	Design 96	47'6"	291
4	Robert Beebe	*Mona Mona*	47'6"	308
5	Jay Benford	*Little Sindbad*	41'7"	406
6	Rod Swift	Willard 40	36'1"	315
7	Chuck Neville	Neville 39	36'4"	372
8	Chuck Neville	Neville 48	43'4"	382
9	James Krogen	Krogen 42	39'2"	293
10	Nils Lucander	3-Point 49	40'0"	488
11	Robert Beebe	Design 105	40'0"	320
12	George Buehler	*Diesel Duck*	36'8"	296
13	Robert Beebe	*Passagemaker*	46'6"	268
14	Steve Seaton	Design 256	53'6"	658
15	Steve Seaton	*Sluggo*	48'3"	322

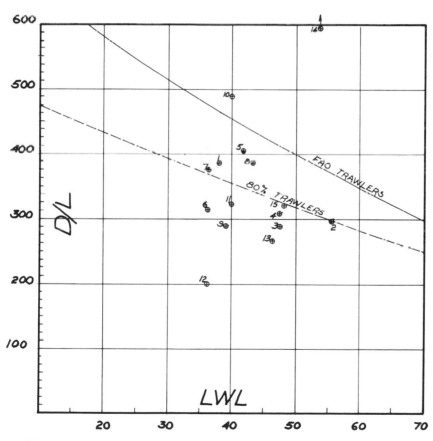

Figure 12-44. *This graph shows how the D/Ls of the listed yachts compare to each other. Put your own vessel on the graph to see what sort of company she keeps.*

A FINAL NOTE

The range graphs presented for each vessel were developed using Beebe's method outlined in Chapter 6. We elected to use this common formula rather than rely on individual designer predictions in hopes of providing more equitable comparisons. Beebe's formula is useful for establishing relative performance, and while the results may be somewhat conservative or understated, the predictions provide a good baseline that can be adjusted after careful ocean testing of particular vessels.

In the case of the Nordhavn 46, the predictions were extremely accurate. The predictions for the 62 were understated by the approximate gains in efficiency resulting from the unconventional bulbous bow. I would anticipate, too, that Seaton's design 295 would perform better than anticipated due to the bulb and moderate PC.

CHAPTER 13

THE BUILDING OF *MONA MONA*

I FIRST MET BOB AND RAMONA SUTTON *during sea trials aboard* Salvation II *off Dana Point, California. The Sinks and Suttons shared common friends on the West Coast, and with Jim and Susy's purchase of a long-range cruiser and the Suttons' intimate knowledge of the subject, we were all brought together.*

It was on that warm spring day in 1990 off Laguna Beach, while discussing cruising motorboats, that Bob suggested Beebe's book was too good to forget and expressed the need to revise and republish it. I had read the account of Mona Mona*'s construction and first attempt at crossing the Atlantic, and throughout that day Bob related their adventures with* Mona Mona *after* Voyaging Under Power *had been published.*

Later, as we reentered the harbor, Bob suggested I should get involved with a revision of Beebe's book and promised a follow-up on their original chapter. Here, then, is the original story, along with "More on Mona Mona*."*

Bob Beebe introduced the Suttons' story with the following note:

I can't imagine a more unlikely candidate for a "do-it-yourself" big-boat-building project than Bob Sutton. When he asked me to design a 50-foot Passagemaker for him to build personally, I'll admit I had some nagging fears that it might turn out to be one more backyard monument to a dreamer who let himself be overmatched.

At the time, Bob was in his early 60s. Thirty years of sitting behind a Columbia Broadcasting System desk had equipped him with a 30-pound spare tire, which was going to get heavier every time he climbed a scaffold. To the best of my knowledge, he had never built so much as a dinghy; he had carpenters put the bookshelves in his home, and he had never used a power tool more complicated than the electric rotisserie on his barbecue.

Later, I'll point out the things that make his backyard-built *Mona Mona* such a remarkably successful vessel.

What prompts a man with such a limited background to take on such a chore? I think Bob can tell it better in his own words.

MONA MONA *AND HOW SHE GREW*
by Robert Patrick Sutton

I got hipped on Bob's Passagemaker concept in the spring of 1967. My wife, Ramona, and I were invited to crew with Bob and Linford Beebe and another couple from Newport Beach, California, to Miami aboard the original *Passagemaker.* On our arrival in Miami, I called the executive VP at CBS to whom I reported and said, "Start plans for an early retirement—I know what I want to spend the rest of my life doing."

I had dreamed the long-distance-cruising dream for many years. But I had also crewed on some ocean-racers, including the *Queen Mab,* a lovely old Herreshoff schooner, 78 feet overall and representing my idea of just about the kind of liveaboard space I wanted on a retirement boat. I had a pretty good idea of *Mab*'s upkeep costs—and I personally knew the amount of backbreaking labor 14 of us expended driving her to Honolulu in the 1955 Transpac. World cruising means sailboat. Comfortable living aboard means *big* sailboat. Big sailboat means lots of money and lots of crew. So forget it. That's how the logic went until the Newport Beach–Miami trip aboard *Passagemaker.*

By September of 1967 I was on the beach, blessed with a few retirement dollars and an understanding wife, ready to go passage-making. But how?

I checked boatyard costs in the U.S. I exchanged some correspondence with Hong Kong and Taiwan. I looked for used boats. The fishing industry in San Diego was having real problems, so I shopped for distress sales in used workboats that I might convert. I did a tour of the Pacific Northwest to check out the ferrocement circuit.

Meanwhile, Roger Bury of Westport, Connecticut, had acquired *Passagemaker* and was looking for a crew for an Atlantic crossing. I jumped at the chance to do some more passage-making and also to search the south of England for converted motor-fishing vessels. I even flew to Malta to look at some prewar gold-platers that were reasonably priced.

Figure 13-1.
Mona Mona *a few days after her launching.*

There were some pretty serious objections to all of them. They just couldn't be fitted into the Passagemaker concept.

About this time, Bob Beebe sent me a clipping from *Boating* about a 65-foot schooner Lloyd Clark was building at his Glas-Dock company in Long Beach, California.

He had come up with a one-off fiberglass building method that started with a big, wooden-batten basket that was then lined with fiberglass sheets. These fiberglass sheets, made right in the yard over a flat Formica form, were secured to the inside of the batten basket from the outside with self-tapping metal screws. Then, using the fiberglass sheets as the exterior skin of the vessel, Clark built an outer hull of four laminations each of mat and woven roving, with extra strength at critical areas.

Then longitudinal fiberglass stiffeners were bonded into the outer hull. They were formed on 2- x 4-inch strips of polyurethane foam placed on 17-inch centers. At this point, his hull was already stronger than the Lloyds 100A1 rules for fiberglass construction.

Clark then went one step further: He filled in between the longitudinal stringers with 2-inch polyurethane foam, faired it with a Sur-form, and laid up an inner hull of the same fiberglass layup used in the outer hull.

The end result was an enormously stiff, reasonably light hull—and at a price substantially below anything comparable being offered by the kit makers.

I climbed all over Clark's hull, looked at the process and thought, "With some professional guidance and a little bit of luck, I can do that."

I prayed earnestly for the luck and made a deal with Lloyd Clark for the professional guidance. The deal included space in his yard to build *Mona Mona*, the right to hire some of his people intermittently, and materials-purchasing service through his firm.

With solid professional support assured, I commissioned Bob Beebe to start drawing.

The design problem we presented to Bob was straightforward: to design a second-generation version of *Passagemaker* for someone with no particular interest in the French canals, who never wants to lay hand on a piece of sail again, and who promises to stay out of the North Atlantic and never go 'round the Horn.

Mona Mona was the result.

We got the drawings from Bob for Christmas 1969.

Bob came south and helped me loft her lines in January 1970.

In February 1970, Lloyd Clark went out of business.

And there I was with plans for a 50-footer, the lines lofted full size, and all the framing cut to build *Mona Mona* by the Lloyd Clark method—but no Lloyd Clark.

In November 1972, at Lido Shipyard in Newport Beach, California, we launched *Mona Mona*.

And in between those two dates were three of the funniest, hardest-working, most frustrating, muscle-straining, expensive, and glorious years that I reckon among the considerable number I have spent on this globe.

I worked with geniuses, hippie freaks, competent professionals, flakes, one man who was as dedicated as I to making *Mona Mona* a great boat, and a jerk who showed up on the job with an American flag sewed to the seat of his pants. I had to keep an eye out for rising costs, material shortages, and a kid with a scraggly beard who took marijuana breaks and tried to float off the end of the scaffolding because a ladder seemed too Establishment oriented.

But it all paid off when we took our shakedown cruise to Turtle Bay in Baja California, in

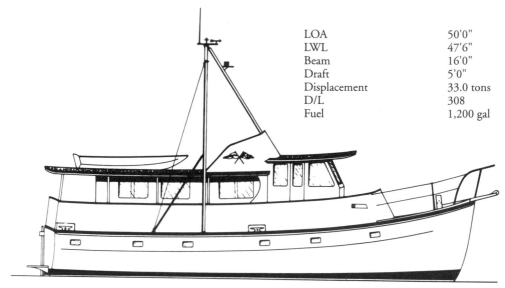

LOA	50'0"
LWL	47'6"
Beam	16'0"
Draft	5'0"
Displacement	33.0 tons
D/L	308
Fuel	1,200 gal

Figure 13-2. *Profile,* Mona Mona.

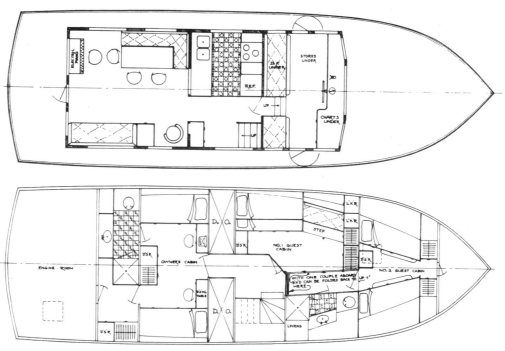

Figure 13-3. *Accommodation,* Mona Mona.

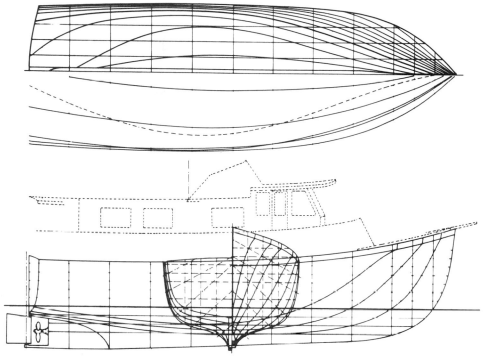

Figure 13-4. *Lines of Beebe 50-foot Design 88,* Mona Mona.

March 1973. The trip of about 500 miles there and our stay were, as our British friends put it, "without incident." Coming back, we left the shelter of Cedros Island and headed into a north-wester that our navigator labeled as a "conservative Force 8." It took us 22 hours to make the 90 miles from Cedros to the shelter behind Punta Baja.

Mona Mona behaved like a lady through it all. With both flopperstoppers out, we seldom rolled beyond 20 degrees. Hour after hour of punching right into the weather produced no creaking and groaning; the hull just simply wasn't working at all. And everything mechanical kept right on doing its appointed thing.

We were convinced we'd gotten our own personal, hand-tooled version of *Passagemaker.*

Later tests confirmed that she was performing to specifications. Stability tests showed her meta-centric height well within the limits set by the designer; she cruised at 8.5 knots using about 70 hp; at our economical cruising speed of 7.5 knots she burned 3 gph, giving us an honest 3,000-mile cruising range on her 1,200 gallons of fuel.

We felt we were ready to go passage-making.

We set our departure date for the big adventure: May 1, 1973.

Actually, about 1500 on April 30 we realized there was nothing more to do: Ship's stores were stowed, the ship was fueled, the crew was aboard, and the good-byes had been made.

We looked at each other and said, "Why not? We might just as well spend the night at sea as here in Newport Harbor." So at 1620 on April 30, we cranked up the main engine and departed Newport Beach on a passage that we hoped would wind up in the Mediterranean.

Starting eight hours early seemed a good omen. You never start a small-boat voyage on time. Always there are delays caused by tardy crew arrivals, supplies that arrive late, or last-minute repairs.

But there we were at sea early. The next morning at 1000 saw us dropping the hook in Ensenada Harbor. We weighed anchor at 1330 that afternoon with the entrance-to-Mexico formalities taken care of and the freezer loaded with a few dozen of the fresh *bolillos* that are an Ensenada specialty.

We had a six-day stretch ahead of us now, with the next stop scheduled in Manzanillo. *Mona Mona* was finally doing what she was designed for: taking six people over a long stretch of ocean with reasonable comfort and privacy.

Reasonable comfort, hell! It was luxury.

The three gals put on a cooking competition that would slow the Galloping Gourmet down to a walk. Each day, two of the ladies were on galley duty while the third one took care of one long daylight watch.

As skipper, I didn't set up a detailed watch list for the ladies; just told them that I expected the three of them to cover cooking, dishes, and the daylight watch from 0900 to 1400. How they did it, or who did what, was up to them.

I realize more authoritarian skippers would be driven up the bulkhead by this attitude, but to me it represented a victory of realism over a new gold-encrusted blue cap. I've spent much of my professional life dealing with creative people. Many of my unprofessional—and happier— moments have been spent around women. And I've never learned how to boss either group.

So I just take them up to the mountaintop, show them the beautiful scene on the distant horizon, and turn them loose. This is known as the Lazy Executive's Shuffle. It's amazing how often it works.

Bob Beebe was our navigator. He took the watch from 0400 to 0800 and was on duty any other time he figured navigating chores needed doing. He was also the man to call in the middle of the night in case of an outside emergency. For an inside emergency I still wanted to get at it personally at the earliest possible moment.

Bob Wendling, with his fine background of teaching auto shop in the San Diego high schools and his years of skippering his own boat, made a wonderful first mate. He and I shared the remaining watches. And if you think having all the males aboard ship named "Bob" doesn't make for some interesting moments, I'll put in with you.

Linford Beebe, Joan Wendling, and my own Ramona—of *Mona Mona*—cooked and cooked. And with a freezer full of food, fresh supplies, and over a ton of canned goods, the major danger on board was instant obesity.

We had all done some cruising before, and with the boat behaving so well, everything soon shook down to the succession of days and nights and watches and meals and miles made good over the bottom that passage-making is all about.

Manzanillo came up on schedule on the afternoon of May 7.

A competent ship's agent there found us cheap diesel fuel, bottled water (500 gallons' worth delivered in the original bottles for $17), and clearance papers for Costa Rica.

Seven more days got us to Puntarenas, Costa Rica.

En route, the Gulf of Tehuantepec behaved just fine—and its waters can get sloppy. Less pleasant was the sea off the coast of Nicaragua: The land just wasn't high enough to keep the northeast trades from coming at us, and butting into 25- to 30-knot headwinds is tiresome after two days.

Figure 13-5. *En route to Panama,* Mona Mona's *F/S gear proves the old adage: "One good tern deserves another."*

On departing Puntarenas, a short visit to Jesusita Island gave us a proper tropical-cruising feeling, and we were off to Panama.

Now the Panama Canal transit, to a small boat, can be a real rump-buster. You get into one of the upbound locks, and the ship ahead of you starts up his propeller, and if you lose a bow line, or if you have been foolish enough to tie up to the side of the lock instead of asking for "center lockage," you go through the trauma of seeing your pretty little boat get beat to hell.

Our *Mona Mona* luck held.

As we reached the first lock, there was a Panama Canal Company tug on the port hand. On instructions from our pilot, we rafted up to the tug and let his crew do all the work of linehandling. As we reached the top of the first lock, the skipper said, "Leave her lashed. I'll tow you to the next one." So we got a free and gentle ride up that one, too. Next lock? Another tug and another free ride for *Mona Mona.* It's got to be the easiest transit a small boat has ever made. We dropped our pilot in Cristóbal at 1445. Fifteen minutes later we were rigged for sea and pulling out of Cristóbal for Florida, all for $90, of which $25 was for a one-time measuring fee. And remember, you must be ready to pay in cash!

The Florida leg had a couple of memorable moments. The radar packed up just as we were approaching the west end of Cuba. The Castroites have been known to get goosey when small unidentified boats approach their island at night. The alternative was to take a big swing around the island, wasting time and fuel, so knowing exactly where you are becomes important. In spite of continuously overcast skies, Bob did some precision navigation, and we stayed just about the right distance off Cuba.

But joining that big stream of tankers that depart the ports of the Gulf of Mexico and make a U-turn around the Florida Keys into the Straits of Florida bound north makes for some tense moments. One night we had six or seven tankers in sight at a time. We were doing 7.5 knots and they were doing 15 to 20 knots. No radar, so you keep up all your relative bearings the old-fashioned way.

But they all did what they were supposed to do, and we did what we were supposed to do, and nobody hit nobody, and Key West showed up right where it belonged.

There was a lot of conversation in Florida and elsewhere about fuel shortages, but not once did we get turned away. An order of 800 to 1,000 gallons of Number 2 diesel didn't seem to upset anyone, and the prices didn't get out of line.

However, neither in Key West, Miami, nor Fort Lauderdale were we able to find anyone to fix the radar, so we took off for Bermuda without it.

The Atlantic decided to get a little less cooperative on the Bermuda leg. We were slowed down a couple of times by some pretty good-size swells from the east.

What with the slowing down for weather, and a few hours off for a cooling-system repair, we were just over six days going from Fort Lauderdale to Bermuda, arriving June 11. And, quite frankly, having done 5,000 nautical miles in six weeks, we were a little travel-weary.

The Wendlings had to leave us in Bermuda; it was all they had signed on for. Our replacement crewmember, due in from the West Coast, got involved in a business deal he just couldn't walk away from. So we found ourselves shorthanded for the Atlantic crossing. We were a week lining up new crew in Bermuda. We were lucky in the ones we found. Ray Wilson and Ron Firth both had seagoing engineering experience in big ships and were glad to take advantage of a free ride to Europe.

So we were off to the Azores—Horta 1,800 miles away—six of us in a 50-foot backyard special.

The June departure was carefully chosen. The pilot charts show that in that month at those latitudes, you're right in the doldrums; you should slice precisely through the middle of the Bermuda High and find 1,800 miles of millpond—ideal weather and seas for a power-driven passagemaker. That's the way we found it when we made the crossing in 1969—the ocean and the pilot charts were in perfect accord.

Not in 1973.

Something pushed the northeast trades way north of their usual limits, and we started slugging into the so-called "reinforced trades" coming from dead ahead at 25 to 30 knots, making for that miserable, tiring, fuel-consuming, hobby-horse pitching.

We were so sure that the easterlies would disappear shortly that we started off at our "fast" cruise speed—8.5 knots. This power setting had checked out to give us about 1.8 nautical miles per gallon. The slide rule showed that we should arrive in Horta with 15 percent of our fuel remaining. We had proven she'd do 1.8 nautical miles per gallon in still water. Only problem, the water wouldn't stay still. Two days out of Bermuda we realized that with the headwinds and seas slowing us down, we were burning too much fuel. So we changed the generator pulleys on our main-engine generator and slowed down to 7.5 knots, running just under a speed/length ratio of 1.1.

At the same time we headed north to try to get out of the misplaced NE trades. According to the pilot chart, about 200 miles north of the Bermuda–Azores rhumb line there should be wind from the west: That is the normal sailing route.

When we got there, the damned easterlies were *still* hitting us right on the bow, and fuel consumption was getting a little dicey. We kept a fuel "How-Goes-It" curve. It kept showing that if everything went on exactly as it was, we would land in the Azores with zero gallons of fuel. If things got worse, we would wind up with zero gallons of fuel some miles short of the Azores. And there was no Coast Guard to come out and get us. If we made the decision now, we could turn back to Bermuda with a good margin of safety.

Or, we could plug on a couple of days, *then* turn back, and if conditions worsened *ahead*, then we could wind up with zero gallons of fuel *before* we made it back to Bermuda. Figuring conservatively, at about 700 miles from Bermuda, we had reached a point of no return.

The older I get, the fewer things I know for sure. But among those certain bits of knowledge is this one: The sea is unremittingly unforgiving of damn fools.

So we turned around and headed back for Bermuda.

And those same easterlies that had been making life so unpleasant blew us right back into Bermuda. And, after a couple of days of R & R in Bermuda, those same easterlies blew us right into Newport, Rhode Island.

Crew schedules got tight; the freak weather conditions of that summer might hold on long enough to prevent an Atlantic crossing that year—and we'd always wanted to cruise the coast of Maine, anyway.

The 610 miles from Bermuda to Newport were made in three days with the help of those easterlies, plus that great sense of lift you get when you and the weather are cooperating. We were only two couples aboard, which made for longer watches but less complicated shipboard routine.

The radar still wasn't working. And the scene of Bob Beebe navigating us right up to the Brenton Reef Texas Tower in 50-yard visibility without proper charts and using the Zenith All-Wave Receiver held in both hands and rotated in an effort to turn it into a radio direction finder, was a lesson in navigational improvisation.

But we found Newport, and after checking in with one of the friendliest Customs-Agriculture-Immigration officials the U.S. career bureaucracy has ever produced, we officially ended the passage-making and started the coastal cruising.

At several points in his articles on the art of passage-making, Bob Beebe has stressed that crossing ocean in a small boat is simply something to be done so that one may enjoy the local cruising. The essence of passage-making is that the great cruising grounds of the world are opened up to you if you can reach them on your own bottom: the maximum of cruising pleasure with a minimum of expense, time, and trauma.

The rest of the summer on *Mona Mona* proved that point beautifully.

The cruise went "down east to Maine" as far as Roque Island and Machias Bay; south through New England, paying particular attention to the Cape Cod area; then a little time in Long Island Sound. Then outside to the mouth of the Delaware and a month spent exploring Delaware and Chesapeake bays.

Nights on the hook back of deserted piney islands in Maine, a week in Boston tied up in a downtown marina, down New York's East River and past the Statue of Liberty, and up the Potomac to Washington—the whole great cruising ground of the east coast of the United States was there for the express purpose of giving three months of enjoyment to a crew of West Coasters.

And that cruise made the building of *Mona Mona*—the three years at hard labor and the spending of too much of the family money—all worthwhile.

So read Bob Beebe and his book on Passagemakers and passage-making with great caution—it may be injurious to your peace of mind.

You see what happened to one couple who listened to Bob's insidious siren song of how the waters of the world can be yours even though you're heavy in the middle, light in the pocketbook, and the reverse of a horny-handed salt.

World cruising for those of middle age and pot bellies?

It'll never work.

ABOUT MONA MONA

Well, that's a good yarn by Bob Sutton. And not too far from the facts, though I thought he helped me lay down the lines. Seriously, the whole thing was a major effort that was remarkably successful. I think the secret of its success was that Bob treated it as a regular nine-to-five job, five days a week, without fail.

One thing that is not in his story is how superbly he and his wife, Mona, decorated the vessel—light and airy and quite superior to several larger and more expensive yachts I have inspected recently.

At the start, I was not too happy about drawing a 50-foot double-decker, but with Bob's promise to stay out of the North Atlantic and to use her as a liveaboard home in the Mediterranean, I decided it could be done, and we could still call her a Passagemaker.

The building method influenced her in two ways: The wooden form made it necessary to design her as if she were to be built of wood; and it made desirable a main deck that ran full length without a break. In addition, the main saloon area aft required an almost flat profile, and we

Figure 13-6. *Building* Mona Mona: *The batten basket in which the hull was laid up.*

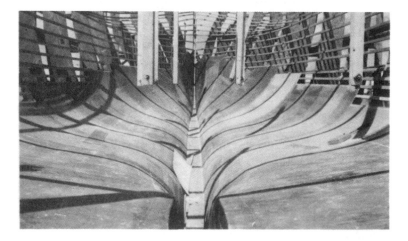

Figure 13-7. *Bottom fiberglass panels laid in the batten basket.*

wanted a higher bow than *Passagemaker*'s for the reasons previously discussed. All this combined to produce a sheerline that didn't look like much on tracing paper, but a scale model showed it would be okay in the round, so we went ahead.

We agreed on the necessity of raising the pilothouse to give vision aft, hence the step-up here. This caused a feeling of insecurity coming out the pilothouse door. If you fell, you could quite possibly go over the side. Hence the pipe rail there, which more than complies with my rule of 4-foot-high rails in any area where the watch-stander can approach the side. It was a blessing while taking sights, too.

Like all *Passagemaker*-trained crewmen, Bob didn't think much of having an outside steering station. But one was drawn in topside if he wanted it. The sheerline was lowered by putting the engine aft. The flopperstopper gear is 39 percent of LWL forward of the stern, instead of the ideal 28 percent, because it had to be placed on the aft galley bulkhead, which is a major structural member, needed to hold it. A slight "double drag" effect was noted.

The lines were made a bit broader in beam at the waterline to make her stiffer—so as to carry the topside weights. One of these was supposed to be a small auto Bob made up. (He has been building and racing sports cars for years.) As none of this topside weight has been installed to date, she turned out to be too stiff, with the results described in Chapter 9.

Her accommodations worked out very well and show how much room is added by double-decking. In Maine, it was interesting to be visited by the crew of one of the better "trawlers," a model 50 feet long with no double-decking whatever, which had actually followed the same track from California that we had. Their expressions of astonishment and downright envy over the difference in crew's quarters, particularly forward, were revealing.

The idea of folding away the partition that separates the two forward cabins worked out very well when only two couples were aboard. Linford and I lived like that in Maine and really enjoyed the feeling of luxurious space. The way to make it perfect would be to arrange the aft top bunk to hinge down and make a settee back.

The first cruise of the *Mona Mona* was really something when you think about it. She had had a shakedown, but a short one. Yet there we were heading out for a destination some 9,000 miles away, expecting to meet some people on the dock at a prearranged time. We would have pulled it off if the weather had cooperated. Everything worked, except the radar. The few troubles we had were minor and easily fixed, and altogether it was a great performance by the "Sutton Shipyard."

Inspection of the weather maps after we came home shows what happened. The pilot chart

Figure 13-8. *Bob Sutton (left) and Bob Beebe on the* Mona Mona's *bow.*

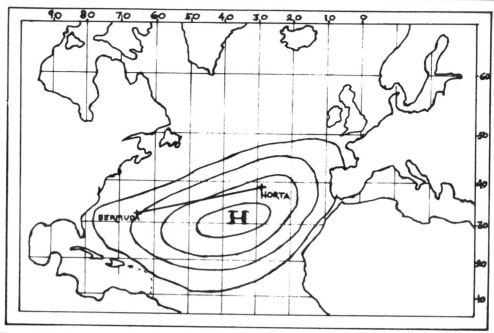

Figure 13-9. *Tracing, weather chart: Average isobars for June, North Atlantic.*

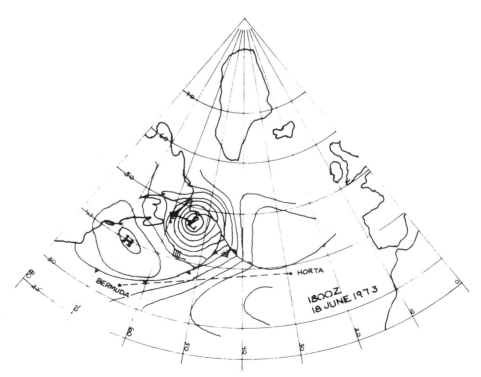

Figure 13-10. *Tracing, weather chart: June 18, 1973.*

Figure 13-11. *Tracing, weather chart: June 20, 1973.*

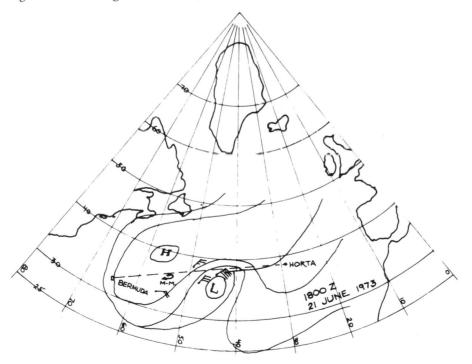

Figure 13-12. *Tracing, weather chart: June 21, 1973.*

shows the average pressures and position of the center to be expected in June in the North Atlantic, and how they relate to the Bermuda–Azores course. In 1969 we had several days of calm. In 1972 the racers from Bermuda to Spain complained about the light airs all the way. But in 1973, a complete reversal.

The day we left Bermuda there was a full-fledged storm up near Newfoundland. Behind this storm, high pressure was forecast to press out over the ocean along Long Island but was not forecast to push down to Bermuda. But it did—early on June 19 we experienced the frontal passage with rain and wind shifts. On June 20 the wind shifted to the east and remained there for at least 22 days, when I stopped checking it. What happened is shown on the map for June 20.

The front pushed down to about Latitude 30°N and then formed waves along its length, at least two of them. With the high pressure north of us, these waves reinforced the easterly winds around the high and kept this up until we had to concede defeat. On June 21, winds of 40 knots were reported ahead of us and we could see swells passing us that looked like the winds were higher than that.

On June 26, when we were back in Bermuda, the map still showed a high center north of our proposed track, producing easterly winds clear to Horta. And, as Bob said, we had southeast winds all the way to Newport, Rhode Island, where we arrived in the evening of July 3. Well, I've always wanted to cruise in Maine!

Author's note (1974): Just before this book went to press we learned from Bob Sutton that *Mona Mona* had made a successful crossing of the Atlantic, from Morehead City, North Carolina, to Bermuda, Horta in the Azores, and Lisbon, Portugal, in June and July 1974. This time they had a few rough days but no problems with headwinds, making the crossing Bermuda–Horta on 795 gallons of fuel in 270 hours running time.

MORE ON MONA MONA *by Robert Patrick Sutton*

In 1974, *Mona Mona* lived up to her designer's description—"an ocean-crossing motorboat"—and truly became a Passagemaker, a personal boat built to cross the oceans that separate the great cruising areas of the world.

Briefly. From 1974 to 1983, we cruised extensively: the Costa Brava of Spain; the French Riviera and the lesser known French Mediterranean coast of Languedoc–Roussillon; the whole boot of Italy; and the Dalmatian Coast of what was Yugoslavia—up and down a half-dozen times. Then a good look at the Ionian and Aegean seas of Greece; plus the jewel in our cruising crown— the southern coast of Turkey from Marmaris to Cypress.

Extensively? We got to know every harbor, anchorage, and gunkhole from Seville, up the Guadalquivir River, to Side, on a Turkish roadstead just above Cyprus.

In 1983, after a wedding ceremony, reception, and party for my son that started on *Mona Mona* and took in the Real Club Nautico and half the town of Palma de Mallorca, we departed the Med. Our new heading: Gibraltar; the Canary Islands; the Cape Verde Islands; Barbados, 2,000 miles to the west; and then a right turn up to Palmas del Mar in Puerto Rico.

In 1984, we took our Caribbean cruise "down island," hitting them all—Windward and Leeward—as far as Grenada. We then took a slant toward the coast of Venezuela, and left the boat in Bonaire, in the Netherlands Antilles.

In 1985, we brought her back to Puerto Rico and did a little soul searching. We took a good

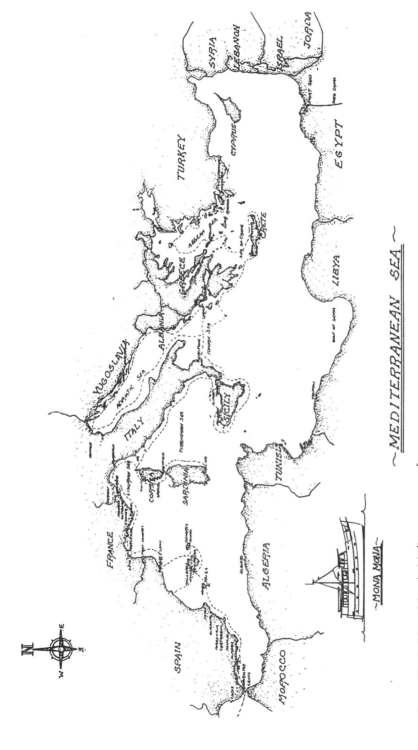

Figure 13-13. Mona Mona's *Mediterranean travel.*

long look at *Mona Mona* and each other: "The years are piling up—and we've had twelve great ones."

"Nothing lasts forever."

"Maybe the time has come to swallow the anchor."

"Let's quit while we're ahead." We did.

What were the lessons learned?

To split our year up into six months cruising and six months in the real world worked for us; good solid cruising, good time for family and friends, and truncated careers and hobbies. For us that was right. I know there are couples who live aboard full time. Some make their marriages work, some don't. There are also couples that leave the boat in a good cruising area and then fly back and forth for a month's cruise now and then—too expensive for us. There are also couples that take three years off for a circumnavigation. I won the war in the Pacific and want nothing more to do with it.

One of the main lessons learned from our cruising pattern was how inexpensive it was: six months on the boat cost us less than six months ashore, and we rented our house for the six months we were gone. In the Med we shopped at supermarkets in the bigger ports or at the farmers' markets, which are required by law in some of the countries. The booze was bought duty-free, and the local wine, what the Limeys call "plonk," was good enough for the natives, and for us.

We allowed our guests to pay for the additional costs they brought with them. A caveat from my tax guy: don't take money from your guests. You'll have to declare it as income and then lay expenses against it—a damn paperwork nuisance. One of the good devices is to set up a "Stewards' Purse," where everybody makes a contribution to a fund and whoever does the ship's shopping buys from that fund; when it runs out—pass the hat again.

Fuel was a minor cost. *Mona Mona* cruises at 7.5 knots. Including lots of generator time, that gives us a conservative average of about 2 miles to the gallon. If we confine our year's cruise to 1,000 to 1,500 miles we've got the best of it; we only have to load up with fuel once a season. And by asking around you find out which countries have bargains in duty-free. Plus a sensible cruise schedule means you can hang around until someone says "whatinhell are we doing here so long?"

The Caribbean is one of the great cruising grounds of the world—but once was enough for us. Just as the Med is a powerboat sea, the Caribbean is a sailor's delight—those trades make you glad for the sticks and strings. Further, the Caribbean is a winter cruising ground—great for the East Coast refugees from winter—not that great for Californians. One of the great advantages of cruising the Med was that we did it in the summer and spent our shoreside time in southern California in the winter, when we're not up to our navels in tourists.

At this point, let's say a kind word for ocean crossing in a Passagemaker type. Bob Beebe says that ocean crossing is the dull interval between being happy cruisers. Not necessarily so. Earlier in the book, Norrie Hoyt has talked about the enormous amounts of time you have to yourself on an ocean voyage, for reading, talking, and just plain goofing off, and the joy—peculiar to a sailor—of crossing an ocean in your bedroom slippers. And Bob Beebe talks about the sense of well-being that comes from the involuntary isometric exercises that you do just moving around and keeping upright.

Well, these were all there in great abundance in our Mallorca–Puerto Rico crossing. We enjoyed them to the quiet rumbling of the big old Cummins turning at 1,150 rpm. Plus the relaxed non-stress that comes when all the gear is working. After all, a 50-foot Passagemaker is a big hole in the water that you can crowd with comfort-giving amenities. Two refrigeration systems, both of which loafed along at half-load. A watermaker that pumped out 100 gallons a day, allowing showering and clothes washing to the max. A freezer full of goodies, including—and this still grabs me when I remember it—ice cream for all hands every night. A good ship's library with a barrel of paperbacks and a Zenith All-Wave radio to keep us entertained, and a satnav that kept us informed within a quarter-mile of where we were and how far we had to go and on what course we had to go that far—rhumb line or great circle.

That, too, was what passage-making is all about.

So may all your cruising be reminiscent of *Mona Mona*'s last ocean passage, and be—in Bob Beebe's phrase—"without incident."

CHAPTER 14

WATCH-STANDING ABOARD THE OCEAN-CROSSING MOTORBOAT

ROBERT BEEBE ONCE WROTE:

> *At long last the weeks and months of planning have come to an end. Everything is done that has to be done to make the ship "fully found and ready for sea." It is time to go, time to leave the shores for the vast reaches of the open ocean. It is also time to think about the duties and responsibilities that lie ahead, the routines to be followed, the preparations for any emergency.*
>
> *Abandoning the land to sail thousands of miles on the open sea has always been a significant occasion. No matter how many times I have done it myself, it has never lost its sense of mystery, of anticipation; there's even a little dread.*

Captain Beebe promoted the concept that watch-standing aboard the long-range motorboat was far easier than the same duty aboard a sailing yacht. The watch-stander under sail is generally exposed to the elements, almost every watch requires sail trimming, and experienced vigilance is required in the face of advancing squalls and changing wind conditions. The penalty for negligence, inexperience, or incompetence can be sudden disaster—jibing booms, torn sails, or worse. On the other hand, aboard the motor yacht the watch-stander is enclosed within a protected wheelhouse, and in lieu of sails and wind his concern is to carefully monitor engine instruments, watch for traffic, and perform other responsibilities requiring less experience and physical effort than the duties required under sail. A sudden passing squall is generally nothing more than a log entry, requiring little or no action on the watch-stander's part.

Referring to passage-making aboard a proper long-range motorboat, Captain Beebe writes:

> *Stabilized against rolling—that curse of the ordinary motorboat—she steams along in the calmest weather she can find at a rate that exceeds the average possible for a much larger sailing vessel. With the autopilot performing all the work, her single watch-stander is essentially a lookout.*
>
> *For this, no experience is necessary, because the only duty, until the watch-stander is qualified, is to call the captain when sighting anything.*

191

*WATCH-
STANDING
ABOARD THE
OCEAN-
CROSSING
MOTORBOAT*

Aboard the motor yacht, Beebe's concept—that with simple training, inexperienced individuals can stand lone watches—is even more reasonable today then ever before. The common use of radar and electronic navigation, and their exceptional reliability (see Chapter 20), make for safer and far easier cruising. With the increasing use of home computers, video cassette recorders, and other household appliances, more and more people are familiar and comfortable with electronic gadgets. Gone are the days when a radar or Loran were viewed by the "landlubber" as mysterious black boxes of incomprehensible complexity and power. It's just another group of switches or a keyboard to be programmed and mastered, really not much different than a simple electronic address book, a garden-sprinkler control, or even the electronic teller machine. These new and user-friendly marine electronics can be operated and understood by the new watch-stander without much difficulty. It is clearly an advantage of this style of cruising as inexperienced crew are always more plentiful than seasoned, open-ocean sailors.

TRAINING WATCH-STANDERS

Introducing a friend to passage-making ranks as one of the greatest pleasures of voyaging. It's an opportunity to introduce them to an activity they can enjoy throughout their lives, and it can add considerable satisfaction to your own cruise. Of course, there are specific qualifications that any person standing a lone watch must meet, including the ability to stop the ship, to disengage the autopilot, and to use its dodger. VHF radio operation, recognition of ship lights and the ability to determine the direction they are traveling at night, and the use of a hand-bearing compass for collision avoidance are also important. The watch-stander must be familiar with the engine instruments and must be able to enter hourly positions into the logbook. Additionally, each new crewmember should be shown the location of each fire extinguisher and how it is used, know the location of life jackets, and understand the procedure for abandoning ship—including the release of the liferaft and the activation of EPIRBs aboard.

These are all simple tasks that can be taught to a receptive student within a few hours. School can start at the beginning of a voyage, but ideally these basics should be taught prior to departure as there's no guarantee that weather and sea conditions will be conducive to teaching. If the new crewmember knows what's expected of him before the voyage and if the skipper can recommend reference material, the basics can be learned shoreside. With a couple of orientation sessions aboard the vessel prior to departure, a responsible yet inexperienced person will be fine crew.

The captain must remember that he is *always* responsible for the safety of the ship, and he will need to treat crew of varying capabilities differently. A new crewmember should thoroughly understand that he *must* request assistance in even the most basic situations. If the captain is the only one aboard with experience, then he should be called. With more experience aboard, another crewmember may be on call as the first to be summoned when specific routine situations arise— ship sightings, rain squalls, changing conditions, etc. If the watch-stander feels uncomfortable with *anything*—if he hears an unusual sound, smells something odd, notes a change in any engine instrument—he *must* report immediately to a designated person. It's far better to err on the side of caution in these situations as the ship will be more safely operated, and other crew can rest without concern.

A nice addition to the layout of any long-range cruiser is a berth in the wheelhouse. With this arrangement, if the captain feels it necessary, he can sleep within arm's reach of a watch-stander who

Figure 14-1. *Watch
berth in the wheel-
house of the
Nordhavn 46.*

might feel apprehensive during a night watch. Sometimes it's actually easier for the captain to sleep in the wheelhouse as he too feels less concerned about the safety of the ship, being so much closer to render help if necessary.

LOGBOOK

Prior to departure, every crewmember should receive detailed instructions spelling out the specific duties required during a watch. Written instructions are preferable, and a logbook should be developed to record specific information on an hourly basis. Keep the logbook as simple as possible, requiring a minimum number of entries. I'm always amused at how complex and detailed most commercially available logs are: there's a box for every conceivable occurrence, all to be filled out with great regularity. It would be like filling out an extensive loan application each hour, leaving no time to navigate the ship.

The essential hourly entries are position, magnetic heading, rpm, engine-coolant temperature, gear-oil temperature, alternator output in amps and voltage, and check-boxes for engine room and bilge inspections. At the end of each watch a distance-made-good through the watch period and speed over the bottom should be calculated. This requires that position be plotted at each watch change, but it offers an immediate warning if there is a problem with the navigational equipment.

While the watch-stander is logging longitude and latitude, experience and some vigilance are required to roughly calculate the hourly distances between sets of coordinates. A sudden 20-mile spread between two hourly entries where there had been a steady seven or eight between previous fixes surely indicates a problem but might go unnoticed until plotted. If the previous plot looked good, then it would be reasonable to assume that the position at the beginning of the watch was

193

WATCH-
STANDING
ABOARD THE
OCEAN-
CROSSING
MOTORBOAT

YACHT "GRYPHON"

DATE: 7-3-93

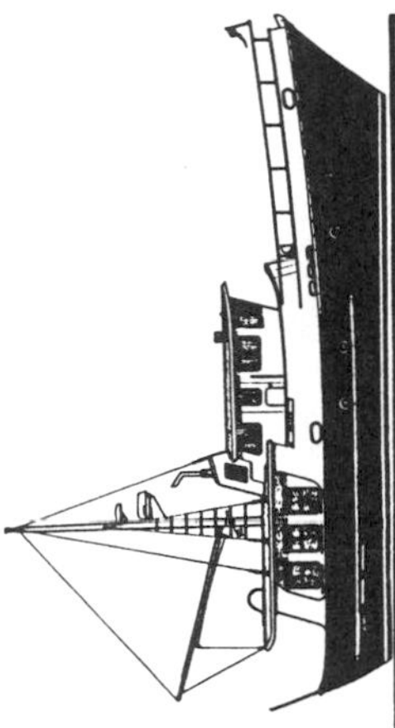

TIME	LAT./LONG.	MAGNETIC HEADING	RPM	TEMP.	GEAR OIL TEMP.	ALT. AMP	VOLTS	ENG. ROOM/BILGE	REMARKS	INTL.
01:00	33.27 117.42	145°	1750	180°	170°	25	13.5	OK	CALM SEAS	
02:00	33.20 117.39	145°	1750	180	170	20	13.7	OK		
03:00	33.12 117.36	145°	1750	180	170	20	13.7	B. PUMP Lt. ON ONCE OK	MOON RISE SHIP TO PORT	
04:00	33.05 117.32	145°	1750	180	170	20	137	CK		

WATCH CHANGE	SPEED	FUEL TANK SETTING	PLOT POS.	BAROMETER	REMARKS	
JEFF	8.1	PORT FWD.	X	10.08	EASY WATCH - NO PROBLEM	

TIME										
05:00										
06:00										
07:00										
08:00										

WATCH CHANGE	SPEED	FUEL TANK SETTING	PLOT POS.	BAROMETER	REMARKS

Figure 14-2. Sample logbook page.

accurate, and a dead-reckoned position could be established using the previous speed (presuming the same rpm had been maintained) and present magnetic heading.

Logging the readings of engine instruments may seem a little excessive, and to a certain extent simply marking the gauges with thin tape to indicate normal readings will suffice; however, I feel logging readings is good practice and worth the effort. The engine is so important—for obvious reasons—and the gauge readings can forewarn of a developing problem and offer helpful information if watched and understood.

For example, a sudden but only slight increase in engine-coolant temperature can indicate a broken impeller blade or a clog in the intake strainer. If noted and taken care of at an opportune time in agreeable conditions, the matter is easily resolved; if the needle-width increase in temperature goes unnoticed, the situation might wait until a precarious time to deteriorate further, requiring immediate action and potentially putting the vessel at risk.

A slight rise in gear-oil temperature can be an indicator that hydraulic fluid is leaking, and sometimes the leak is out the oil-cooling heat-exchanger, so it's not noticeable in the bilge. Catching this early gives the opportunity to take action before the situation turns into a significant problem.

Of course, there is always the possibility that warmer water has been encountered, or that the engine may just be working harder driving into a head sea. Having a continuous log of previous readings at different rpm and in varying sea conditions will allow the situation to be accurately assessed. An abnormal change in a gauge reading can warn of a problem sometimes hours or days in advance.

Voltage, too, should be carefully monitored. With our reliance on electronics, a complete loss of electrical power can be serious; and if the failure of an alternator is not caught early, this is a very real possibility.

On a modern 50-foot yacht with electronics, lighting, electric autopilots, fans, inverters, etc. it isn't uncommon to be drawing in excess of 100 amps of DC power. The alternator is being asked to produce substantial and continuous amperage to replenish the current drawn by the yacht's accessories, and the draw will vary throughout the day—as will the ship's voltage. I have noted that when running at midday, with lighting demands low and without heavy inverter use, voltage will show in a normal high range of about 14 volts; yet before midnight, when everyone is awake, lights are on, and loads are high, the voltage can drop down into the 12-volt range. It's important to understand this and learn to compare voltage readings with previous readings taken under similar load demands. Obviously if a midday reading is noted at 12 volts, a problem is present and action must be taken. Herein lies the need to log these readings.

Logging engine room and bilge inspections ensures that the job is being done by each watch-stander. There won't be much to report, but the box must be checked.

Barometric pressure should be logged regularly, along with other weather conditions. Leaving plenty of room after each series of entries for remarks will allow a variety of other information and data to be logged. Each vessel may have additional specific logging needs, such as day-tank fillings, pyrometer readings, fuel vacuum, stabilizer deployment, etc.

LONE WATCH-STANDING

Open-ocean watch-standing aboard the long-range motorboat is often a passive role. Instruments are monitored, log entries are made, and sometimes the ship will proceed through many watch shifts without a single adjustment to course or speed. The comforting pulse of the easy-running

195

*WATCH-
STANDING
ABOARD THE
OCEAN-
CROSSING
MOTORBOAT*

diesel undertones life aboard. The watches pass with relaxed routine. It is easy traveling. The rested watch-stander is awakened by alarm or summoned by the concluding watch, and often simply rolls out of a warm bunk and reports to a cozy wheelhouse. There's no donning of heavy jackets or rain gear, and the watch-stander is often still half asleep when the ship's con is handed over. The hourly entries serve to discipline each crewmember into maintaining a higher level of vigilance, making for safer passage-making, and helping to pass the hours of the watch.

Sleeping on duty is no small problem and cannot be tolerated at sea. A good captain should watch for this with any new crewmember, and if found napping, he should be confronted and the problem discussed. Sometimes it's necessary to open windows, stand during watches, or step outside every 15 minutes for air. Hand-steering is also a good way to stay awake and pass the time. Usually the embarrassment of being caught just once will eliminate the problem. A captain who makes a habit of occasionally visiting the wheelhouse during his off-watch will usually find an alert watch-stander.

The watch-stander often needs to step outside to get a clearer view of a distant light to visually locate a blip on the radar screen. If the vessel isn't equipped with a Portuguese bridge or very secure rails of appropriate height—outboard of the wheelhouse doors and completely surrounding the space the watch-stander will occupy when outside—then a safety harness should be required, or a second crewmember should be summoned to ensure the watch-stander's safety while outside the protection of the wheelhouse. I've been surprised by how many vessels are designed such that an open wheelhouse door combined with a stumble or a fast roll induced by an out-of-sync wave could result in a person actually flying through the door and flipping directly overboard. If there is *any* possibility of this, a lifeline gate should be used across the door when it's left open.

Figure 14-3. *Hank Schuette on watch at night in the Atlantic.*

Falling overboard and watching the vessel's stern light as it steams off over the horizon is every mariner's worst nightmare. Without belaboring the point, more men are lost overboard while relieving themselves than for any other reason. This is easy to imagine as the procedure requires a sometimes-precarious stance and leaves only one hand available to hang on with. Generally this happens at night when no one is around to see, and it can be an extremely dangerous alternative to using the onboard wc.

Watch schedules are always the subject of debate. Various approaches can be taken, with the only real requirement being proper rest for everyone. No single watch system is perfect for every vessel, and coming up with the best one requires taking into account the number of persons aboard, their levels of experience, and their talents and desires.

One thing is for sure: no matter how long the passages are, the night watches are more difficult than those during the day. I've always had good luck with a schedule that recognizes this distinction. Four- to six-hour watches are easy during the daytime and evening, but late-night watches—between 2100 and 0600—should be limited to three hours if possible. With three watch-standers a schedule like this will work:

0600–1200	1200–1700	1600–2100	2100–2400	2400–0300	0300–0600
(B)Jim	(L)Dan	(D)Jeff	Jim	Dan	Jeff(B)
Jim(L)	Dan(D)	Jeff	Jim	Dan	Jeff
(B)Jim	(L)Dan	(D)Jeff	Jim	Dan	Jeff(B)

Each 24 hours: Jim 9, Dan 8, Jeff 8

(B) breakfast, (L) lunch, (D) dinner

This schedule would be agreeable to me as I would not be responsible for any dinners—only breakfasts and lunches—and I would not be up after midnight. Were I the captain of the ship, this would still be acceptable as I could complete my added work during my watches, which would not be a problem. It's safe to assume that someone would be awake before lunch time, and I would plan my engine room inspection and fuel checks then. This plan requires volunteers for meal clean-up, but that generally doesn't present a problem.

For offshore use where insurance is involved, three crewmembers are generally the minimum acceptable—most insurance companies require this number. Three is fine if everyone can chip in; with four aboard and each standing a separate watch, it's absolute luxury. Four aboard allows many schedule variations, including a duplicate of the three-man plan above where each watch-stander is freed from watch-standing and becomes cook every fourth day.

Some watch schedules vary from day to day. I've used these and really don't mind them, but there is some logic to daily repetitive watches. For me at least, it is easier to get into a routine of sleeping during specific hours, and I find I can adjust to the repetitive schedule quite well after a few days. Adjusting to a rotating schedule—where a crewmember sleeps between 2400 and 0600 one night and then must be awake the next—may be harder than adjusting to a fixed nightly routine.

During passages where time zones are crossed, it has worked out well simply to make the adjustment at midday. Someone always gets a hour cut off or added to his watch, but during the day no one seems to mind much. Whenever calculations are made for fuel burn and daily plots, Zulu time (GMT) should be used as changing the clocks can cause confusion with added or lost hours.

As conditions change during a voyage, the watch schedule may need to be adjusted. For instance,

197

*WATCH-
STANDING
ABOARD THE
OCEAN-
CROSSING
MOTORBOAT*

during heavy weather it may be necessary to keep more experienced crewmembers on duty because more activities need close attention: changes to course and speed may be required, depending on the sea conditions; extra vigilance is important because of poor visibility and the reduced effectiveness of radar in high seas; and fuel-filter vacuum and water-separator bowls must be watched due to the potential for stirring up debris and water inside the fuel tank (discussed in Chapter 7).

OPERATION OF ELECTRONICS

Much of the operation of the ship is left to the captain or an experienced, designated crewmember; fuel management, engine maintenance, routing, and many other operating responsibilities and decisions are not a part of the watch-stander's duties. As each member of the crew gains experience, he or she can take on more responsibility, but the captain must be prepared to limit authority to ensure it does not exceed the crewmember's capability.

An example of this is the adjustment of electronics such as radar, sonar, autopilots, and radios. It's standard procedure to constantly tune gain, range, and filtering adjustments on radar and sonar, which allows an *experienced* operator to enhance the picture and improve the information gathered from the unit. If this isn't done properly, however, the instrument could be left in a state that yields inaccurate information; i.e., showing nothing when a ship, shoreline, or underwater hazard actually exists.

Radios require adjustment, and they can be left with the volume too low or gains too high to receive important information. Autopilot adjustment can result in inadvertent course changes, and many vessels have been destroyed this way. Hourly log entries of magnetic heading should help reduce this risk. The point is that every person authorized to make any adjustment to any piece of equipment should be certified by the captain to do so. Complete familiarity with the equipment is essential, and it's best for a green watch-stander to request assistance if these types of adjustment seem necessary. It is important, however, for the new person aboard to understand the basic function of electronics that might have to be used in an emergency—turning on the VHF and using channel 16, activating the EPIRB, or hitting the *save* button or *man-overboard* function of the Loran or GPS. A broader examination of the electronics available to the Passagemaker is found in Chapter 20.

Offshore operation, especially on a voyage of sufficient duration to require scheduled watches, is the essence of this whole passage-making activity—rivaled only by the arrival at and enjoyment of the chosen destination. It takes two or three days to adjust to the sea, to the motion and sounds of the ship, and every time I have experienced it, I have noted that a transition takes place. The worries of shoreside life temporarily disappear, and any concerns over putting to sea fade away as confidence in the abilities of the ship and crew grow. Midpassage is the best time—you are completely adjusted, well rested, absorbed in the operation of the ship, focused on the duties of the moment. Enough time has passed to enable you to gain a more healthy perspective on responsibilities and problems left ashore, but it's still too early to worry about arrival procedures or details of homeward-bound crew.

I am reminded of a vacation commercial showing the five-day metamorphosis of a battle-fatigued, shell-shocked businessman into a relaxed guy wearing a Hawaiian shirt and sipping a coconut drink; an ocean passage on a good yacht has the same effect. But before we cast off, some voyage planning is essential.

CHAPTER 15

VOYAGE PLANNING

VOYAGE PLANNING IS A LARGE subject, one that space limitations will not allow us to cover fully in this book. It consists largely of absorbing the experience of others and applying it to your own prospective voyages. Sailing Directions and Pilot Charts are pure experience distilled over hundreds of years, for example. All books on cruising, even if under sail, will have bits and pieces of what to do and what not to do.

The bible for this sort of thing is without doubt Eric Hiscock's *Voyaging Under Sail* (International Marine, 1981). In it the Dean of Circumnavigators has set down the essentials of the business in clear and concise form. As a departure for more detailed planning, it is invaluable, and I strongly recommend it as part of any serious planner's library.

In addition to the type of file recommended later, the planner should be aware of the specialized information available from the Seven Seas Cruising Association, P.O. Box 1598, Fort Lauderdale, Florida 33302; 305-463-2431. This unique organization's members are all liveaboard, cruising sail skippers, and to become a member one must meet those criteria. When the group was formed in 1952, the primary purpose was to exchange cruising tips and information on ports, etc., which were circulated to the members in a monthly bulletin. Over the years, the original mimeographed sheet has expanded to a monthly pamphlet of 20 pages or so. To meet the increased cost, the SSCA allows nonmembers to subscribe to the bulletins. This has been so successful the subscribers now outnumber the members, and the association is actively seeking information from subscribers as well as from its members. In effect, it is a pooling of experience that can only improve as more people become involved. Back issues of each full year are available from 1957 on. Write for the current subscription price.

One of the first things I did when planning a west-to-east crossing of the Pacific was to get a complete file of these bulletins. They were a tremendous help and well worth the cost.

While much planning is common to both sail and power, the two types do differ in certain respects. And it was to these differences that I addressed myself in writing an article on voyage planning, using a passage across the Atlantic as a guide. This article appeared in *Boating* in May 1970, entitled "*Passagemaker* Across the Atlantic." Now, some years later with more cruising under my belt, I find myself hard put to add anything of value to what I said then. Here it is.

PLANNING THE OCEAN PASSAGE

PLANNING THE OCEAN PASSAGE

The growing interest in long voyages by seagoing motorboats of modest size is soundly based on the advantages a power approach has over the more conventional sailing cruiser. Many of the problems in planning long voyages are common to both types, of course. Provisioning and medical, for instance, would be the same, also navigation. But the seagoing motorboat differs from the sailing cruiser in several major respects that must be considered separately. Taking our voyage across the Atlantic in the summer of 1969 as an example, let us see how the planning was done—and how it worked out.

After some 50,000 miles of deep-water cruising in the 50-foot seagoing motorboat *Passagemaker,* I sold her to Roger Bury of Westport, Connecticut. Roger and his wife, Marion, had made a passage from Hawaii to Seattle with us and remained ever after interested in the whole concept of long voyages under power. I agreed at the time to help him take *Passagemaker* across the Atlantic to Scandinavia and complete his checkout of problems faced by the captain of such a vessel.

Here are some extracts from our correspondence on the approaching cruise:

(September 1968) "Dear Bob: I think it is time we started planning next summer's trip to Europe. I'd like your comments on the following: (*three pages of topics*)."

"Dear Roger: You're right, September is not too soon to start planning. When we went East to Expo in Montreal in '67, I didn't decide to go until January, and when we left in May we still had annoying gaps in our planning. Here is what I think should be done: (*five pages of suggestions*). In view of the fact you have a secretary, I hope you can handle the correspondence!"

To BBC, London: "Gentlemen: We are interested in having the frequencies and times of your weather broadcasts for our forthcoming. . . . "

"Dear Al: In view of your interest in *Passagemaker,* I wonder if you and Kitty would care to join. . . .

"Dear Roger: Your spares list is okay. But I think it needs a few additions. If the oil cooler fails you will need a piece of copper pipe with a 90° elbow the same length as. . .

And so on and so on, until the lists, letters, and printed information filled two thick ring binders. Not a day passed on the voyage that these files weren't consulted for something, from the location of a spare part to the address of the next mail drop. In the end, nine months of planning proved to be none too much for our cruise!

Looking over the problems involved in voyage planning, we find three areas in which the difference between the motor and the sailing approach to cruising is most apparent. These are: track selection, mechanical spares and repair, and watch-standing/crewing. Chapter 14 includes a thorough discussion of watch-standing, so only the first two will be discussed here.

Track Selection

The natural habitat of the seagoing motorboat is the calm areas of the oceans. Unlike the sailing cruiser—which avoids calms as much as she can—the motorboat regards a calm day as a jewel, a day she can make her cruising speed unhindered by wind or wave. When wind cannot be avoided, she will of course seek reaching and running winds, as does the sailing cruiser. Going to windward under power in the open ocean is a frustrating exercise at best. In certain areas, such as the fully developed monsoon of the Indian Ocean, it would be impossible. In the trades it is possible but hardly worth the effort when your range under power enables you to get out of the trades into areas of lighter winds.

The literature on small-boat voyaging is concerned primarily with sail. Thus what might be called the "standard tracks" for sailing vessels making worldwide cruises are well known. What is not generally appreciated is how much of the ocean has calms and light winds for the powerboat to exploit. The Azores High, the Pacific High, and the Doldrums are conspicuous examples.

What can be done is shown by past experience in *Passagemaker.* On a voyage from Honolulu to Seattle, we spent 6 of 12 days in glassy calm or light airs. On 10 out of 12 days, Azores to Bermuda, we had very light conditions with favorable winds. On a crossing of the Indian Ocean at the change of the monsoon, 7 of 14 days were ideal for a motorboat. There are other areas waiting to be tried. For instance, it would be possible to cross the Atlantic westward with light airs and no fear of hurricanes any time of the year between Latitude 6° North and the equator. Another route that has intrigued me since wartime service in the area is Singapore to Hawaii via Rabaul and Canton islands. If you were a good enough navigator to stay in the Equatorial Counter Current, you would have lots of motorboat weather plus a "free" boost of some 25 miles a day from current.

The tools for studying this matter are the wind and weather charts of the oceans, called *Pilot Charts,* plus a text on cyclonic storms, such as *Bowditch.* They will repay months of study, providing not only tracks but proper starting dates for various areas, a most important part of planning. In addition, the serious student of voyaging will maintain a file of magazine articles on cruising from the yachting press, tourist bureau literature, and the like for the important bits of information they contain. For instance, in a British magazine bought in Bermuda, we found for the first time that yachts *do* moor to the quay wall at Horta in the Azores.

The track chosen must be within the capabilities of the vessel. The heavy-displacement motorboat operates under conditions where slight changes in speed make large differences in fuel consumption. The practical speed/length ratio (speed in knots divided by the square root of the waterline length) is 1.1 to 1.2. On *Passagemaker* (46-foot waterline) this speed range is from 7.5 to 8.2 knots. We planned on the basis of 1,000 miles a week to allow for possible adverse weather, and always did better than that. An assured range of 2,400 miles at an S/L ratio of 1.2 means ample fuel for the longest passages. If fuel runs low, speed can be dropped to a ratio of 1.0 to give you about 50 percent more range on what is left. If the wind comes ahead, as it is certain to do on a voyage from the East Coast to California, the only thing to do is go slowly until green water stops coming over the bow, and wait it out. We found that even with a 30-knot wind we still kept forging ahead and that fuel consumption was negligible.

Applying theory to the proposed voyage worked out like this. The objective was to take *Passagemaker* to Europe with sufficient time available to cruise in Scandinavia that summer. The *Pilot Charts* show that the most settled weather in the North Atlantic is late June and July, but such a late start would seriously restrict the opportunities for further cruising overseas. We finally determined, all things considered, that leaving the East Coast on June 1 was a pretty fair compromise, particularly since we would have to spend a week in Bermuda for personal matters.

Passagemaker carries enough fuel to make a run from Newport, Rhode Island, to Ireland, direct. But this track was rejected for several reasons. Not only was the weather better farther south, but also we have found that, considering the type of crew used, it is best to break up a voyage into several stages whenever possible, even if it does take longer. The final decision, then, was to leave *Passagemaker*'s yard in Virginia in late May and start down the Intracoastal Waterway toward Charleston. The purpose was twofold: Before going to sea, to get south of Hatteras to an area where the winds should be lighter and more likely to be favorable, and to give the boat a shaking down before departure in an area where anything that needed attention could be taken in hand. On June 1 we would leave for Bermuda. From Bermuda we would steer a rhumb line for Horta in the Azores, deviating from it north or south as necessary to spend as much time as possible in the center of the Azores High. From Horta to Ireland we would venture into a region influenced by low-pressure areas, resulting in winds predominantly from the west. By standing west of the rhumb line when the weather was good and running off to the eastward when it was bad, we hoped to finish off this leg with reasonable aplomb.

How did it work out?

Well, it worked out fine. In fact, it worked out better than we had reason to expect. We actually left one day early, on May 31, from Cape Fear, North Carolina. Three of our four days to Bermuda were flat calm. Only the last day was marred by the wind coming in from the southeast, somewhat to our surprise, with a velocity sufficient to cause us to slow to 5.5 knots for some hours.

From Bermuda to Horta, the Azores High was in great shape. We got into it shortly after leaving and basked under clear, sunny skies with light winds or calm for 9 of the 10½ days on the 1,850-mile leg to Horta. At the end, the wind gradually came in from the northwest, indicating that we had reached the high's eastern limits. Only in the last six hours before arrival did it become strong enough to suggest using the whole stabilizing gear. It was the best example of the virtues of seeking out the calm areas of the oceans that *Passagemaker* has produced to date, a most enjoyable cruise.

We left Horta on June 25. Our trepidation over the last leg, to Ireland, was wasted. Although it was completely overcast the whole way, with some rain and fog, the winds remained light and in the main favorable. The passage ended with a bit of excitement at 0130 on July 2 when we sighted Fastnet Light through thick fog. As we coasted the green shores of the Emerald Isle to Cork, we were able to look back on a most successful track selection and timing.

Mechanical Spares and Repair

Unlike the sailing cruiser, where you often observe shocking neglect of the auxiliary power, the main engine of a seagoing powerboat is the heart of the ship and must be treated with the respect it deserves. Reliance on one's own resources is fundamental to offshore work. In particular, there must be alternatives for all vital systems. Main propulsion can be provided in various ways. It can be a sailing rig *(Passagemaker)*; twin engines on twin shafts; twin engines on a single

Figure 15-1. Passagemaker *leaving Monterey, California, for her passage to Hawaii with a crew of two men and four women.*

shaft; a single shaft with auxiliary drive, or a wing engine (Nordhavn 46). There is only one long-range cruiser known to me that has actually returned to port under alternate power. Others have had trouble but have been able to reach port for repairs with their main engines functioning in one way or another.

After the provision of alternative drive, what other spares and repair equipment should be provided? I have often been asked this question by persons hoping to profit from my experience. My answers may not have helped very much. The truth is, of the large stock of spares on board *Passagemaker* very few were used except in the course of routine maintenance. But combining my experience with that of other owners and maintenance men shows a pattern worth thinking about:

1. Feed the engine absolutely clean fuel. *Passagemaker* had three filters ahead of the engine. A motorboat that circled the world had no fewer than five. Certainly the single filter supplied with an engine is not enough.

2. The basic block of the diesel is very reliable. It is the equipment external to the engine that causes trouble. The only satisfactory way to handle trouble inside the block is, apparently, to have duplicate engines. It would be bad luck indeed if one of them could not be kept going by using parts from both.

3. An outstanding culprit is the heat-exchanger. Careful provision for alternative sources of this vital service must be made.

4. Rubber impeller pumps should be viewed with suspicion and extensive spares provided.

5. There doesn't appear to be a satisfactory wet exhaust system that will stand up under thousands of hours of running without replacement. This is particularly true of the Monel muffler. At the conclusion of her present trip, *Passagemaker* is in need of her fourth. However, this area responds well to emergency repair with epoxy compounds.

6. Belts must be constantly checked for condition, tension, and alignment. Numerous spares of correct sizes must be carried.

7. Electric tools can be vital. In particular, a small drill press has been most useful.

8. The brushes and commutators of electric equipment should be the subject of routine maintenance and not ignored until they cause trouble.

9. Be prepared as well as possible for the unexpected because it is bound to happen. Our worst trouble of the cruise happened this way. The fuel high-pressure line to No. 5 cylinder fractured at the injector one morning. Since we had a spare set of fuel lines on board, we replaced No. 5 and went on

Figure 15-2. *Al Willis works on a new alternator mounting in* Passagemaker's *cockpit "shop," which fitted conveniently on the after deck.*

our way. Much to our horror, 24 hours later the replacement fractured in *exactly the same place,* a most astonishing occurrence. Finally, after much trial and error, we managed to bend the remnant of one of the other lines so it bridged the space from pump to injector fairly well, and reinstalled it using spare "olives" we had on board. This had to be redone several times, the last time 13 hours out of Cork. But we did enter port with all six cylinders firing merrily.

10. Take a jaundiced view of any items of equipment for which the only repair instructions are: "If it does not work, return it to our nearest service station." This is cold comfort when the nearest land is 1,000 miles away. The light, compact, streamlined equipment designed for weekend boating has no place in the long-range cruiser if it is possible to find something heavier, simpler, and more fixable. This applies particularly to such items as reverse-reduction gears, horn and refrigerator compressors, steering gears, and autopilots. Although our hydraulic reverse gear has performed perfectly to date, I have always worried that there is no way to get into it and jam it ahead for "come home" ability. (There are gears with this facility). At any rate my policy has been not to hesitate to break into anything. If it isn't working, you can't make it worse by operating on it.

As it turned out, we had an unusual amount of mechanical trouble. Much of this was in convenience features that had been added to the boat in the spring and not had a proper shaking down. In the end we managed to fix everything so it functioned well enough for us to keep going. We replaced a broken exhaust valve in the generator, fixed the fuel lines as previously mentioned, stopped an oil leak by replacing a defective gasket, redesigned and rebuilt the mounting of the newly installed 40-amp alternator. We left port with the SeaStill not working and managed by trial and error to adapt it to *Passagemaker's* rather peculiar cooling system.

We replaced a defective SeaStill control panel with a simple manual on-off switch, reworked the belting of its pumps, and made enough water to more than satisfy our needs. We gave the autopilot a complete overhaul when, understandably enough, it refused duty after someone spilled a glass of beer into it. We did a lot of other things, too. In fact, the "daily crisis" became something of a joke. The log shows the main engine was stopped for one reason or another during nine of the 21 days underway. But we kept going and made our ETAs. That's the important thing. And Roger Bury surely got a good checkout in coping with mechanical trouble.

Figure 15-3. Passagemaker, *well stocked for her Atlantic passage. What do you need besides soft drinks, beer, and bananas? We always carried an oversupply of canned beer. It was considered our emergency water supply. Canned beer is cheaper and keeps better than canned water. Besides, it improves morale.*

CHAPTER 16

CRUISING IN
EUROPE

IN A LETTER DATED JANUARY *1, 1993, Jim and*
Susy Sink write from aboard Salvation II:

It's New Year's Day here on the Turquoise Coast
of the Aegean Sea, near the ancient city of Ephesus, not far from three great cradle-lands
of civilization. . . .

Salvation II logged 10,000 miles, Texas to Turkey, in 1992. Crossing the mighty
Atlantic. Cruising the south coast of England. Up the Thames to London—two glorious
weeks at St. Katherine's Dock. Parading Parliament on the fourth of July, captain of the
Queen's barge on board as our guest. Across the English Channel, the North Sea, the
IJsselmeer, Frisian Islands, Keil Canal, Baltic Sea to wonderful Copenhagen. Then south
on the Mittelland and other lovely canals through the spectacular heartland of Germany.
Up the fabled Rhine and the meandering Main to the summit of the new Main–Danube
Canal (1,332 feet above sea level), at the front of the line for first locking on opening day.
Finally, carefully down the troubled Danube through central and eastern Europe ...thus
laying claim to the first ship in history to transit the inland waters (2,223 miles and 93
locks) Baltic Sea to Black Sea!

Onward through the Bosporus to fascinating Istanbul, Sea of Marmara, the
Dardanelles, into Kuşadasi for a Thanksgiving feast, and Christmas holidays with new-
found friends in this most congenial country.

I still can't believe that less than 30 months earlier, using a handheld VHF from Salvation II*'s*
inflatable tender, I had supervised the captain's first solo docking, coaching Susy on line handling and
ready to talk Jim out of a botched mooring attempt. We've become good friends since then, and it's been
a pleasure to watch Jim and Susy evolve from inexperienced newcomers to virtual experts, with more than
30,000 miles under the keel of their Nordhavn 46.

I asked Jim and Susy to review the original "Cruising in Europe" chapter and give me their thoughts
on any revisions that might be beneficial. Jim's response:

"Cruising in Europe," and I believe it is so well written and still so valid that it would be an injustice to rewrite it or revise it. My own knowledge of French canal cruising is limited to our analysis of the Moselle–Canal de l'Est–Saône–Rhône route from Koblenz to Marseilles, which we considered as an alternate route to the Mediterranean in view of the Yugoslavian situation on the Danube. I found that the controlling height above water is now 11 feet 4 inches and by stripping *Salvation II* down to the top of the muffler, removing our searchlight, and adding fuel to at least three-quarters full, we could clear with several inches to spare. Draft appeared to be no problem with almost 6 feet clear.

We did have problems in Europe with draft on the uncanalized Danube River due to shifting shoals, poor to nonexistent buoyage, and low water as a result of drought conditions. Our full keel, dry exhaust, and keel cooling made it easy for us to work our way off groundings without damage . . . except to our pride.

So here is Bob Beebe's look at this fascinating aspect of voyaging under power, as he originally penned it.

Author's note (1974): This chapter originally appeared in *Boating* in May of 1971, and I am indebted to the editors for permission to reprint it here. It does give the basics of cruising in Europe and in the canals of France. And nothing I have learned since indicates the need for any changes.

The world being what it is, I cannot guarantee that all the article says will still be correct at whatever future date you may cruise in the fascinating areas across the Atlantic. The careful planner will make certain of the facts pertaining to canal regulations, customs, fuel, electricity, and water before leaving by referring to the latest information available from the sources shown in the bibliography.

When *Passagemaker* and her stout crew arrived in Greece direct from Singapore, we were certainly a fresh-caught bunch of innocents. And it would have been nice then to know what is in this article. But by greeting everyone with a smile, doing what we were told, and in case of doubt, exhibiting an eager but uncomprehending willingness to cooperate if somebody would only explain, we had a ball—and no trouble to speak of.

My discussion of voyage planning for seagoing motorboats in *Boating*, May 1971, used for its example a crossing of the Atlantic to cruise in Europe. This was done deliberately. For I do find the greatest interest of the long-range cruising fraternity is in yachts capable of spanning the Atlantic to sample the fascinating waters that stretch from Scandinavia to Greece and Turkey. In the past, such expeditions have been largely the domain of the sailing cruiser. But a growing number of owner-operated motorboats of modest size have made this trip and laid down a track for others to follow. The voyage of *Passagemaker* showed how such an Atlantic crossing should be done.

So, once you decide to join this group of ocean-crossing motorboaters, are there any special considerations peculiar to the European area that will affect your boat's design and equipment? The answer to this question is, Yes. There is one major point and several minor ones.

First, let's tackle the minor problems. To start with, in the Mediterranean, and to some extent in other areas, you "Mediterranean moor" routinely. To "Med moor" means an anchor is dropped ahead and the stern backed into and secured to the quay wall. This is great sport, especially with a beam wind and a single-screw vessel. The other yachtsmen, already secured, will sit smugly on deck and criticize your technique. After you are safely moored, you will find yourself quite willing to join them and do likewise to the next newcomer.

Without telling you how to handle your vessel, a few pointers may be useful. Obviously, a good view of the stern from the pilothouse should be designed in, if possible. If this is not possible, a well-trained member of the crew, able to judge distances and communicate with the skipper, will have to do. This is how we did it on *Passagemaker,* and it worked very well—after a few early disasters.

Large cleats astern with a good lead aft are essential (the hardware on most American motorboats is shockingly inadequate). And you should provide lengths of chain shackled to your mooring lines to take the chafe from the rough seawalls.

After you are moored, your next problem is to get ashore. Some people use a plank, or launch the dinghy and pull themselves back and forth. But we soon found this was inadequate for handling stores and visitors. What is required is a real gangway, complete with lifelines, a swivel fitting on the stern, and small wheels on the dock-end to allow for the boat's movement. A design about 12 feet long is good.

And, finally, it wouldn't hurt to practice a few Med moors!

While there are a growing number of marinas abroad that approach U.S. standards, in general the facilities are adapted to commercial work, especially in their extensive inland waterways. A really big, strong guardrail is a necessity and will save you much worry about your topsides. The rail provided on most American-built motorboats is little more than a bad joke.

Electricity is available to some extent. But the multiplicity of voltages and cycles, coupled with a complete lack of standardization of connections, makes it simpler for the vessel to be capable of supplying all its own needs on a continuing basis. An exception to this would be wintering over. In our winter berth in Greece, we ran in a 220-volt line for heat and light and managed to find a 3,000-watt 220/110-volt transformer that enabled us to use our electric tools during overhaul.

Water is always a problem. Not only is it suspect in some areas, but it seemed to us there were not two faucets the same size on the whole continent. We got around this by using clamps on various sizes of hose feeding into 150 feet of lightweight hose, a length that proved none too long.

A relatively minor problem that caused us some trouble: Customs will sometimes want to seal up any "bonded stores" (liquor and cigarettes) that exceed their rules. The first time this happened to us, the only suitable place I could find was a big locker in the stern. It wasn't until the liquor was in and sealed that I realized some tools and spares that we badly needed were also in the locker. It took me several hours to figure out how to jimmy the locker and get the gear out without breaking the seal—but I finally managed it! *Passagemaker* now has two lockers devoted exclusively to bonded stores.

Now for the major question: Should your vessel be capable of entering the inland waterways of Europe? More specifically, because of the French canals' smaller size, should your vessel be capable of entering them? There is a good deal to be said on this point.

In contrast to the United States, Europe is literally laced with busy inland waterways, which carry a large part of its commerce. They form a magnificent cruising ground in themselves. I certainly remember warmly the impressive scenery of the Caledonian Canal across Scotland, the Göta that crosses Sweden, the myriad canals of Holland, the fabled gorges of the Rhine. All of these have passed under *Passagemaker*'s keel. But it is the canals of France, which provide a link from the North

Sea to the Mediterranean, that have at once the greatest charm and the greatest utility. A compelling argument for being able to traverse this network is that it enables you to cruise in Scandinavia and then retreat for the winter to the Mediterranean later than would be sensible if you had to go down the North Sea and across the Bay of Biscay to Gibraltar. Many yachts use this route every year in both directions.

Useful as such a route can be, we also found from our own experience that canal-cruising has such charm that we would like to do a whole season of it. So, in my family, the answer to this question of being able to cruise the French canals is, Yes! It is interesting to note, however, that among my clients the vote is about 50-50. Designing in a French-canal capability raises certain problems. If you don't desire to take them on, then any craft able to make the ocean crossing is well prepared for coastal cruising in Europe and for going into the larger canals. Let's discuss, then, the various pros and cons of being "French-canal-capable."

The French canals have the smallest limiting dimensions; clearance of these is critical for any vessel planning to travel through Europe. Length is not critical; it can be as great as 126 feet. But draft should be no more than 5 feet, beam over the guards 16 feet 4 inches, and height above water no more than 10 feet 10 inches. Can we meet these restrictions and still have the living room we need?

In designing a vessel capable of crossing the Atlantic under power, we find certain basics. First, these vessels are of such a size and cost that they don't make much sense unless they are used a greater part of the year. My own feeling on length is that 46 feet is about the minimum, with 50 feet a good comfortable size. With such lengths, the limit on beam and draft match well with the usual vessel proportions, and the canal capability looks attractive.

But it is the height that causes trouble. In a boat of fairly short fixed length, trying to provide excellent living space depends largely on the ability to double-deck. In the size we are talking about,

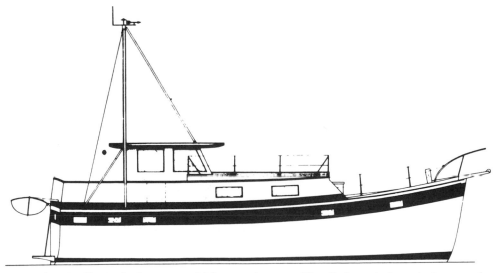

Figure 16-1. *Profile, Beebe Design 93, 46-foot canal runner. The pilothouse is shown in its normal position.*

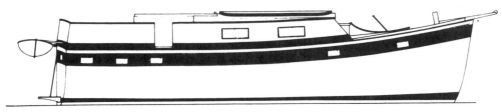

Figure 16-2. *Profile, Design 93, showing pilothouse demounted for canal work.*

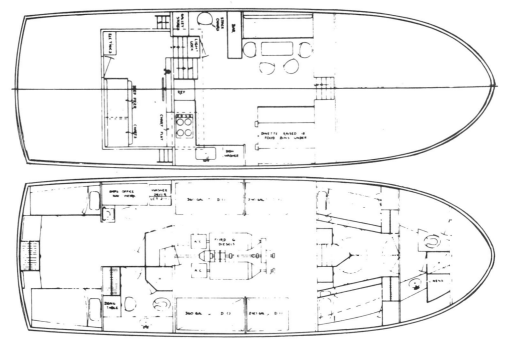

Figure 16-3. *Accommodation, Design 93.*

it is impossible to have fixed double-decking and still go through the canals with a vessel properly shaped for ability at sea. But there is a way to lick this problem, at least part of it.

The solution comprises two steps. First, we arrange the pilothouse so it can be *broken down* for the canal passage. And second, we go to a full-width cabin for the galley/lounge area. Figures 16-1, 16-2, and 16-3 are sketches of a 46-footer with this arrangement. The 13½- x 14½-foot galley/lounge area provides 196 square feet of floor space for any arrangement you may want. The owner's cabin is 15 feet long in the full-width stern. And the pilothouse breaks down at the level of the forward cabin, the top is stowed forward on deck, and the sides in a rack on the stern. This isn't as difficult as it may sound. The cabin is put together with bolts instead of screws. A tent can be provided for the night. And, of course, the installations in the pilothouse should be treated as if they were on a flying bridge.

The effect of double-decking is illustrated in the sketches of the 50-footer. As Figure 16-4 shows, she doesn't break down the pilothouse; there is no double-decking. In spite of her greater

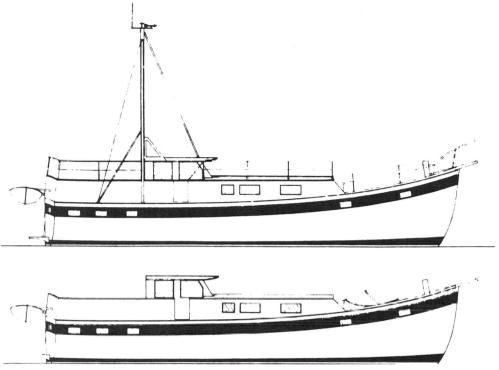

Figure 16-4. *Two profile views, Beebe Design 92, 50-foot canal runner. This design does not break down at the pilothouse as there is no double-decking.*

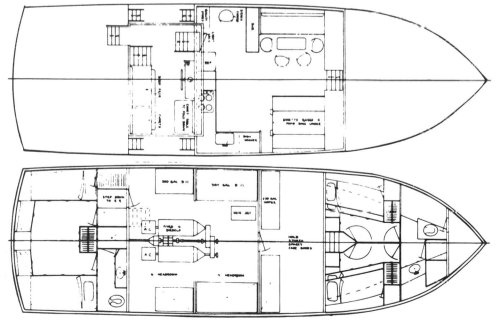

Figure 16-5. Accommodation, Design 92

length, we find the owner's cabin must be much smaller (see Figure 16-5). Whether this is acceptable is up to the individual. It can be seen that for this type to have the same room as the 46-footer she would have to be longer by the amount of the smaller model's double-decking, or a length of 53 feet, with its attendant greater costs.

But a comparison of room alone doesn't tell the whole story. As a matter of fact, the canal runners, due to the restrictions under which they labor, come much closer to the ideal layout for unrestricted ocean work. Their pilothouse is properly placed aft, their silhouette and center of gravity are lower, and their freeboard is higher. They are quite suitable for making a direct passage to northern Europe. So there is something to be said for both designs.

The choice must be a personal one, depending on the preference of the owners and the type of cruising they propose to do. As I said, in my family there is no doubt we want our boat to be "French-capable." For those who want to explore this more fully, let me add a few remarks on what is involved in running the canals, a highly specialized nautical activity.

In the size of vessel we need for the ocean crossing, it would be inadvisable to make the beam small enough to be sure of entering the locks without touching the sides, say about 13 feet. You might as well go to the maximum, to have a roomy hull, and just ease her through. Fenders *cannot* be used. The lock walls will just cut the lines. And we found that if an air fender hits one wall hard, it can bounce you over against the opposite wall harder than the first hit. A heavy and well-shod guardrail is a must. Another advantage of the full-width boat is that once she is inside the lock she can't charge about. In fact, we found the small French locks easier to go through than wider ones, such as those on the Caledonian Canal, and used only a single spring line with the engine idling against it.

This may sound difficult but isn't really, after you get used to it. The solution to entering a lock with only an inch or two clearance each side is "inch-calling." This is used in tunnels as well. Here's the drill: An "outside man" takes station right outside the pilothouse next to you. As you head into the lock, he leans over the side until his eye is right in line with the wall of the lock. Then he glances down at the guardrail and makes an estimate of how far out he is leaning, and calls it off in inches. He can also tell if you are "opening" or "closing" with the lock wall. In the meantime, you concentrate on how the boat is moving and watch the wind on your bow pennant; even a slight breeze makes a perceptible difference when you are moving this slowly. With this inch-calling, it is surprising how often you will slip into a lock with the barest touch on the wall, or none at all. Of course, just after you have done several masterful jobs in a row—*wham!* But you can't win 'em all.

We had a crew of five on board *Passagemaker* and were fortunate to have available as "outside men" two who liked the exercise and spoke good French. The outside man has a very active life. After he finishes his inch-calling and the boat comes to a stop, he leaps up on the lock wall, drops the spring line on a bollard, runs to the gate opposite the lock operator and closes his half of the gate by winding on its crank. (The crew is always expected to help in locks.)

Then the outside man goes to the other end and helps open the paddle valves to let the water in or out. On board, in the meantime, your crew puts over thin fenders, *forward* on the side that has the spring line and *aft* on the other side. The helmsman then goes ahead against the spring and the boat rests on these two fenders, sliding up the moss-covered lock walls easily. As the boat rises, the French-speaking outside man offers the locktender a cigarette and gossips about what's ahead and how the traffic is, sometimes gathering most valuable information. When the boat is up, he again goes to the side opposite the *éclusier* and opens his half of the gate. As the boat passes

Figure 16-6. Passage-
maker *moored for the
night at 1,200 feet
elevation in the Voges
Mountains. Note use
of* quant *poles to hold
the vessel off the bank.*

Figure 16-7. Passage-
maker *in an "up" lock
in France. Note the
close fit. The "outside"
man, on the port side,
is Rob Poole, a
Canadian medical
student.*

*Figure 16-8. With
the "outside" man
standing on the
starboard midship
deck "inch-calling"
for the helmsman,
Passagemaker slides
through a 3-mile
unlighted tunnel in
France. (Photo taken
by flash arrangement
devised by Ralph
Arndt)*

him, he swings on board, shouts, *"Bonjour,"* to the locktender, and prepares for the next lock, which may be only 100 yards away when you're going up and down hills. It's a high-speed operation, taking about four minutes when the crew is in the swing of things. Down locks are somewhat easier on everyone but the outside man.

When I called it a high-speed operation, I referred of course only to the passage through the locks; you should do this as rapidly as possible to cooperate with the waiting traffic. There's almost always someone waiting, either behind or ahead of you. The rest of the time your progress can only be called leisurely—delightfully so. The 4-mile-an-hour speed limit gives you time to savor the countryside in a way that is impossible by any other means of locomotion. The ancient towns and churches, to say nothing of castles and forts, are a constant invitation to stop and explore. And, in fact, a trip planned with plenty of time to do this offers the most pleasure.

If your trip must be made quickly, as a "passage," it can still be fun, if a bit wearing. Working a full day everyday in the locks keeps all hands busy. We had to do this, passing from the Mediterranean to the North Sea via Strasbourg and the Rhine, in 22 days. With two days off in Lyon and two more in Strasbourg, we had 18 days underway, passing through 224 locks. This time could be cut several days by using the new canal from Nancy to Koblenz, but this would eliminate the Rhine gorges passage, the highlight of that river.

If you have an objective to reach and want to keep going, it is a good idea to have some kind of land transportation on board. We bought a Solex motor-driven bicycle. At a likely spot the off-duty French-speaker would roll this ashore as the boat sank below the level of the wall and go shopping for delicious French bread and local wines and cheeses. He would then hunt us down four or five locks later and roll back on board.

Notice in the sketch of the boat rigged for canal-running that the lifelines have been removed. They are just a nuisance in canals. Tell your crew that if they fall overboard, they can darn well swim ashore and run to the next lock in time to do their duty!

The locktenders quit for the day promptly at 7 P.M. Whatever "pound," or water between locks you are in then, becomes your harbor for the night. About half the time, we found some place to lie alongside *something.* The rest of the time we had to tie to the bank, holding the ship off on *quants,* long poles that can be purchased along the canals. To use the quants, it is necessary to get a hand ashore. It is for this reason that, as shown in the sketches, a dinghy is carried over the stern, where it can be used with the mast down. In our case, we couldn't use the dinghy in this condition and bought a two-man rubber liferaft that did the job well enough. If a barge is in the pound with you, its crew will invariably be agreeable to your tying alongside. We made some very pleasant acquaintances this way.

All in all, it was a most interesting experience and we would like to go back. The canals reveal a different France from the one seen by the ordinary tourist! It is off the beaten track and occupied by a distinct breed of people who spend their entire lives on the waterways. Without exception we found the canal people charming. When one locktender found we had a woman on board, he went to his garden and picked flowers for her. My wife, Linford, became thoroughly enchanted with the French canals. And I am sure you will, too.

CHAPTER 17

INLAND VOYAGING
by Jim and Susy Sink

WE WERE TWO HAPPY VOYAGERS on our own little yacht, moored at North Cove Yacht Harbor on Manhattan Island at the very heart of New York City. It was just before Labor Day 1991. New York Harbor was quiet and almost abandoned—except for the Hoboken Ferry, which pushed an uncomfortable surge into our corner of the tiny marina each time it landed at the Esplanade outside.

Rising from the landscaped plazas immediately surrounding us, the familiar twin towers of the New York World Trade Center and the slick new facades of the World Financial Center presented a spectacular view straight up through our hatch.

This marina is to the World Financial Center what the ice plaza is to Rockefeller Center: a little open space for people to help make the dense urban development tolerable—in this case the largest real estate development in the history of the United States. Being there was a bit like being at the center of the universe, and we paid dearly for the privilege: $4 per foot. The tab, including power and phone, was more than $200 a night for our Nordhavn 46. . . about 10 times the average of the more than 100 marinas we've visited and several times more than the next most expensive.

It was worth every nickel—for one night—as it was the auspicious beginning of our inland cruise through some of the most exciting waters in North America. Ahead lay the Great Lakes and the mighty Mississippi, the majestic Hudson River and the pastoral waters of the Erie Canal; we would pass through some of the most beautiful land in America at the height of autumn. The Chicago River, the Chicago Sanitary & Ship Canal, and the Illinois Waterway would carry us south from the Great Lakes, linking us to the Mississippi River above St. Louis.

For *Salvation II* this would be the last half of a 6,000-mile circumnavigation of the eastern United States. Beginning in our home port of Houston in early summer, we had powered eastward through the Gulf of Mexico to Florida, north off the Atlantic coast to Cape Lookout, turned inland for a brief cruise of Chesapeake Bay and the Potomac to Washington, down the Delaware to Cape May, then straight up through Cape Cod to Eastport, Maine, for an August cruise south along the New England coast. Including the inland cruise yet ahead of us, we would call at 127 ports in the waters of 28 states during this six-month voyage.

All was mostly on schedule and according to plan. We had to leave New York City by September 1 to clear Chicago by October 1. This would get us out of the Great Lakes ahead of the winter storms, down the Mississippi River and back to Houston about November 15, after hurricane season. It gave us precious little time for cruising the Great Lakes, but better little than none at all. We had set our pace to stay ahead of the weather since our cruising had begun the year before. In less than 12 months we managed to "semicircumnavigate" the North American continent, coasting the

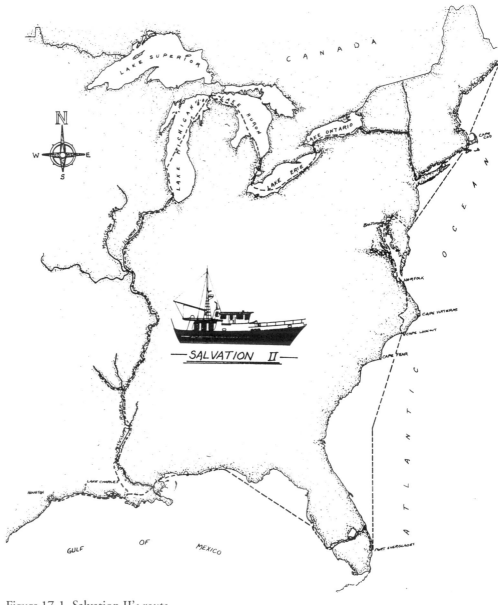

Figure 17-1. Salvation II's *route.*

Figure 17-2. *Jim and Susy Sink aboard* Salvation II.

Pacific south from Alaska to Panama, then the Atlantic north from Panama to New Brunswick in Canada. This included a detour into the Gulf of Mexico and a stop in Houston to dispose of our house, put our business on hold, and plan an agenda for our new life afloat.

Actually this East Coast and inland cruise was a substitution for a planned transatlantic crossing that, for several reasons, we had decided to postpone a year. We wanted to transit the Rhine–Main–Danube Canal when we arrived in Europe, and its opening was delayed until 1992. We felt we could use the Mississippi River experience as a training ground for the great rivers of Europe; we needed additional time to take care of business before leaving the U.S. for an indefinite period; and we both considered the Mississippi River part of our "roots." Susy was born in St. Paul, Minnesota, on the Upper Mississippi, and Jim was born in Little Rock on the Arkansas River but raised in the Lower Mississippi Valley. Like everyone of our era, we had grown up with Tom Sawyer and Huckleberry Finn, and our own adventure on the Mississippi seemed ordained.

We left that morning from a guest mooring at the Seawanhaka Corinthian Yacht Club in Oyster Bay, Long Island, carefully timing our departure to clear the Throgs Neck Bridge and arrive at infamous Hell Gate at slack tide on the nose. We hardly felt a ripple as we passed and paraded on down the East River. There was the Empire State building, the Chrysler building, the United Nations, South Street Seaport—an astounding view.

Nothing comes close to the thrill of approaching Manhattan from the deck of one's own yacht. Space was available at North Cove, and we were quickly ushered alongside.

After a night on the town at the nearby Hudson River Club, we spent the next morning exploring, shopping, and waiting for the afternoon tide up the Hudson to Tarrytown, where we were to meet our longtime friends the Ames for dinner. Shortly after noon we were underway, with time for a trip across the harbor to pay our respects to the Statue of Liberty—another experience not to be missed by cruisers, and we lingered awhile to absorb it all.

The Hudson River was as majestic as promised, lined with mansions and rich in history. The cold, gray walls of West Point, FDR's final home at Hyde Park, Bear Mountain Bridge, the lovely white swans—all left indelible memories.

At times we had the river to ourselves; at others there was traffic of all kinds. On Labor Day we stopped in Catskill to unstep our mast. Later that day we toured the state capitol at Albany, then left the Hudson through the Federal Lock at Troy and anchored off Green Island for the night.

When the New York State Lock opened early the next morning, we were waiting, ready to begin our four-day transit of the Erie Canal. Completed in 1825, the Erie Canal linked the Great Lakes and Midwest with the Atlantic seaboard and quickly made New York the nation's most important port. Today it is operated on a limited budget by the State of New York mostly for pleasure boats, excursion boats, and some commercial traffic. Much of the canal winds through the Mohawk River Valley, with strikingly beautiful outlooks, varying countryside, small towns, and distant vistas of the Adirondack and Catskill mountains.

There are 83 locks rising 676 feet to Lake Erie. To gain a few more cruising days on the lakes, we decided to take the alternate 30-lock route via Oswego to Lake Ontario, but next time we might opt for more days on the Erie Canal. Friendly and helpful, the locktenders seem to compete in landscaping their grounds. There were no marinas, but none were needed; we tied to the locks and quays along the way in exquisite surroundings.

In Herkimer, New York, we tied to bollards at the terminal dock next to a field of flowers alongside Interstate 90. Eastbound truckers honked and waved, and late in the afternoon we were visited by a yachtsman named Bill Gould, who had been driving home to Ontario, Canada, when he saw us. Missing the exit, he drove 15 miles out of his way to come back, enthralled by the vision of *Salvation II* sitting out there in the countryside.

We were larger than the few other yachts we saw on the canal, but our size was never a problem. For a couple of days we ran in tandem, lock to lock, with two overnight excursion boats. The fourth day was clear and calm, and we saw only two other boats on the 21-mile crossing of Lake Oneida. We entered Oswego Canal at Three Rivers Point, and, after 24 more miles and a total of 12 locks for the day, we reached Oswego on Lake Ontario, the first and easternmost of the Great Lakes.

It was September 6, and although we were ahead of schedule, we make no pretensions about "cruising" the Great Lakes; we were making passage, staying ahead of the weather, following an alternate way home after a wonderful summer, anxious to make the Mississippi before winter. Those with an appetite for seriously cruising the Great Lakes will want months to explore these extensive cruising grounds. We barely touched them.

We followed the most direct route—along the south shores of Lake Ontario and Lake Erie and the west shores of Lake Huron and Lake Michigan. This also promised to be the easiest going weather-wise, with the shortest fetch for seas to build in the prevailing winds. Avoiding the temptation to cruise the Thousand Islands, the Bay of Quinte, and Georgian Bay, we would save our lay days for some of the pretty spots along the way, certain to include Michigan's Mackinac Island. Nor would we cross into Canada to call at Toronto, limiting ourselves to Detroit, Milwaukee, and other cities along our direct route to Chicago.

We restepped our mast at Oswego, then made the short trip to Sodus Bay, running a half mile offshore in about 5 fathoms of calm, green water. Searching for space amid the congestion of small boats off the village at Sand Point, we suddenly developed a strange vibration. We discovered we were towing a huge glob of weeds, and it took us an hour to work out of them, turning and backing until they fell away. We pulled up another big glob with our anchor the next morning. We were glad to get out of Sodus Bay.

We arrived midday at the Rochester Yacht Club and spent a pleasant afternoon watching the

Sunday racers barreling past and enjoying the double-takes caused by our Houston home port. We left early the next morning for a long haul through a weak cold front to reach the Welland Canal at Port Weller, Ontario, before dark. We couldn't raise St. Catherine's Marina on the VHF but continued cautiously through tight quarters to the transient dock, where we found barely 5 feet of water. A couple from another boat helped us in.

After we tied up, Wally and Blanche told us we were required to have at least three in crew for the next day's eight-lock lift up the canal, and Wally offered to help for the going rate of $100. We had failed to read this point in the pilot book and initially resisted but decided to sign him on. It was the best $100 we ever spent.

The locks average about 40 feet in height, the upbound lift is fast to keep commercial traffic moving, and the incoming water is extremely turbulent. It was a tough test of physical endurance to keep things under control. Wally was a jewel to have aboard, and we couldn't have made it without him.

After an exhausting 12-hour day, we layed over in Port Colborne, renting a car for a magnificent drive through the autumn colors to Niagara Falls.

Lake Erie's south shore was easy going—calm and clear for three days running. We cleared back into the U.S. at Erie, Pennsylvania, anchored peacefully in the industrial harbor at Ashtabula, Ohio, and put in to Put-In-Bay in the Erie Islands for a pleasant night ashore. On the fourth day we entered the Detroit River in a chop, paraded past the impressive skyline of Renaissance Center, and moored at the Detroit Yacht Club. It was September 15 and we were about halfway to Chicago.

Above Detroit we passed through Lake St. Clair and the St. Clair River, and in the swift current below Port Huron we had one of our more serious mechanical difficulties, though it ended without disastrous results.

We had cleared through two lift bridges into the Port Huron city marina on Black River, just off the St. Clair, and spent a pleasant evening walking the town. There was a small-craft warning earlier in the day, with a possible gale to follow in a day or two. We telephoned friends in Minneapolis confirming we would meet them in Chicago in 10 days, which meant we had to keep moving along, despite weather conditions.

The next morning broke clear, calm, and gorgeous. When we were ready to depart, the bridges were up and we moved out quickly to beat their closing, cutting short some of our usual checks before getting underway. We made it with time to spare, but Jim commented that the hydraulic steering seemed sluggish. By then we had passed the Coast Guard station at the mouth of the Black River and were back into the St. Clair, moving against a 2- to 3-knot current toward Lake Huron. We decided to go through a full check of the steering system before proceeding any farther and at that point lost it completely. We quickly found we had no fluid at the steering pump, and the system was totally disabled.

Jim moved aft with lightning speed to throw open the lazarette, pitch out things on top, find our huge manual tiller, and turn the hydraulic bypass valve. Within 30 seconds we had the tiller installed on the rudderstock, Jim was back in the wheelhouse notifying the Coast Guard, and Susy was aft at the tiller, blindly following helm commands from Jim, who could see ahead and control the engine only from the bridge. We made a few short turns for practice before heading back into the narrow, twisting bend at the mouth of the Black River. We had to hail some small boats to stand clear, then made our approach and glided gently in for a perfect landing, loudly applauded by the Coast Guardsmen standing by at their dock.

It didn't take long to locate the offending leak at a flair fitting in a short section of pipe. After consulting Jim Leishman in California by phone, we found a nearby plumber in the Yellow Pages, took a taxi that waited outside, and in 20 minutes had a new fitting—at a cost of $7 including the cab. By afternoon we had installed it and bled and checked the system. All we had lost was the day.

A gale warning was up the next morning, with westerly Force 7 to 8 winds expected. Rather than lose more time, we decided to take a long leap north across Lake Huron, staying close to the western shore—except for a 25-mile run across Saginaw Bay, where the 50-mile fetch gave us rough going for a few hours. *Salvation II*'s Koopnautic stabilizers earned their keep that day. The wind and seas began to moderate about midnight, so we continued to Presque Isle Bay, then on to Mackinac Island the following day. This 200-mile leap was an effective way to make up time that could be better spent in the days ahead.

Mackinac Island is one of the great destination resorts of America. Its century-old Grand Hotel is renowned for its ambiance, service, and graceful columned porch—the longest in the world. The little 19th-century village is well preserved and full of delights. Motor vehicles are banned from the island; the clippety-clop of horses' hooves are heard all over. We spent two fine days there at the government dock in the shadow of historic Fort Mackinac, riding in a horse-drawn carriage, walking, resting, eating, drinking, enjoying the life of the touring yachtsman.

We left on the 22nd, counting the days now to reach Chicago by the 27th. We had planned to run overnight from the Straits of Mackinac directly across Lake Michigan for 150 miles to Sturgeon Bay. This would get us across the lake to the western shore where we would have a clear shot south to Chicago. At 0600 it was dark, and we left the harbor using our searchlight and radar to find the way out. A small craft advisory called for 15 to 20 knots, diminishing later. We had 3- to 6-foot seas to the Mackinac Bridge, building by 1000 to 8 to 12 feet with no sign of diminishing, and the wind on the nose. The Coast Guard issued a gale warning at 1100, and by 1200 the seas were 12 to 15 feet from the northwest, and the wind was 25 to 35 mph from the southwest. We were at a point where we could turn east for shelter or leave the eastern shore behind us and buck into the weather for 24 to 30 hours to cross the lake. Good instincts took charge and we turned southeast for Charlevoix. It proved a wise decision: Charlevoix was a terrific little town, we met new friends Svend and Marjorie, former members of the Houston Yacht Club who noticed our burgee, and the weather continued to worsen for the next two days.

On the 24th the weather turned fair and we set off straight for Milwaukee, 200 miles southwest. It was a glorious day crossing Lake Michigan, although the weather started to build that evening, and at midnight a gale was forecast for the next afternoon. We were making good time, estimating arrival in Milwaukee about 1130, and we beat the weather there.

Gale warnings were in effect the next day, but we decided to head on south, staying close inshore and riding comfortably. It was extraordinarily clear, and by early afternoon we had our first sighting of the dramatic Chicago skyline more than 30 miles ahead. The tallest buildings started showing their upper floors above the crisp, hard horizon of the lake, then others appeared. The scattered tops of buildings looked more like a convoy of hull-down ships, and we were confused at first. It was a strange panoply that we have not seen before or since, seeming to rise out of the lake, looming higher and higher as we drew nearer.

By now we were abeam the Great Lakes Naval Training Center. We wanted to stop for the night, giving ourselves a full day the next day for approaching and arriving in Chicago. We pulled alongside the Flag Dock and were welcome to stay for a transient fee of 20 cents per foot. A fellow navy retiree offered his car, and we loaded up at the navy commissary with all we could manage in the hour he gave us.

On the 27th, our appointed day of arrival, we were underway early. Just outside the harbor we diverted to the right to enter the tight west entrance just off Lakeshore Drive, practically at the heart of the city. We paraded around the Navy Pier to Monroe Harbor, taking it all in, and found the tiny channel leading to the Chicago Yacht Club.

Chicago was a major milestone for us, about halfway home to Houston. It was hard for us to leave, but after four activity-packed days we tore ourselves away and entered the Chicago Lock. We unstepped our mast at the quay to pass under the downtown bridges and through the city on the Chicago River, then into the stretch called the Chicago Sanitary & Ship Canal and through the Illinois Waterway to Brandon Road Lock in Joliet, where we moored at the government dock in a rainstorm.

The Des Plaines River led into the Illinois River, which would take us the rest of the way to the Mississippi. There would be eight locks in the 288 nautical miles between Chicago Harbor and the Upper Mississippi, with 2- to 3-knot currents pushing us much of the way. A paucity of suitable moorings for a vessel of our size made it important to stage our running days. Also, when we restepped the mast, we found the radar inoperable, evidently due to a frayed antenna cable, and we didn't like the idea of navigating rivers at night without radar.

On the third day this loss led to one of our hairiest nights ever. Earlier in the day we had been running in steady rain helped by a 2- to 3-knot current, passing only three tows all morning and no pleasure boats. About noon the rain stopped and there was absolute solitude—we owned the river. Approaching Peoria in the afternoon we smelled the weather turning sour again and called the Illinois Valley Yacht Club for a mooring. The only one available was deep inside the harbor with a tricky approach they tried to explain to us on the radio, but we grounded at the entrance. We managed to back free, and on down the river we were invited to enter Detweiler Marina by a fellow who heard us on the radio, but we grounded again.

We continued to Peoria Lock in hopes of finding a place to moor, but there was none. Locking down with a towboat in heavy rain, we were out of the lock by 0930, sweeping the river for buoys and markers with our searchlight, and greatly missing our radar. At 2000 we were having serious difficulty but managing, though we shuddered at the thought of having to do this all night. We attempted to anchor at a likely looking turn on the chart below Turkey Island at 2200 but had no luck and left. An hour later we tried at a place called Liverpool with the same result. We were discouraged, to say the least, about the night ahead and worried about getting in the way of the now-heavy barge traffic.

Then, as we rounded the next turn, we were hailed by a towboat captain who had pushed his barge into the bank. He asked if we were going to continue all night through this mess. Jim's quick answer was: "Not if you'll let us tie up to you, we won't." He helped us alongside his barge, and after we got secured he came aboard for a visit. A kind and fascinating fellow, he stayed until the wee hours, telling tales and giving advice about the river ahead and the Mississippi below. At dawn the next morning a man on the riverbank screamed for us to get off his barge: it was carrying residual waste from the Chicago Sewer Treatment Plant, it was dangerous stuff, there was no insurance, and we had two minutes to get clear. We made it but were grateful for the good deed of our friend on the river. At some risk to himself, he may have saved our necks that night.

The remainder of the southward run through Illinois was uneventful. We had planned to stop at Père Marquette Marina, just above the junction with the Mississippi, but we were unable to raise them on VHF. The cruiser *Free Spirit* answered our call and advised us against entering there as the entrance was shallow. We accepted his suggestion to follow him 4 miles up the Mississippi River to a yacht club on Dardenne Slough, where there would be no charge for docking.

Woodland Yacht Club at St. Charles, Missouri, turned out to be our happy home for the next three days, though we bounced crossing the marina entrance and were aground when we pulled up to the fuel dock. We backed away easily, decided against deepening our draft by refueling, and tied alongside the floating clubhouse barge that was moored outside with a gangway ashore. One friendly club member offered to splice our radar cable; electronics repairman "Gemini Joe" took the better part of a day installing a 16-wire junction box. It was better than a new cable at half the cost, and our radar was back in business.

On October 9 we were underway again for our first day on the Mississippi. We were soon passing the massive and graceful Gateway Arch looming above the city of St. Louis. Two huge paddle wheelers, symbols of the Mississippi, lay along the bank.

We regretted there were no facilities for us to go ashore at St. Louis. In fact, we had been warned there would be no stopping along the river in the 70-mile stretch from St. Charles down to Hoppie's Marina at Kimmswick, Missouri. This section includes the mouth of the Missouri River as well as the Illinois, which add massive quantities of water to the Mississippi and push the current to more than 4 knots in places, even when the river's not in flood stage. We made the 70 miles to Hoppie's in less than seven hours.

Hoppie's consists of a series of moored barges and pilings in a fairly quiet section of the river, fronting on the restored old town of Kimmswick. We spent a lay day to take on fuel, service our engine, and dine in the historic "Old House."

The helpful manager called ahead and found there was no room for us at the next marina, 100 miles downstream at Cape Girardeau, so we were advised to anchor in the Little River Diversion Channel there. We covered the distance in less than 10 hours with almost no traffic, the current pushing us along smoothly at 11 to 12 mph. We spent a quiet, pleasant night with one other boat anchored in 10 feet of water.

The next day, where the Ohio River joins the Mississippi at Cairo, Illinois, we passed into the Lower Mississippi. The Army Corps of Engineers makes this distinction because the character of the Mississippi changes, now being burdened by the waters of the Ohio and Tennessee rivers below Cairo. This is also the juncture where many passage-making yachts from the Great Lakes turn east to get off the Lower Mississippi and into the less exciting Tennessee-Tombigbee river system to reach the Gulf of Mexico.

The traffic on the Lower Mississippi is much heavier, the tows larger, and the current swifter—2 to 4 mph at its slowest, as much as 8 to 9.5 mph in constricted reaches during flood stage. A navigable channel 300 feet wide and 9 feet deep is maintained by dredging and snagging operations to keep it clear, and we found no problems with buoyage.

At Hickman, Kentucky, we turned off the channel into a backwater, finding a Coast Guard buoy tender moored at its base just inside. We called on VHF to ask about conditions for anchoring upstream from them. The response came from the USCG Group in Memphis, who advised us that the cutter was secured for the weekend but he would contact the watch officer by landline phone. In less than two minutes he was back with a message saying we were invited to go alongside the cutter for the night. At that moment the duty section appeared on deck, standing by to take our docking lines and plug our electric cord into their power.

Later we traded tours with USCGC *Chena,* and it was the first time Susy had seen *that* kind of engine room. They invited us for breakfast the next morning, and we left a case of beer for them to find. It was hospitality of the finest kind and we commended the crew in a note of thanks to the Group Commander.

Our last stop before Memphis would be an elevator chute at Caruthersville, Missouri, about 70 miles downstream. We were there by midafternoon, anchored in a clearing above the elevators. When a towboat came in a few hours later and asked us to tie up to one of their moored barges, we happily complied.

Approaching Memphis was exciting. In the distance we could see the huge double arches of the "Dolly Parton" bridge, and the massive new pyramid-shaped sports arena just being completed. We turned at the foot of the bridge up Wolfe River to Mud Island Marina, home of the Memphis Yacht Club. The few pleasure craft here were the first we'd seen on the Mississippi.

Relatives of friends took us on tours of this revitalized city. We especially enjoyed the Mud Island Mississippi River Museum, the riverwalk showing the entire Mississippi in three-dimensional scale from the head of navigation to its mouth below New Orleans. When we left, the marina manager told us the next logical stop was a towhead above Helena, Arkansas, about 70 miles from Memphis. She then rather sheepishly added that only two weeks before, a cruising couple and their dog were murdered on a sailboat anchored there, but not to worry—the murderers had been captured and jailed. When we arrived, we anchored well offshore and locked all our hatches and doors. We had a quiet night, but it was a spooky place and we were glad to leave it.

On October 18 we turned off the Mississippi into the White River mouth of the Arkansas Post Canal, leading into the Arkansas River system. Completed in 1970, its 17 locks lift boats 390 feet, and the river is now navigable all the way to Tulsa, Oklahoma. We would negotiate 7 of the locks in the 127 miles to Jim's birthplace at Little Rock.

The Arkansas River is not as pastoral as the Erie Canal, perhaps, but the locktenders are almost as friendly. When Jim told the one at the D. D. Terry Lock he had grown up with Congressman Terry's son, the locktender called ahead to arrange space for us at Little Rock Yacht Club. We had visited Little Rock many times when Jim's parents were still living, so it was a homecoming for both of us.

By the last week of October we were back on the Mississippi, and by the 31st we had reached Vicksburg and moored at the Marina Barge on the Yazoo River, taking time out to tour the Vicksburg National Park and Cemetery. We were considering the Atchafalaya River as an alternate route home below Natchez, so we also visited the Army Corps of Engineers office, which seems to be the only source of the necessary charts.

The weather was growing noticeably colder, though clear and pleasant most of the time, and the days were growing shorter. Traffic was continuing to build on the river, and at one point below Vicksburg we counted 14 36-barge tows passing upbound in succession in one hour. No pleasure craft could be seen anywhere.

The paddle wheeler *Delta Queen* had arrived in the night at the ramp just astern of our barge. Late that afternoon we watched from our boat deck as she pulled away from the riverbank to the accompaniment of three hot-air balloons drifting slowly across the river, her calliope playing as she paddled on down the Mississippi, and literally faded into the sunset. It was a climactic end to our voyage on the Mississippi, for the next day we confirmed that the Atchafalaya River was open, and we left to enter the Old River Lock.

The Atchafalaya route would avoid the tumultuous traffic from Baton Rouge south to New Orleans and save us several days. It was an easy few days in the Intracoastal Waterway, with a short detour up the Calcasieu River to call at Lake Charles, and we were home in Houston on November 14. As it was we had a hard freeze with ice on the decks at anchor one morning: It was time to be off the river.

A summary of *Salvation II*'s log from New York–Houston shows:

Calendar days	77
Ports of call	53
States of the U.S.	14
Locks	68
Nautical miles	3,032
Engine hours	464
Gallons diesel fuel	870
Mpg	3.49*
Gph	1.88*
Average speed in knots	6.53

*These are exceptional due to the effects of river currents and low engine rpm.

Summary of the waters and locks transitted by *Salvation II*, New York–Houston 1991

	Miles	Days	Ports	Locks
Hudson River	175	4	3	1
Erie/Oswego Canal	186	5	5	30
Lake Ontario	175	3	3	
Welland Canal	30	1	1	8
Lake Erie	290	4	3	
Detroit River/St. Clair River	75	1	1	
Lake Huron	250	4	2	
Lake Michigan	390	12	7	
Chicago River/Illinois Waterway	327	4	4	8
Upper Mississippi River	230	6	3	2
Lower Mississippi River	650	18	8	
Arkansas River + return	280	7	5	14
Atchafalaya River	115	2	2	2
Gulf Intracoastal Waterway	252	4	4	1
Calcasieu River + return	30	1	1	2
Houston Ship Canal	30	1	1	
Totals	3,485 SM*	77	53	68

*3,485 SM × .87 = 3,032 NM

CHAPTER 18

ROUND-THE-WORLD PASSAGE-MAKING

THE ULTIMATE VOYAGE FOR any vessel is around the world. But in this chapter we will also consider under this heading the problems of long voyages in general, voyages of some months that are clearly more ambitious than a trip, say, from New York to the Caribbean.

At the very beginning of this book I said, ". . . a very good case could be made for the power approach over sail for all long voyages." Here is that case. First, there are people who, for various reasons—mostly physical—cannot make long sailing voyages. This group could certainly use the power approach to their advantage. Another group, small but likely to grow, might also find the power approach the ideal solution to their long-distance voyaging ambitions. This group consists of people, by no means get-away-from-it-all types, who would like to make a world voyage in their own boats if the time away from home and work could be limited to a reasonable span. The period of two years is often mentioned as the goal in cruise books; this seems reasonable enough. But many who have tried it under sail didn't make it in that time; or, if they did, wore themselves out in the attempt.

In contrast, a vessel with an assured speed of 7.5 knots could circle the world in six and a half months steaming time. This leaves 70 percent of the two years for local cruising and enjoying the ports along the way. When this time saving is combined with the crew arriving in port fresh and ready to go again, as described in Chapter 8, a power voyage should be a relaxed and enjoyable experience.

To point this up, let's turn to Hiscock's *Voyaging Under Sail* (International Marine, 1981) and, in its tabular record of voyages, follow a vessel that is listed almost all the way around. In fact, it was reading Hiscock and using a slide rule on his list of passages that first convinced me it was possible to do better. His book abounds with hints that more range under power would be desirable in a world-voyaging boat, though I doubt if he, himself, would ever adopt the full power approach. His leading design example, for instance, is *Beyond,* a 41-foot cutter that had a range under power of 1,500 miles, autopilot, and covered steering station and did a "very workmanlike circumnavigation in two years."

Another example was *Omoo*, a 45-foot ketch with a waterline of 37 feet, which would give 6.7 knots at an S/L of 1.1. Her listed voyages actually show speeds from a high of 4.9 knots for the run from the Canaries to Barbados, to a low of 3.46 knots, crossing the Indian Ocean from the Keeling Cocos Islands to Mauritius. The total time for the nine listed voyages (about 70 percent of the distance around) is 215 days. If she had averaged a speed/length ratio of 1.1, as *Passagemaker* proved was possible, she would have made these voyages in 126 days, leaving 89 days—almost three months!—that could have been spent in port or exploring other places. If the whole voyage were made at these averages, the extra time available would be a bit more than four months. As cruising is done essentially to enjoy the ports, the people, and the scenery of the places you visit, such a gain in time is impressive. And this time advantage persists, in proportion, on less ambitious voyages, of course. The question is: How valuable is this advantage to individuals?

To a young crew in a well-found sailing vessel with no particular deadline to meet, it would seem to have no advantages. However, even here a couple of items need consideration. First, as John Samson noted in his book, *A New Way of Life,* which is dedicated to such people, going under power might very well turn out to be cheaper. Food cost at sea, where you consume expensive canned and prepared foods until you can get the cheaper native foods found in ports, can be a big item. Second, the care and upkeep of a sailing rig is a constant expense, with a heavy cost such as a blown-out sail always possible.

For the "man-and-wife teams," the appeal of the power approach would vary depending on their devotion to and experience with sail. It appears, from what little data there is on this free-wandering mass of individuals, that many of them are interested in voyaging for a definite period before moving ashore. They, too, could extend their range with power.

ROUTES

It is interesting to speculate on the best routes for world-girdling power passages. Going west, it appears the departure schedules and tracks of the sailing voyager would also be the best for the power cruiser, with two exceptions. One is that the long distances from Panama to the South Seas make it practically mandatory that the power vessel select the Acapulco–San Diego–Hawaii route before heading east to the islands. A trip to Tahiti would take a 7.5-knot boat 16 days longer than would going direct. And in the Indian Ocean, using the Suez Canal both to shorten the voyage and to make possible a cruise of the fascinating Mediterranean is attractive to the power vessel. Generally, sail voyagers avoid this route due to the difficulties of negotiating the Red Sea and timing conflicts with the monsoon seasons. If the power voyager elects Suez, his departure date for leaving the Pacific would be different from that of the sailing cruiser.

Occasionally a book will mention the possibility of a circumnavigation made eastward via Suez and the North Pacific to Panama. To my knowledge it has not been done to date. It looks quite practicable for the power vessel. Without investigating the route in great detail, it looks as if it would go like this, from California:

1. Leave Southern California about November 15 and go to Grenada in the West Indies, then cruise the Caribbean to June 1.

2. On June 1 leave for the Mediterranean via Bermuda and the Azores. Cruise in the Med until October 1.

3. Transit Suez about October 1 and proceed as directly as possible to Singapore during the change of the monsoon from SW to NE, arriving Singapore about November 15.

4. Leave Singapore about December 1 for the Indonesian islands of Bali and Timor. Then go around Australia from the west, checking in at Darwin, then via the new western ports to Perth, Adelaide, Melbourne, Tasmania, and up the east coast (including cruising along the Great Barrier Reef), reaching Port Moresby about March 15.

5. Cruise through the Solomons to the Carolines and Guam. Then enter Japan at Nagasaki, arriving about May 1. Cruise in Japan and its Inland Sea until July 1.

6. On July 1, leave Hokkaido for Prince Rupert, B.C., Canada, fueling at Dutch Harbor, Alaska, if necessary. Cruise in British Columbia until September 15.

7. With due regard for weather, about September 15 run down the coast to San Francisco for a couple of weeks, then south to Southern California about October 15—to end a world-girdling voyage one month short of two years.

The crux of this routing is getting through the Indian Ocean on the fall change of the monsoon. The rest is straightforward, following the best tracks and times, and should provide good weather all the way. The only exception is the passage from Japan to Canada, where a good deal of fog and some wind can be expected. Radar would be useful in this stretch, as the area abounds with fishing vessels.

Crossing the Pacific is quite a problem compared to crossing the Atlantic. The route suggested above is fine in summer but prohibited in other seasons. You can go east by an equatorial route, seeking out the countercurrent where possible, stopping at Rabaul or Honiara, Tarawa, Christmas Island, and Honolulu. But here again the passage from Honolulu to the mainland should be made in the summer, as one must go well north to get out of the trades. To make a winter passage, the only possibility seems to be from Christmas Island to Acapulco, if your vessel could make the 3,715 miles of this leg. This is quite a distance, of course, and would probably

Figure 18-1.
*Linford Beebe
enjoying the perfect
weather in the
middle of the Pacific
High. There is no
land in any direction
for 1,000 miles!*

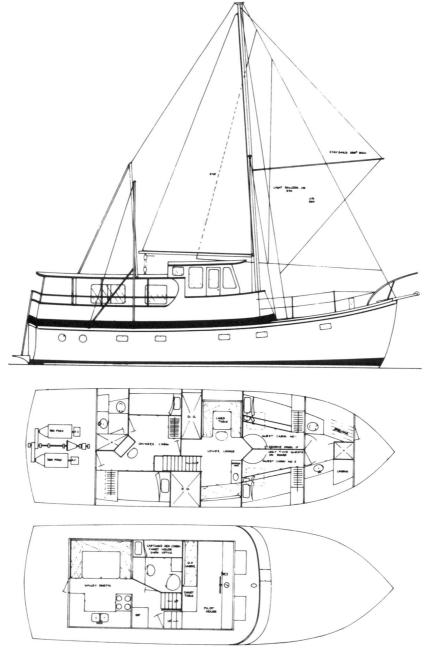

Figure 18-2. *Profile and accommodation (both decks) of Beebe Design 90, a proposed 50-foot motorboat for round-the-world passage-making. Note the rig for reaching and running in the trades, captain's sea cabin, twin engines on a single shaft, and lounge spaces on the lower deck.*

bar this route to smaller craft, though use of rubber fuel tanks below and some drums on deck might make it possible. The distance would be somewhat shorter if fuel were laid on in the Marquesas. Some of the advantages this has would be lost by your having to get out of the southeast trades immediately and return to 6° or 8° North, where the countercurrent runs strongly to the eastward.

At these isolated islands, negotiations to lay on a supply of fuel should be undertaken 10 months to a year in advance. There is a ship from Suva to Christmas Island twice a year, for instance. If such a refueling job from drums is attempted, the vessel should be equipped with its own electric pumps, hoses several hundred feet long, plus excellent filters and funnels.

DESIGN CONSIDERATIONS

What design features would characterize a round-the-world passage-maker? Figure 18-2 shows a sketch I made as a start on this problem. Besides fuel and propulsion (two engines coupled to one shaft), she has two features specifically added for the world voyage: a sailing rig designed for reaching and running to give the crew something to do, and a layout designed to provide the maximum number of places the crew can spread out into and find some privacy when they wish, coming together only for meals. I think this is important.

Tales of crew trouble abound in sail-cruising literature, and undoubtedly many more incidents go unreported. Of course, certain personalities should not go to sea in small craft at all. But most people can handle the enforced intimacy of a voyage if it is kept within reasonable limits, as it hardly can be in a small sailing cruiser. In a Passagemaker, where each person has his own bunk, with no more than two in a cabin and several spaces to "get away" to, the situation is much easier.

The sketch takes these ideas about as far as they can go in such a small vessel, 50 feet overall. The above-deck space shows a galley-dinette where everyone gathers for meals and the cook is part of things. Forward of this is a captain's sea cabin that doubles as a charthouse for navigation work, keeping this operation out of the dinette and pilothouse. And of course, the pilothouse is the domain of one person all the time. Below, there is a built-in card table, and across from it a small seat and belowdecks coffee bar. There is plenty of space for friendly gatherings. But if people are not in a sociable mood, they are not restricted to a single public space as in so many vessels.

So, let's visualize this craft cruising through the isles of Greece, entering Malaysia at Penang to celebrate the end of the passage across the Indian Ocean, anchoring in the little harbor at Benoa on Bali, skindiving along the Great Barrier Reef, visiting fishing villages in Japan, and mooring in that perfect spot—Princess Louisa Inlet. Then, at last, passing under the Golden Gate Bridge, and getting home again to look back on the cruise of a lifetime.

CHAPTER 19

THE LONG-
RANGE GALLEY

AUTHOR'S NOTE (1974): The care that goes into provisioning and the dedicated labor that produces fine meals day after day are as important to successful passage-making as the operation of the vessel itself.

No one is better at these duties than my wife, Linford, for years a gourmet cook of reputation. She came to boats late, and probably never in her wildest dreams did she imagine she would be preparing meals on a plunging small boat a thousand miles from land. I think it would be interesting, particularly to families contemplating taking to the sea, to say a few words on how she came to join *Passagemaker*'s crew.

We had both lost our spouses some years previously. When Linford and I met, *Passagemaker* was a sheet of tracing paper on my drawing board. When we finally decided to get married, I was in Singapore finishing up *Passagemaker*. It took something of a logistic miracle to make all the pieces fall together, but they did, and we were married in the American Church in Athens, Greece, on July 6, 1963—six weeks after *Passagemaker* had arrived there.

When Linford came aboard, her seagoing experience was limited to globe-circling steamer trips—her small-boat experience was nil. She took to it like a duck and has been *Passagemaker*'s most ardent fan ever since. She knows her watch-standing, handles the wheel for anchoring, does stern coaching, and handles lines for Med mooring. She can lay a boat alongside the dock if she has to and has stood her share of night watches. As noted in Chapter 15, she doesn't care much for this last activity, preferring to be permanent cook.

At this duty she is superb.

Linford Beebe's original chapter "The Long-Range Galley" certainly illustrated her expertise in the ship's galley, but she makes it clear in this new galley chapter that much has changed in the intervening 20 years. I was particularly pleased when she agreed to provide this new chapter as a greater authority on the subject would be difficult to find.

PROVISIONING AND GALLEY TIPS
by Linford Beebe

It was strange going aboard *Passagemaker* at the Vouliagemeni yacht harbor in Greece, not only because I'd had no experience with such a life but also because *Passagemaker* on paper hadn't prepared me for her three-dimensional enormity. Suddenly there she was—those half-inches grown to 50 feet, a full-scale seagoing home. I loved the commodious master's quarters. I enjoyed the raised dinette where we could look out the window-size ports at the harbor, and I was delighted with the more than adequate food storage space beneath the dinette. I took pleasure in her comfort and felt secure in her dependability.

Chapter 4 described how *Passagemaker* was equipped for the voyage from Singapore: a two-burner Primus stove, cold-water hand pump, and an icebox in the cockpit. That was my first galley. I didn't find it too difficult to cope, however, and I learned a great deal more about food preservation, recipe adaptation, and food substitutions than I would have if I had come to a fully equipped galley.

We spent the winter of 1963 in Greece, cruising throughout the islands and up the Yugoslavian coast. Our shore base was just 2 miles from the Vouliagemeni yacht harbor, where we kept *Passagemaker*. Much of our time was spent decorating and finishing the boat's interior. We painted a frieze around the wall of the dining area, inspired by a Greek vase. On a trip to Athens, we purchased a frying pan, wok, pressure cooker, and an oven, all electric.

We visited many outlying islands in search of local crafts. We scoured the markets for fresh and canned foods of Greek origin and checked out the tastes and quality of prepared foods and local wines in the restaurants and taverns. Each island seemed to have a specialty uniquely its own.

In Rhodes we found handsome blue-and-white hand-painted dishes for the galley and table. In Mykonos the beauty of handwoven place mats, napkins, curtain fabrics, and bedspreads was irre-

Figure 19-1. *Linford and Bob Beebe on* Passagemaker's *deck in Kotor Gulf, Yugoslavia, in 1963, stopped for lunch.*

sistible. The boat was looking very fine. Those were splendid days, as were the days and months to follow as we visited the many ports and harbors written about in foregoing chapters.

Ten years and 60,000 nautical miles passed under *Passagemaker*'s keel from the day she left Singapore until we sold her. We cruised in all kinds of weather conditions. We went through rough seas and had green water over the wheelhouse numerous times. A condition not to be enjoyed but never feared, for I'd learned to have confidence in *Passagemaker*'s ability to survive. The story of her beginnings and years of testing was first published in 1975. Now, 20 years later, *Voyaging Under Power* enters the nineties.

Fortunately for the cook, the intervening years have made time in the galley less burdensome. Many labor-saving electrical appliances, some with a brain, have taken on work the cook had to do in the sixties. Today's *Passagemaker* would certainly be equipped with an electric cook-top and oven, refrigeration, and a generous freezer. My nineties' galley would also have an eye-level microwave oven. A Jet-Stream oven (sold in many department stores) would be in use for most meals. This handy appliance can boil, fry, toast, broil, and bake, and it is compact enough to leave on the counter (in a vertical position).

A mini food processor that chops and purees, with a separate head for shredding and slicing, is a daily necessity for making salads and soups—a must in any seagoing galley. An electric ice-cream maker is a great answer to the "What's for dessert?" question. They come in different sizes and are easy to operate.

The latest bread makers are a joy. It takes only a few minutes to toss in the ingredients and push *Start*. Choose a model that produces a sandwich-shaped loaf; it cuts to better advantage. Some brands can be preset for any selected time. To have a hot loaf for breakfast is a special treat at sea. Just the aroma of baking bread coming from the galley tantalizes the senses, and sharing a loaf with neighboring yachtsmen will make the cook queen of the anchorage.

There are other small appliances I have found useful and time-saving. Braun makes a hand-held blender that can puree soups, especially lentil, split pea, or bean. It mashes potatoes, beats eggs, makes pancake and waffle batters, mayonnaise, and sauces.

Krups gives us a fine coffee and spice grinder. Coffee beans and spices are far more flavorful if ground just before use. Preground herbs and spices lose their zest in a relatively short time, especially under seagoing conditions. Processing torn pieces of bread after each use clears the grinder of lingering flavors.

An electric juicer is handy, as well, if storage space permits.

Storage and Provision List

On *Passagemaker*, storage areas were planned for long-range cruising without ports of call on the way. The space beneath the dinette was divided into 21 bins of 2 to 3 cubic feet each. We kept an inventory of supplies held in each of the numbered bins and a record of the foods each bin actually contained, recording daily withdrawals for future shopping lists.

What to buy and how much of each poses a full-scale problem for a long voyage. My best approach was to plan menus for breakfast, lunch, and dinner multiplied by the estimated number of days at sea. A two-week menu plan, repeated, seemed satisfactory. This provides a basic provision list. Before buying, however, make sure the bulk of anticipated purchases will fit into available storage space by estimating the cubic size of these items compared to total space available.

Figure 19-2.
*Passagemaker's crew
returns from grocery
shopping in Lyon,
France, on the
Rhône River.*

Dried Goods and Condiments

canned milk, whole and nonfat

dry milk powder, whole and nonfat

flour, all-purpose

flour, whole wheat

baking powder

cornstarch

baking soda

cake mixes

brownie mixes

Bisquick

muffin mixes

pancake mixes

pancake and waffle syrup

butter

margarine

cooking oils

olive oil

Butter Buds

PAM (for spraying pans)

crackers

cookies

tortillas

popcorn

potato flakes

spaghetti

lasagna

other pastas

rice

bulgur wheat

dried split peas

lentils

pinto beans

navy beans

cereals

rolled oats

nuts

raisins

dried fruits (apples, bananas, apricots, peaches, prunes)

jellies

jams

peanut butter

chocolate for cooking

ketchup

mayonnaise

Worcestershire sauce

Marukan rice vinegar

Marukan seasoned vinegar

mustard

coffee

tea

sugar

salt

onion flakes

garlic powder

salt-free seasonings

selected spices and herbs for planned menus

various package mixes for soups

vegetable and fruit juices

gravy and sauces

dry, mixed salad dressings (Knorr, Spice Islands, Lawry, and Good Seasons are all good choices)

Knorr Chicken Bouillon

beef cubes

Suggested Provisions

Oriental markets and some supermarkets stock Japanese products: *Panko*—excellent for breading chicken, fish, and other meats for baking or frying; *Dashi-No-Moto* fish stock is a good base for fish soups and chowders. A light soy sauce and teriyaki sauce are a nice flavor change, splendid especially with chicken or fish. Chinese water chestnuts and bamboo shoots, dried mushrooms, chow mein noodles, and various packaged soups and sauces, such as sesame, plum, black bean, soy, and five-spice seasoning give variety to the Western menu.

Canned Vegetables. Canned vegetables are available in great variety in almost every country. The basics are tomatoes; whole green beans; baked beans; white, red, and black beans for soups, salads, and casseroles; corn, cream and whole kernel, for chowders and a variety of uses; okra, sliced and whole, and shredded beets for salads, borscht, or Harvard style; and jars of artichokes to add to salads and casseroles for great taste and texture.

Canned Fruits. Canned fruits can be quite good, especially if given a lift by adding lemon juice, liquor, or brandy, with perhaps a custard pudding mix.

Canned Meats. Canned meats are not offered in great variety. However, small hams—1 to 1½ pounds—need not be refrigerated if kept in a cool place. Rath Black Hawk Honey Glazed and Dubuque Royal Buffet are quite good. Italian dry salami is another meat choice.

Canned Seafood. Salmon and tuna make excellent salads, soups, casseroles, and sandwiches. Both are good in quiche and with many pasta dishes. We found one or two such meals a week acceptable. Also include shrimp, crabmeat, lobster, salt cod for Finnan Haddie, and sardines for hors d'oeuvres and for a great, hearty Scandinavian dish called Johnssen's Temptation:

This dish is traditionally made with fresh anchovies, but a good substitute is to mix sardines packed in oil with whole anchovies in equal amounts. Layer sliced potatoes, onions, parsley, and fish in a well-buttered casserole, starting and ending with potatoes. Drizzle oil on top and pour cream over all. Bake at 325°F for about 1½ hours or until potatoes are done and top is browned. Can be made ahead and reheated in a 350°F oven.

Food Preservation

Vegetables and Fruit. There is scant information on the subject of preservation and provisioning for long-range voyaging. Most galley cookbooks seem to assume you'll be going to the market every three days. Lists of what has proved satisfactory on long voyages are hard to come by, yet knowledge of the subject can mean the difference between enjoying fresh fruits and vegetables for weeks at sea or depending entirely on canned stores.

Some fresh foods last best under cool, moist conditions; others need dry, dark, and cool. Some may go on the deck topside, others in shaded places or in the hold. Bins and lockers designed and located for preservation of fresh stores should be prepared before the stores are taken aboard.

Covered deck lockers with louvered sides can be used for those foods that travel best in moderately moist conditions. Some of these are: cabbage, cauliflower, Chinese cabbage, and lettuce.

Figure 19-3. *The
fascinating market-
place at Ponta
Delgada in the
Azores. (Photo by
Norris D. Hoyt)*

They should be wrapped separately in burlap and dampened from time to time. Choose cabbage that is solid and heavy for its size. Cauliflower should be white with no yellow tinge. Lettuce must be firm, the outer leaves green, and the core end white and sweet-smelling. Lettuce should not be stored next to fruits, for many fruits give off gas as they ripen, causing dark spots to develop on green, leafy vegetables. Wrap oranges and grapefruit and store the same way. If heat is so intense that these items start to sweat, shade the bin, but allow air to circulate.

A box of moist sand kept out of the sun is a good place for many root vegetables. Choose all as fresh as possible with crisp, green foliage. Trim foliage to within an inch of the base, as it drains moisture from the root. Small carrots with small cores are sweetest. Bury celery in the sand so only the leafy tips are exposed. Beets and leeks, with roots left on, keep best in *dry* sand in a cool place.

Wrap potatoes in newspaper and store in a cool, dark place; they can stand some moisture, but light causes green areas to appear and turns them bitter. They should be separated from onions, which steal moisture from them, and sprouting results. Keep onions dry and dark. Watch all vegetables for sprouts and remove these from time to time. Pumpkins and hard-shell squash last indefinitely and do well in warm weather if kept in a dry, airy place.

Buy tomatoes while still green or with a slightly pinkish cast, wrap in tissue paper, and keep in a cool spot—they should last six to eight weeks. Bring them out a day or two before planned use, but do not place them in the sun. After ripening they are good for two to three days only.

Select small mushrooms with tightly closed caps, and store where it's dark and humid. Broccoli should have compact heads with tightly closed flowers; it will last about two weeks if wrapped in a damp cloth and kept cool.

Purchase avocados still hard with a firm stem end and free of bruised spots. Wrap separately and bring out to ripen. Ripening can be accelerated by placing avocados in a paper bag for a day or two. Never refrigerate before fully ripe as chilling stops the ripening process.

Apples, peaches, apricots, pears, and plums last longer if wrapped in tissue paper and kept dry. A box of sawdust stored inside the boat helps preserve them if they are free from blemishes and completely dry before covering. Or wrap in paper and store in a covered crock with paper between each layer. Firm, small apples keep better than large ones.

Select hard, green pears—they will ripen quickly when you bring them out. Color doesn't always indicate ripeness, but a slight "give" at the stem end shows they are ready to eat.

Peaches, apricots, and plums should be firm but not green. Enjoy these less durable fruits at their best as they won't last long.

Buy lemons and limes with thin skins and slightly green. They will last indefinitely if wrapped in plastic and kept in an airtight, plastic container. The limes you buy in the tropics are fat, juicy, and delicious.

Many tropical fruits don't travel well and should be enjoyed as you go. Pineapple, though common in our markets, tastes sweeter and more flavorful on native soil; for export, they are picked before entirely ripe. This stops the ripening process. We bought a crate of specially selected ones in Hawaii, kept them on deck under a tarp, with good air circulation. They lasted six weeks.

Cheese. Hard Italian cheeses such as Parmesan, Provolone, and Romano are least perishable because they contain the least amount of moisture. They freeze well, too. After defrosting, keep wrapped in a salt- or vinegar-saturated damp cloth in a cool place.

Cheddar, Gouda, and Swiss should be sealed with paraffin and refrigerated, then coated again after cutting. Processed cheese keeps until opened if kept relatively cool. If mold appears on any cheese, just cut it off—it doesn't affect the taste, nor is it harmful.

Cakes and Cookies. Cakes, cookies, and crackers should be purchased in tins, if possible, or removed from cartons and stored in airtight containers sealed with Scotch tape.

The Magic of Wine and Herbs

Adding a touch of wine or liquor and/or herbs or spices can often lift an otherwise mundane dish to a gourmet level. Primitive knowledge of such culinary magic brought savor to the staple fare of

Figure 19-4. *Ralph Arndt returns to* Passagemaker *in a French canal after one of his forays on the Solex bike for cheese, wine, and bread.*

peasants and elegance to the dining of kings. A judiciously used accent can mark you as a sophisticated cook and master chef.

Most canned foods are dismally undistinguished unless some imagination is used in their preparation. I consider my bin stores only as a starting point for a meal and am constantly experimenting. Here are a few selections from my "Sea Fare" cooking file.

Welsh Rarebit. To ½ can Aged Cheddar Cheese Sauce (available in the gourmet section or at specialty food stores) add 1 to 2 tablespoons Worcestershire sauce, a few grains of cayenne pepper, and 1 teaspoon dry mustard. Cook over low flame, stirring until smooth. Slowly whip mixture into 1 lightly beaten egg and return to pan. Add ½ cup beer. Reheat, but do not boil.

With tomatoes. Gently sauté one 12-oz. can of sliced tomatoes in garlic-seasoned butter (or margarine) until just heated through. Cover toasted English muffin half with rarebit, top with tomatoes and sprinkling of freeze-dried chives. For a more hearty dish, put a slice of lightly browned ham under rarebit.

With green chilies. Add ½ can chopped green chilies (Ortega brand) to rarebit.

Spinach Soufflé. Partially defrost 1 package of Stouffer's Spinach Soufflé, stir, add 1 cup of fresh white bread crumbs, 2 tablespoons finely sliced green onions or yellow onion minced, 2 teaspoons lemon juice, and 2 tablespoons shredded Swiss cheese. Bake in preheated oven at 325°F until browned.

Rosemary Potatoes. Peel 4 large baking potatoes. Cut across in 4 pieces each. Coat casserole with PAM and add potato slices in single layer. Cover with Campbell's Beef Consommé (1 cup) plus ⅓ cup water. Sprinkle with 3 to 4 tablespoons finely chopped rosemary leaves. Dot with 3 tablespoons butter, diced. Bake at 400°F until tender, about 30 to 40 minutes. Cover lightly with foil if becoming too brown.

Orange-Mint Cooler. Bring 2½ cups water with 1½ cups sugar to a boil. Put 1 cup crushed fresh mint (or ½ cup dry mint leaves) in a jar and pour boiling sugar syrup over. Add 1 teaspoon orange zest, 2 cups fresh orange juice or reconstituted frozen orange juice, 1¼ cups lemon juice. Cover and let stand 2 hours. Strain, cover tightly, and refrigerate. To serve, use ⅓ cup juice to a tall glass, add ice cubes, and fill with chilled ginger ale. (Mint extract can be used if fresh or dried leaves are not available.)

Coffee Mousse. Combine 6 oz. semisweet real chocolate bits, 2 beaten eggs, and 2 tablespoons rum. Blend and slowly add 3 tablespoons hot strong coffee plus ¾ cup scalded milk. Process, using on-and-off technique for 2 to 3 minutes. Top with toasted nuts and whipped cream or whipped cream substitute.

Mock Sour Cream. Blend 1 cup creamed cottage cheese with 1 tablespoon lemon juice. Let stand overnight.

Chili Sauce. One cup chopped tomatoes, ½ cup chopped onions, ¼ cup chopped fresh cilantro leaves or parsley, 1 teaspoon salt, 1 teaspoon vinegar, ½ cup chopped Ortega canned green chilies.

Hot Tea Mix. Combine 1⅓ cups orange Tang, ½ cup sugar, ⅓ cup instant lemon-flavored tea, ½ teaspoon cinnamon, ¼ teaspoon cloves. Store in tightly sealed jar. To serve, add 1 teaspoon of mix to 1 cup boiling water. Add ice for a cold drink.

Chinese Marinade. For chicken, beef, fish. Keeps in refrigerator 3 to 4 weeks: ¾ cup soy sauce, ¼ cup sugar, ¼ cup dry sherry, 2 teaspoons minced fresh ginger.

Herb and Spice Mixtures

Fine Herbs. Three tablespoons each of dried leaf thyme, basil, savory, dried lemon peel, marjoram, and sage. Shake to blend.

Five Spice (for Chinese dishes). One-quarter cup ground ginger, 2 tablespoons ground cinnamon, 1 tablespoon allspice, 1 tablespoon crushed star anise (Oriental markets), 1½ teaspoons ground cloves. Blend.

Creole. Two tablespoons each of ground pepper, garlic powder, and lemon peel. Three tablespoons sweet paprika, ½ teaspoon red pepper, 1½ teaspoons onion powder, 1 tablespoon lemon peel. Blend.

Curry. Seeds from 12 cardamom pods and 2 tablespoons coriander seeds, ground; 1 tablespoon each ground turmeric, ginger; 1½ teaspoons each ground allspice, cinnamon, pepper, and cloves.

Garlic Herb Seasoning. Two tablespoons each marjoram, oregano, rosemary, basil, and parsley. One tablespoon each onion powder, black pepper, thyme; 2 teaspoons garlic powder.

A Couple of Hearty Soups

Borscht. Two cans Campbell's Beef Consommé or Beef Broth. Add 1 can of water, 1½ cans of dry red wine, the liquid from canned beets, 2 cans shredded beets (add last), 1 small onion (chopped), 1 clove garlic (minced), 1 carrot cut into ¼" slices, 2 medium potatoes cut into ¾" cubes, ½ teaspoon salt, ¼ teaspoon ground pepper, 2 teaspoons sugar, ½ teaspoon ground celery seed. Cook onion, garlic, carrot, and potato in consommé, water, wine, and seasonings until just tender. Add 1 tablespoon vinegar, beets, and beet liquid. Simmer until hot but not boiling. Garnish with sour cream or its substitute (see Mock Sour Cream recipe on page 235).

Fish Chowder. Mix 2 cups Japanese fish stock (Oriental markets) with 1 can Campbell's Mushroom Soup and 1 can Campbell's Celery Soup, 2 cups powdered whole milk prepared as directed, ¼ cup dry white wine or vermouth, 4 tablespoons butter, 1 chopped onion, ½ teaspoon ground celery seed, 1 teaspoon dill weed, 2 potatoes cut into ½" cubes. Bring to boil, then reduce to simmer until potatoes are tender. Add 2 cans solid pack white tuna (albacore) in water, separated into bite-size pieces. Dry potato flakes may be added to thicken. Garnish with small shrimp and freeze-dried chives.

Quick Soups

1. To a can of green pea soup, add ⅓ cup whole milk powder, 1 cube Knorr's chicken bouillon, 2 cups water, curry, chives, and bacon bits to taste.

2. To Top Ramen chicken soup with noodles and vegetables, add a little sherry and soy sauce with 1 tablespoon of dried parsley leaves.

3. Combine cream-of-chicken soup with cream-of-mushroom soup, season with tarragon or curry. This soup mixture is also a good basic cream soup for additives such as cream-style corn and chopped ham, bacon, or chicken.

4. When thickness is needed for soups, add potato flakes instead of flour.

Three Sauces

Using French's White Sauce as a base:

1. Add 1 cup clam juice (instead of water), butter, capers, a little anchovy, and some parsley. Serve with fish.

2. Add ½ cup dry white wine, ½ cup chicken stock, butter, and ½ cup grated cheese. Serve on vegetables and poultry.

3. Make a mustard sauce by mixing onion juice, ½ cup milk, ½ cup white wine, 1 teaspoon Coleman's mustard, a squeeze of lemon, and a little sugar.

Gravy

Envelopes of gravy mixes are a good start from which some delicious gravies evolve. Instead of the water called for on the package, try using Knorr's beef or chicken stock, or dry red or white wine, and always add some butter. Seasonings can be tarragon, a little lemon juice, and bourbon; or curry, soy, and bourbon; or a tablespoon of tomato sauce, some sour cream or its substitute, tarragon, and bourbon. Bourbon seems to give a great lift to gravies. Gin is good as well, especially with beef, but don't overwhelm other flavors by adding too much..

Desserts

A great deal can be done with packaged dessert mixes. Certainly, most cake mixes are improved by adding fruit juices, such as lemon, orange, apricot nectar, or sherry instead of water. Rum and instant powdered coffee are delicious in chocolate cake or brownies. Sherry, rum, and many liqueurs give pleasing flavors to pudding mixes. Add lemon and orange zest to fruit pie fillings. For a real treat, try this one:

Brandied Peach Pudding. Soak canned peach halves overnight in a syrup made from the canning liquid boiled down to half the original volume. Add ½ cup brandy. Flavor vanilla pudding mix with sherry and spoon into dessert dishes. When ready to serve, sprinkle peach halves with a little orange and lemon zest mixed with brown sugar and put under the broiler long enough to melt the sugar. Put a peach half in each dessert dish and top with sliced almonds.

Galley Tips

1. Cover pan with colander to keep frying foods from splattering.

2. Put damp towel under bowl to keep it from turning or sliding.

3. Make a dark roux for chowders or gumbos—spread flour thinly over cookie sheet and bake at 350°F until desired color is reached.

4. Macerate dried fruits in fruit juices, brandy, spiced wines, or sherry.

5. To freeze 6 eggs, separate yolks from whites. To yolks add 2 teaspoons sugar for sweet dishes and ½ teaspoon of salt for savory dishes. Bottle and mark. To use, allow 8 to 10 hours to defrost in refrigerator. One tablespoon yolk plus 2 tablespoons white will equal 1 egg. The whites need no additive.

6. Cottage cheese lasts longer if stored in refrigerator upside down.

7. Have all ingredients at room temperature when baking breads or cakes. They will rise better.

8. Freeze cakes without frosting and they will keep indefinitely.

9. To preserve fresh ginger, select with tight, shiny skins. Slice into ⅛-inch pieces. Place in bottle, cover with sherry, or red or white wine—will last up to one year.

10. Make up white sauce mixes: 2 tablespoons Butter Buds to 2 tablespoons flour, ½ teaspoon salt for medium sauce. Reduce by one-half for thin white sauce and increase by half for thick white sauce. Each recipe calls for 1 cup of milk.

11. Cheese sauce: Add 1 cup shredded Cheddar cheese to cooked white sauce. Stir until melted. Do not boil.

12. Steak sauce: 1 cup butter, room temperature; ¼ cup Worcestershire sauce; ¾ teaspoon anchovy paste; ¼ cup dry parsley flakes; ⅛ teaspoon paprika; ⅛ teaspoon garlic powder; ⅛ teaspoon ground pepper. Roll in bag and freeze.

13. Mock Olive Oil: 24 unpitted brine-packed green olives. Cover with 1 quart vegetable oil. Let stand one to two weeks in a cool, dark place.

14. Drying in the microwave. *Herbs.* Wash and dry, place on double paper towel, cook about 4 minutes uncovered or until thoroughly dry. Allow to dry overnight and put in glass jars with tightly fitting lids. Store in a cool and dark place. *Zest.* Use vegetable peeler to obtain zest from one orange and two lemons on a double sheet. With one covering sheet, will dry in about 2 minutes. *Mushrooms.* Clean with a damp cloth, slice thin and place on double paper towel, covered by a single towel—should dry in 3 to 4 minutes. Check after 2 minutes.

15. Refresh wilted vegetable in salted water for 1 hour; drain and pat dry.

16. Frozen and canned shrimp are best if washed briefly, covered with ice water, and refrigerated 1 hour.

17. Fill new pan with vinegar. Bring to boil and allow to stand ½ hour to make it stick-free.

18. Bananas may be frozen for cooking if peeled, mashed with lemon juice, and packaged in plastic bags. They will keep fresh in the refrigerator for about two weeks although skin will darken.

19. Nuts may be toasted in the microwave. For 1 cup walnuts and pecans, 3½ to 4 minutes on high; for 1 cup almonds, 4½ to 5 minutes on high (check during last 1½ minutes). Keep in sealed containers.

20. Allow frozen ground turkey to drain in refrigerator 1 hour before cooking or freezing.

21. To make a pastry bag: put food in plastic bag and tie top securely, snip off one corner and pipe out food, such as mashed potatoes, cookie dough, and so forth.

22. Brown sugar may be softened by placing in microwave for a few seconds.

23. Crystallized honey will liquefy by placing in microwave for a few minutes.

24. Lemons or limes will give more juice if placed in a microwave for 15 to 20 seconds. Pierce and put in a cup to keep juice from escaping.

25. Chicken parts washed and placed in salt water to cover for 1 hour will be white and free of discoloration.

The beginning of this chapter tells how I came as a novice to the cruising world and how I became happily and incurable committed. I attribute my gentle introduction to first going to sea on *Passagemaker*. Our voyages have taken us across thousands of miles of oceans and seas and into dozens of harbors. They have been a blend of many pleasures: the joy of being at sea . . . the thrill of a landfall . . . the fascination of personal discovery in each new port . . . and always, the continuing gastronomic adventure of savoring the exotic in cooking pots of the world.

Landfall

For the long-distance voyager, there is a special magic to a landfall: not just excitement, more like enchantment, as a vision dissolves into focus and becomes reality. Even men who have worked with stars and horizons for many years acclaim the wonder of this moment.

For two or three weeks you have been at sea, crew settled into jobs, ocean vast around you, high sky above, living the arts and work of the sailor. Then at some unlikely moment someone shouts, "Land ho!"

At once the crew assembles on deck, first to find the tiny speck on the distant horizon, then to identify it indisputably as land, finally to watch it grow. Abruptly, you are terrestrial creatures again, eager to see your native medium, wondering about all the mysteries of the land ahead.

Awed, you see the speck swell into a mountain, stare harder as the mountain takes shape and throws out a headland, takes on a fringe of palms, acquires a coral necklace of crashing waves, and finally reveals a village—boats, people, cars, houses, shops. . . .

At last, a few hours after the speck appeared, your little ship passes through a gap in the reef, curves across the harbor toward the town, slows as it nears the seawall, and then—as always and remarkably—through the smiles of welcome, several pairs of willing hands reach for your lines and make you fast to the land. . . .

Tomorrow you will explore the busy streets; hear the chatter; soak up the color; be startled by noise and surprised by scurry; discover the tang, aroma, fragrance, and spice of a native market. But for the rest of today, it is enough to sit and watch and marvel at being back on land again.

CHAPTER 20

OPERATING A SEAGOING MOTORBOAT

*O*PERATING" IS A BROAD TERM that covers just about every activity aboard a seagoing vessel once it gets underway. We cannot even begin to list *all* that the captain and crew should know or should have done before they leave the dock. Instead, we will comment on certain activities and functions that experience has shown to be important, or in which we differ from the standard texts, or where we can offer a better way of doing things.

The great majority of yachtsmen who acquire a motorboat with real seagoing ability have already had years of experience. Many have switched to power after years in sail. At any rate, they have long since graduated from "basic training."

But some skippers are coming into the field without this basic training and without prior experience at sea. What advice can we give them?

While there is no substitute for time at sea in the making of a competent seaman, the vast store of knowledge built up over years of experience by mariners of all nations is available in books. These books should be part of the boat's "equipment" from the start. The skipper should be so familiar with their contents that he knows just where to look for any information he needs. Courses in navigation and seamanship are available commercially and for free from such excellent organizations as the U.S. Power Squadrons and the Coast Guard Auxiliary. By volunteering for and becoming proficient as an observer in predicted log racing, a good deal of "underway time" can be acquired quickly. This activity is particularly valuable for the example experienced operators will give in operating at the highest standards of navigation, steering, and speed control.

As for sea time, there is just no substitute for getting out there. Experience as a crewmember should be actively sought. If a power voyage is not available and a sail voyage is—grab it. You will learn much on either. Four of the people who have made long voyages in *Passagemaker* now skipper their own little ships.

With the commissioning of your own vessel, you should lay out a definite program for advancing your experience, doing a little more each time you go out, until a passage of several days is no longer a novelty or a cause for concern.

In observing neophyte skippers, I've noticed that they generally show wisdom by starting slowly, with respect for the sea and an understanding of their own limitations, but when finally they are qualified to take off on a passage of some days, they are somewhat reluctant to do so. This is largely a reluctance to trust their navigating ability out of sight of land.

Author's note (1994): The following sections on navigation and communications have been completely revised. The remainder of the chapter, with a few minor changes, is as Robert Beebe originally wrote it.

NAVIGATION

One of the biggest challenges faced by the long-range cruiser is navigation, and until recently this has been primarily accomplished through the use of a sextant. The mariner measured the height of the sun and various other celestial bodies and then, through a fairly complicated series of calculations, could accurately fix his position. It was commonplace for a vessel, its navigator hindered by heavy overcast, to run for many days without a "fix," only able to calculate her position based upon dead reckoning—estimating speed and course made good. During most of Beebe's voyaging career this was the way, and I admit to great admiration for those who have really mastered that dying art.

Today various forms of electronic navigation have developed into extremely reliable systems. Loran, which utilizes land-based transmitters, has been in operation for quite some time. For many of the developed areas of the world, this system can provide accurate navigational information at affordable prices. The drawback to Loran is that it can be adversely affected by heavy precipitation and, because of the limited number of Loran stations, cannot be depended upon worldwide.

The most exciting new form of electronic navigation is the Global Positioning System, which utilizes orbiting satellites to give extremely reliable and accurate information worldwide. The signals are not affected by weather, and recent price reductions of GPS units have made them very attractive.

Without getting into the technicalities of how GPS works, we can review some of its features and how easy it can make the process of navigation. The most basic information it offers is a digital readout of the vessel's longitude and latitude, which can be converted to a point on

Figure 20-1. *GPS receiver with navigation readouts for course over ground (COG), speed over ground (SOG), cross-track error (XTE), course to waypoint (CTW), and an off-course graphic. (Photo courtesy Trimble)*

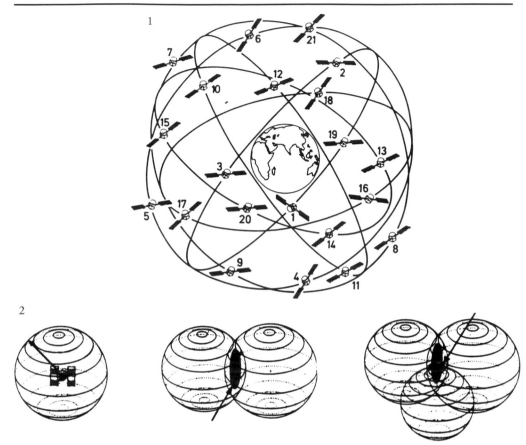

Figure 20-2. *(1) GPS satellites are not geostationary—they have inclined orbits that take them over any point on their ground track once every 12 hours. (2) GPS uses ranges from satellites to determine the only possible position of the receiver. (Illustrations courtesy Trimble)*

a plotting chart. The importance of transferring this information regularly is detailed in Chapter 14.

GPS units can instantly provide additional information such as speed and course over the ground. All have the ability to hold waypoints, allowing you to enter the longitude and latitude of your destination or points along the way, and the system will tell you how far you are from any waypoint, what the magnetic course is, and how long it will take you to get there at the present speed. If you're trying to maintain a very accurate track, a course deviation indicator can tell you how far you are from a course line between your starting point and destination. In the 1991 Transpac we used a GPS aboard *Ariel* (one of our Mason 53s) that could graph our steering course over as short a distance as ½ nautical mile. The graph clearly showed which of the crew could maintain the straightest and fastest line.

Any prudent skipper must question the reliability of the electronic navigation system—and rightfully so. We've been taught that safe navigation requires careful consideration of all the navigational aids and information available, and we're not to rely totally on only one source or method.

The GPS aboard *Salvation II* quit on us between Fort Lauderdale and Bermuda, showing the message "ROM Failure." Fortunately the problem was quickly resolved with an SSB phone call to the GPS manufacturer. A technician walked us through a reprogramming procedure, and the system has worked perfectly ever since.

Had we not been able to get the GPS working, we did have a portable, hand-held Loran that operated from its own internal batteries. Using the little unit was inconvenient, requiring a trip to the bow to erect the antenna clear of the deck obstructions, but we could get a fairly accurate fix all the way across the Atlantic. We also carried a sextant, along with the current almanac and required tables, but none of us was totally proficient in its use. Had the Loran not worked and the sextant failed to give a credible position, we could have dead reckoned until we picked up Bermuda on radio, then used a direction finder and finally the radar to bring us in safely.

To conclude then, GPS simplifies navigating across oceans, but prudence requires an alternative system. Hand-held GPS units are widely available, and most of the vessels we've delivered lately have had one aboard as a backup. A GPS failure due to a satellite malfunction is not really possible due to the redundancy of multiple satellites. The hand-held has the added appeal of not being dependent on ship's power to operate. Recording and plotting hourly positions, as recommended in Chapter 14, will immediately expose an incorrect GPS reading, and dead reckoning can then begin until the problem is sorted out or another navigation method is implemented.

COMMUNICATIONS

VHF

The most basic equipment used aboard yachts and ships for communication is the VHF radio. Designed for clear and reliable transmission, the range of these radios is generally limited to well under 50 miles, with 10 to 20 miles being normal. The very-high-frequency (VHF) signal is referred to as a line-of-sight transmission, which is the primary limiting factor in useful range.

In the open ocean, channel 16 on the VHF radio is continuously monitored. Turning up the *squelch* will silence the radio, and transmissions will only be heard if the sending vessel is fairly close by. Any time a ship is sighted, a call on this frequency will generally get a reply, and it is most useful to discuss course, speed, and mutual intentions with any vessel where a collision is even remotely possible.

Close to shore, VHF can generally receive weather information, and a network of radiotelephone operators can *patch* your signal through the land-based telephone system. Channel 16 is also monitored by all shore-based Coast Guard stations and by marine and harbor patrols.

SSB

Single-sideband radio has been in operation for many years and really works quite well. Unlike VHF, SSB frequencies are such that they are reflected by or bounce off the upper atmosphere, or ionosphere. This bounce and propagation of the transmission allow the radio signal to reach out

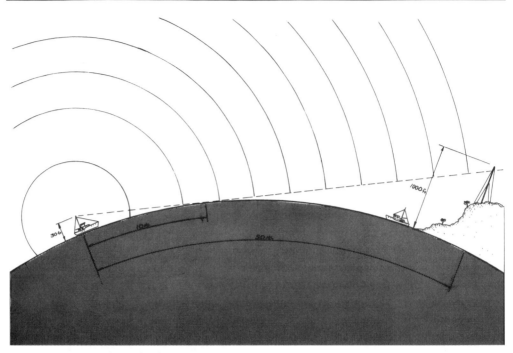

Figure 20-3. *VHF line-of-sight transmission.*

around the curvature of the earth. While crossing the Atlantic aboard *Salvation II,* we all made numerous calls using U.S.–based high-seas radiotelephone coast stations, which, like the VHF, also interface with the land-based telephone system. SSB can also be used for ship-to-ship communications, to contact the U.S. Coast Guard, and to receive valuable weather and *Notice to Mariners* information.

Operating the SSB is always a challenge. Appropriate frequency selection is determined by a combination of factors. Close-range communications require a lower frequency; as distance increases, the appropriate frequency becomes higher. Also, the behavior of the signal changes throughout the day and night and can be dramatically affected by weather and conditions within the ionosphere. A typical radio conversation might involve numerous frequency changes to maintain the least amount of static and the best signal. Despite these problems, SSB is and will probably remain the system of choice for the cruising yacht due to its long-range effectiveness.

Ham

Another form of long-range communication used aboard yachts is amateur radio, or Ham, equipment. Operating generally within the same frequency range as SSB, and with the same kind of tuning and adjusting required, the Ham radio can prove very useful to the long-range cruiser. Unlike VHF and SSB radios, Ham is considered an amateur band by the FCC and requires a specific license of its users. To get a novice-class Ham license, a moderate amount of study is required to pass a simple written exam and a five-words-per-minute test in receiving Morse code.

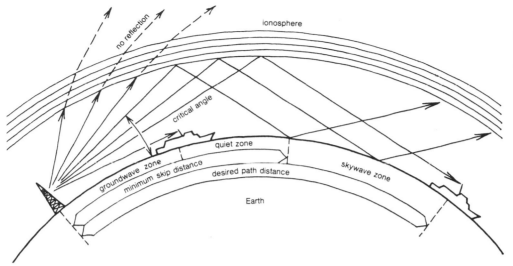

Figure 20-4. *SSB skywave and groundwave paths. (Illustration by Jim Sollers)*

A novice license authorizes voice communications on the popular 10-meter amateur bands. A general-class license is required for operators wishing to use voice on the standard high-frequency amateur bands, including the 20-meter Maritime Mobile Net. General-class exams entail a slightly more difficult written test and 13-word-per-minute code reception, but 10-year-olds frequently pass this test; it should prove no obstacle to anyone seriously interested in getting a license.

Once licensed, the Ham operator can use the gear aboard ship, with its greatest appeal being the easy and cost-free ability to phone home through the land-based telephone system. There are Ham operators that sit down every night and hope for the opportunity to pick up a ship's call and use their patching equipment, like SSB radiotelephone operators, to help the mariner place his call. The reward? Simply the thrill of speaking to a ship at sea and the enjoyment of operating their radios. They place the call "charges collect," and oftentimes you can reach a Ham operator who is close to the person you're calling to minimize the charge.

A phone call placed through SSB is quite expensive; $40 to $50 per call is about the minimum. With Ham it's almost free, but there are some restrictions; most notably, the amateur status prohibits any conversation that can result in financial gain. This rule is strictly enforced by most Ham operators and FCC monitors. A very well equipped cruiser would probably want to have a Ham system in addition to SSB equipment.

Weatherfax

Operating within the same frequency range as SSB and Ham radios, the weather facsimile machine offers the yachtsman the ability to receive printed maps that provide useful weather information—locations of high and low pressure areas, along with pressure gradients, wind direction and velocity, wave heights, cloud cover, an ocean-current analysis, and storm tracks. In addition, *Notice to Mariners* information is printed, along with high wind and sea warnings. During a 1991 delivery trip to Panama, the GPS system was shut down for about four days for one of the final position

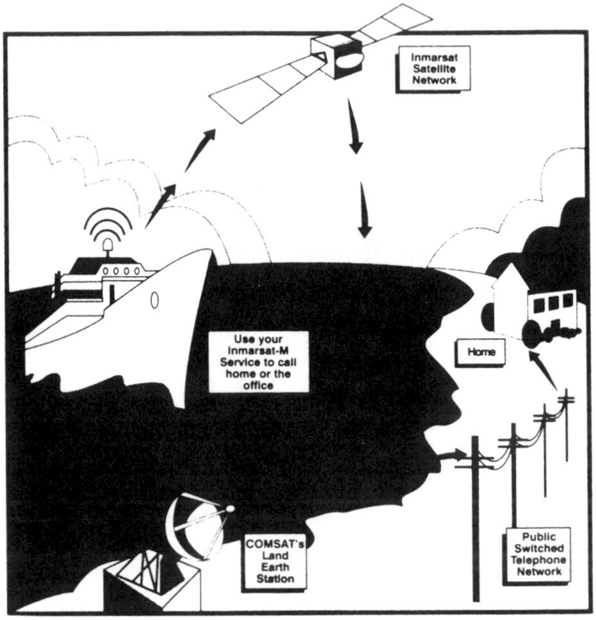

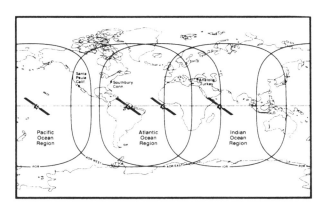

Figure 20-5. *Typical transmission path for Comsat's Mobile Link Service. (Illustration courtesy Comsat)*

Figure 20-6. *Comsat's earth stations for Inmarsat 4 ocean coverage. (Illustration courtesy Comsat)*

adjustments of the satellite network, forcing us to dead reckon the last 560 miles. But we knew ahead of time the specific date and time this would happen from the *Notice to Mariners* information we received on the weatherfax.

Satcom

VHF, SSB, and Ham equipment have been around for years, and while offering good communication, they do have limitations. As with navigation, the biggest breakthrough in communication is a result of satellite-based equipment. Unlike SSB and Ham, Satcom, or Inmarsat, uses satellites in lieu of the ionosphere to propagate its signal. The system is unaffected by changes within the ionosphere or any weather phenomena and provides a completely reliable communications link, free of distortion or static.

Satcom A, or, more correct, Inmarsat A, has been in operation for quite some time and has been used primarily by ships and the largest of luxury yachts. Aside from high cost, the antenna is almost 50 inches in diameter. Cruise ships use a variation with the ability to operate multiple phone lines, called Inmarsat A/4, and its antenna is a whopping 105 inches in diameter. These exotic systems have not been popular among cruising yachts, but now two new variations are being offered that may be of greater interest.

Inmarsat M, like the A system, provides voice and facsimile communications. The M antenna is a manageable height of about 30 inches with a 24-inch diameter and, although significantly less expensive than Inmarsat A, the current price of about $25,000 is still difficult to swallow. Inmarsat C was recently demonstrated to me, and it impressed me as being extremely useful and reasonably affordable at about $7,000. The C system does not offer voice or fax communication but sends and receives telex messages of type only.

To give an example of the usefulness of the system, I found I needed to contact Bruce Kestler aboard his vessel *Zopolote* for clarification on some of the information he provided for this book. Bruce had completed his circumnavigation and was bringing *Zopolote* back to the West Coast from Fort Lauderdale, but I had no idea where he was or how to contact him. I simply typed up a normal fax and sent it to Comsat (the U.S. affiliate of Inmarsat) in Washington, D.C. Bruce had given me *Zopolote*'s identifying number, which I included on my fax to Comsat. The text of my fax was sent from the land earth station and, via the satellite, relayed to the ship earth station aboard *Zopolote*.

Bruce was actually not aboard and the bridge was not manned. When he returned to the vessel after a morning of skindiving, he noted a message light on the Inmarsat C receiver. He turned on his laptop computer, which interfaced with the receiver, and the message—stored in the receiver's memory—was transferred to the computer where it could be read from the screen, stored on a disk, or printed if necessary.

Zopolote was in British Honduras, and Bruce simply went ashore and phoned me. Had he been at sea, he could have responded via the Inmarsat by typing out a message on the computer and pushing the send button. A few minutes later he would have received a confirmation from Comsat that his message had been received and relayed on to me in the form of a facsimile. Cruising may never be the same!

I recently saw a demonstration of a system combining GPS with Inmarsat C that offered some really fantastic features from the standpoint of safety. If in distress, an emergency message can be sent to Inmarsat's *Safety Net*. The nature of the distress can be stated, and the exact location of the vessel and its present course and speed automatically appear on the message. *Safety Net* also broadcasts notices of impending bad weather or other safety conditions to vessels within a specific geographical area; the system knows from the GPS what area it's in and collects the data pertinent to that specific area.

One last thing: By programming the onboard system to send a report at regular intervals to Comsat, the owner at his shoreside location can be kept apprised of the vessel's position, along with course and speed, without the crew's knowledge. As I said, cruising will never be the same, and that applies, too, to professional crews with absentee owners!

SAFETY AT SEA

Collision Avoidance

Anyone who goes far to sea these days should be aware of two things: First, the number of ships transiting the oceans is increasing by leaps and bounds; second, the speed of ships is increasing.

What does this mean to power voyagers running at 8 knots in a 40- to 50-foot boat? Obviously, it means the watch-standers must be more alert as the time available for evasive action is shortened, and there is the real possibility that the ship you've spotted will not sight you at all.

All this is compounded because many ships of all nations are running with a one-man watch, a watch that has other duties besides looking out. Even following good procedure—before taking his eyes off the sea to do something like writing up the log, the watch-stander should sweep the sea ahead very carefully with binoculars—the lights of a yacht most probably will not be visible from the distance the ship will cover while the watch-stander is not on the lookout.

You will have no trouble seeing the ship; the range lights of ships these days are much brighter than the law requires. They come up over the horizon looking like searchlights on a clear night. What is needed is some way *the ship* can see *you* as soon as possible. There is only one light available to a yacht that will do this—the Xenon flasher. I strongly recommend that you equip your vessel with one. The flasher should not be used except for its intended and legal purpose: as the "flare-up light" allowed by the rules "in order to attract attention." On *Mona Mona*'s cruise, the first I made on a flasher-equipped yacht, it was not used at all.

Even with this equipment, the only safe policy is to assume *nobody* can see you and act accordingly. This means staying out of everyone's way by early and extensive changes of course if there is any possibility of another vessel coming close. In fact, any changes in course or speed should be large so they will show up quickly if you are being watched on radar.

For radar and reduced visibility it is essential you have some really good radar reflectors. It is not generally appreciated how sensitive "corner reflectors" are to the slightest deviation from a 90-degree angle. The sides must be rigidly held to this. The folding type of reflector is hardly more useful than a big tin can.

During *Passagemaker*'s cruising days, radar was limited to use on large, expensive vessels. Today's cruising yacht will probably include a radar system, and many reliable, economically priced units are available. One of the most stressful cruises I've endured was aboard one of our 44-foot sailboats on a springtime delivery from Los Angeles to San Francisco. We experienced pea soup fog along the entire route, with visibility rarely exceeding 100 yards. While Loran kept us current on our position, three days of constant peering into the mist for fear of being run down by the extensive freighter traffic proved extremely fatiguing and unpleasant.

In lieu of radar, a piece of equipment that would have been useful during that trip is the radar detector. This device is essentially an upgraded version of the common automobile "Fuzz Buster" and can warn you if your vessel is under surveillance by marine radar. With the most basic models, an alarm will sound and the crew can then go on a traffic alert that would include careful scanning of the horizon and probably require pulling the engine back to idle; stopping the yacht; and listening for a fog horn, bow wave, or engine sounds from an advancing ship. While this method might not seem too comforting, you could be somewhat sure—in the absence of an alarm signal—that you're not on the verge of being run down.

More sophisticated radar detectors are available that not only warn of a radar beam being received but will indicate the direction from which the radar signal is being transmitted. The cost of these sophisticated units is reasonable—comparable to the cost of a moderately priced VHF marine radio.

The Husband-and-Wife Boat

The probable use of the seagoing motorboat for more husband-and-wife cruising in the manner of the many sailing cruisers was mentioned in Chapter 10. Here, we are concerned about the safety of this type of operation.

Sailing yachts with crews of two, or even one, have been sailing the seas for many years. By and large, their casualty rate has not been great enough to cause concern, but they do go missing occasionally. There are good reasons to suspect some of these casualties were run down by large ships that never saw them. The problem of taking evasive action in a small sailing vessel can be compounded by sudden calms or wind shifts. So from this point of view the full-power craft is safer.

The danger of being run down varies in different parts of the oceans. For instance, from Los Angeles to Panama, the coast has an almost constant curve toward the east, causing everyone to hug the coast most of the way. On a passage I made in 1973 there was almost always traffic in sight. In the South Pacific the traffic is still quite light. In the North Pacific, and to a lesser extent in the North Atlantic, new routing services to take advantage of weather have resulted in some scattering of shipping away from the traditional (and direct) great-circle routes, so ships can be found all over these areas.

With only two watch-standers, alertness is bound to deteriorate when a passage lasts more than a few days. There are some things that can be done to assist in this matter. Small radars sound an alarm if there is any contact within a certain minimum distance of the vessel. A less expensive alternative is a radar detector, as described above. As another possible alert, a clock could be rigged to sound an alarm at any interval desired unless a reset button were pressed regularly. If this is rigged also to stop the engine, believe me, it will bring all hands up, all-standing! The idea that a fully alert watch should be stood in the dark with less alertness during the day has been advanced in several places and appears to have some merit as making the best of a bad situation. Of course, a full watch list of at least three watch-standers is even better. It is worth some inconvenience and added expense to achieve this on long passages.

MANEUVERING

Some prospective owners, while conceding the superiority of the single-screw vessel in range and propeller protection, still want twin screws to make the vessel easier to maneuver around docks. The twins do this, of course, but not by much in a proper vessel, and by proper vessel we mean one without an excessive A/B ratio. The chief use of twin screws is to neutralize maneuvering problems caused by windage. Many popular makes of coastal motorboats have A/B ratios of 4.5 and higher and are practically unmanageable in a good breeze of wind; *their* twin screws are a necessity.

But a seagoing vessel with an A/B ratio of about 2.6 should handle easily with a single screw under all conditions. The owners of single-screw vessels who I know all have developed great competence in putting the ship right where they want it, and they take considerable pride in this ability. As one said to me, "Twin screws take all the sport out of it."

HEAVY-WEATHER HANDLING

The literature of sail cruising is loaded with advice and examples about handling vessels in heavy weather. For power voyaging there is not nearly as much advice available, and what there is seems largely concerned with coastal motorboats and "recreational" boats—such as fishing launches. Some of this advice is applicable, particularly about running inlets and handling in thunder squalls. But for a small motor craft a thousand miles at sea, not much has been written—the experience is just not there.

Passagemaker's experience may be of some use, though her gales were not too severe. Her first hit us at the south end of the Red Sea with winds of just about gale force, around 30 knots from astern. The problem was that we had to head about 20 degrees across the wind to avoid going ashore somewhere near Mocha. And we were uncertain about how far off downwind we could safely go without tending to broach. It soon became clear that we could head as far off as we needed, except before the very biggest waves. As a matter of prudence, we took these from dead aft. It was not until this wind died out after sunset that I realized it had never occurred to me to slow down: We ran at 7.5 knots the whole time.

Our hurricane off Bermuda was a strange experience. The sky became overcast and it started to rain, the barograph went down like a rock, and the wind increased. The trouble was that to us the wind appeared to be from the wrong direction for a tropical storm. It turned out later the storm had formed over Bermuda and headed northeast so it was already north of us. At the time we had sail up and ran off with the wind on the port quarter, which of course is the wrong tack for a tropical storm. The rain was so heavy it flattened the waves, but as closely as we could determine, the wind reached 55 knots. It had been 85 knots at Bermuda but was dying rapidly. We eventually entered what must have been the remnants of the storm's center because the barograph started back up as rapidly as it had gone down. We were able to go to power only and head directly for Bermuda in a dying sea.

A day ahead of us, a yacht (a 77-foot motorsailer) had a very hard time of it, but she came through undamaged.

Our second hurricane was encountered on the passage from Sandy Hook, New York, to Delaware Bay; this storm was coming up the New Jersey coast. The weather bureau said we could beat it if we started *right now;* but what they didn't tell us was that conditions were building up for a typical nor'easter, in addition. The result was plenty of northeast wind all night as we ran down the coast. At about 0200, when I took over, we took down the sail and continued to run with the wind and sea on the quarter, our only choice. She rode the big swells easily, and we had no real problems in wind velocities as high as 50 knots.

Our worst gale, which I noted earlier, was encountered off Cape Mendocino, California. After a summer in British Columbia, we were going down the Pacific Coast toward San Francisco, where we had an onboard party planned for the next day. The night before, the wind started to increase from astern. By 0300 it was bad enough for me to be called. I was on the bridge for the next 27 hours. Conditions were not too bad until dawn. After that, the winds gradually increased in strength until they reached full gale. This was not a storm but a gradient wind, powered by the hot interior valleys of the West making a "thermal low," while the cold ocean air rushed in to fill the vacuum. It soon became so strong I felt it advisable to take the wheel and head off directly before the waves at low speed. Around sunset, the waves began to "roll," giving them a most frightening aspect. I was concerned about being able to stay dead before the waves after dark on a moonless night. Much to my relief, I found this was no problem: The waves could be seen well enough to manage that.

Thus we kept on southward. The trouble was San Francisco was southeast, getting more easterly the farther we went. I had visions of the gale sweeping us right past the Golden Gate and putting us back in Monterey again. But after midnight the wind gradually started to slacken, and we could steer across it a bit more each hour, until the course was attained for San Francisco. Shortly after dawn we were steaming through a windless sea. The party was a great success. We were on schedule despite a difficult night.

Now, in all these incidents we ran off before the weather; in the last, dead before it, in the others, across the wind to varying degrees, at all times using flopperstoppers. Would it be possible to do this in winds of higher velocities, say in the 65- to 75-knot range? The answer is, I don't know. I rather suspect that in those conditions, the recommendations for sailing vessels under such "survival conditions," found in books on the subject, would be applicable to power vessels as well. But the essence of the argument—and there is an argument—about the best methods of meeting heavy weather is that running off raises the danger of "broaching," while lying "a-hull," that is, with engines stopped and the drifting vessel allowed to take what attitude she will to the seas, raises grave danger of heavy damage from breaking seas because, in this situation, almost every vessel will lie broadside to the seas.

Broaching means the boat turns uncontrollably beam to the wind and sea. It is caused by going too fast down the face of a wave that is coming up from astern. The bow buries deeply with enormous increase of resistance forward. The rudder is unable to provide the force necessary to stop the turning motion that results. The turn is so quickly made that large centrifugal forces are generated that, combined with a breaking wave pushing against the side, can capsize the vessel. The same forces in extreme conditions have also caused some vessels to "pitch-pole," or turn end-over-end.

It is these end results of broaching that have caused some experts to urge lying a-hull. They point out that the forces acting on a hull lying broadside to the seas are very much less if the vessel is stopped than they are with the addition of centrifugal forces from the sudden broaching turn. This should make the vessel less liable to capsize. If it does, it would be better to be rolled over from the broadside position, with inertial forces helping to bring the vessel upright through a full roll, than it would be to chance the damage from pitch-poling. Actual incidents are cited to show the difference in danger and damage.

All of this sounds quite grim, and of course it is. Although many professional seamen have gone to sea all their lives without meeting such conditions, nevertheless one must realize that it can happen. What is really needed in this case is something like a submarine. Vessels going far to sea should have extensive preparation for preserving their watertight integrity under any condition. The roster of sailing vessels that have pitch-poled or been capsized, yet righted themselves and returned safely to port, is quite lengthy. So we can see such an incident need not mean certain death—no matter how traumatic the experience. The key, of course, is keeping the sea out of the boat. It is this concern that inspired my earlier remarks on glass areas.

Returning to broaching, our experiences with *Passagemaker* showed she had less tendency to broach than I had hitherto experienced. The "rooting" tendency was there—you could feel it as she put her bow down and accelerated before a wave. But her big rudder proved to have enough "command" to keep her from actually running off course. The drill was to watch the waves astern, and when a particularly vicious one appeared, to put the stern dead before it. As the bow went down, the helmsman's line of sight was shifted to dead ahead. If the bow showed the slightest tendency to turn to either side, the rudder was immediately slapped hard in the opposite direction. This always worked, yet I hesitate to imply that it always would, the sea being so full of surprises.

PAPERWORK AND OFFICIALS

"Going foreign" means inevitable contact with the maritime officials of countries much different from your own. This is nothing to worry about, provided your papers are in order and your heart is pure.

For a vessel built abroad, a consul may issue a "Certificate of American Ownership." If he does not remember what this is, tell him it is in his form book. Ordinarily, permission to issue the certificate must be obtained from Washington after the sale is completed. But for a brand-new vessel obviously being built for an American citizen, it is possible to obtain permission in advance from the State Department for the consul to issue the certificate when he is satisfied all conditions are fulfilled. We did this, and were able to leave Singapore immediately after completion of the sale. Be sure to invite the consul to your christening party.

See that the consul binds all your papers with yards of red tape and the biggest seal he has. I think this does more good than anything. You will often be asked for gross and net tonnage figures.

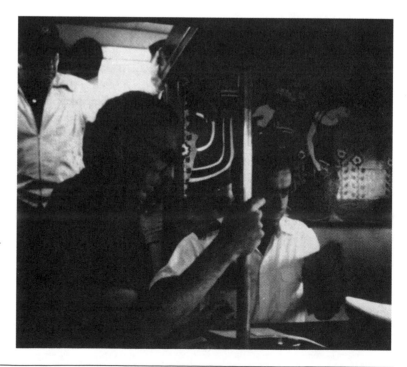

Figure 20-7. *Customs check-in at Ponta Delgada, Azores Islands. While the captain answers questions, Colonel Bibb stands by to assist if necessary.*

If you don't know them, give displacement for gross and half that for net. I had *Passagemaker* measured by the British, and although the paper was clearly marked "not for British Registry" this impressive form seemed to do a lot of good. The yard's hull number was mentioned on this form and in the certificate and was successfully pointed out as the "registry number" more than once. A consul can issue a "Temporary Certificate of Registry," but this document is only good for six months and hardly any owner would want to return home in that short time.

All hands should have passports; don't fool with "seaman's papers" on a yacht. The only place we went where a visa was required in 1963 was Yugoslavia. That country, Greece, and possibly other countries have a restricted list of ports where a yacht can enter and clear. If there is any doubt, you should plan your entry into a country at a port that has facilities for regular shipping.

Every port will want crew lists with passport numbers, dates of birth, and so on. Make up plenty of them in advance on a typewriter. I have been asked for as many as six. Be sure all hands have International Immunization Certificates and that shots are up to date. Have a locker where "spirits" and cigarettes can be sealed up in case Customs thinks you have too much.

The best time to enter port is 0900 on a working day. I had reason to regret the occasions we did not follow this rule. Overtime charges are quite high in some places.

Flying a good-size national (not merchant) flag of the country, steam right into the port. If no one tells you what to do, it is always legal for the captain to go ashore and make his presence known. But *only* the captain.

If, as is usually the case, the officials come on board for check-in, have everything ready in advance: all papers and passports laid out in an area such as the dinette where writing can be done. The area should be cleared of all crewmembers except the captain, with one other member prepared to come if the captain summons him to serve coffee or beer. During the time the officials are on board, no crewmembers other than the captain should speak to them. If questions are asked, they should be referred to the captain. He alone should speak for the ship, and he should limit himself to answering questions. After all business is concluded, it is in order to offer some refreshment. It is surprising how often this will be refused. Even if no one on board smokes, it is a good idea to have cigarettes on board to offer to the officials.

This may all sound a bit formal and stuffy, but it is a good idea to exhibit a brisk, businesslike manner, be dressed in clean clothes, and have the yacht all ship-shape in order to make a good impression. Unfortunately, there are enough sailors who *don't* make a good impression to raise suspicion of yachts among customs officer, and to lead to remarks like this in an SSCA bulletin: ". . . and find some freaked-out creep in a sailing pasteboard box has queered it for everybody else."

FIRE

Fire is an ancient terror of seamen. Many of the sea's great tragedies have been caused by fire, not by the sea itself. The possibility of fire must always be present in the captain's mind and every precaution taken against it.

What I want to emphasize here is something these books neglect: the diesel-driven vessel, while much safer than gasoline, is *not* immune to fire caused by fuel. Carelessness in handling diesel fuel or control of leakage is no more tolerable than it would be with gasoline. Under certain conditions the fumes from diesel oil *can* explode. And high-pressure fuel-injector leakage that can drain into the sump has caused "base explosions."

I personally know of two small vessels that were destroyed by diesel-fuel fires. A 50-foot twin-engine (in the stern), long-range yacht burned and sank while underway in the Mediterranean when it was about three months old. During the short period the crew was able to fight the fire with ordinary fire extinguishers, before they were driven off the vessel, no investigation could be made of how or where the fire started.

In the second instance, the engine room was equipped with a CO_2 flooding system. It was also equipped with powerful engine-room blowers, which were in operation. The cause was a fuel-line break right over an uncooled section of exhaust line, a situation that should have been foreseen. The CO_2 automatically functioned—and the engine-room blowers automatically blew the CO_2 out the vents! Result: an uncontrollable fire. This gives you something to think about.

Diesel-fuel fires can be fought using techniques the navy developed during the war. The principal reliance was on the "fog nozzle" at the end of a "wand," a section of pipe about 7 feet long. The fog nozzle can be approximated by the ordinary adjustable spray nozzle used on rubber hose. The main point is to get it into action as quickly as possible. On *Passagemaker,* the hose with nozzle was always hooked up with the valve open. Full pressure could be obtained instantly by flipping a switch that was outside the engine room in the galley. Some such arrangement is recommended.

Its undeniable convenience has made propane cooking much more popular over the past few years. With absolute adherence to safety regulations and proper operating technique, propane *can* be quite safe. However, propane is heavier than air, and if accidentally released within the confines of a vessel will settle and accumulate in the lowest part—likely the bilge—creating a terrific fire and explosion hazard.

Current regulations require that propane fuel be stored in a locker sealed from the rest of the vessel and vented overboard. All valves, regulators, and pressure gauges must be contained within the propane compartment; a single run of approved reinforced rubber hose (no joints or couplings) or seamless copper tubing must carry the fuel to the stove.

General practice is to install an electric solenoid valve within the propane locker. The valve is controlled from the galley, allowing the operator to turn the fuel on for cooking and off when not in use. A red light illuminates when the solenoid is open and should be clearly visible within the galley. These electric valves are "energized to open" and are very reliable. When the circuit is interrupted, or if the solenoid fails, the valve closes.

Electronic sniffers are also available that sound an alarm or shut off the propane at the tank if gas is detected within the vessel. A pressure gauge installed between tank and regulator allows periodic leak checks. With the manual valve on the propane bottle shut off and the solenoid valve open and all stove burners off, the system should hold a constant pressure for 15 minutes with no noticeable drop on the gauge. This test should be conducted at least every two weeks. While these safeguards have been designed to enhance the safety of propane, the most important aspect of dealing with this fuel is a thorough understanding of the system and cautious operation.

KEEPING TIME

Your vessel should be run on zone time, using the numbered zones as described in *Bowditch.*

The time we use to regulate our own routines is called *local time* and usually corresponds closely to the ancient idea that noon is when the sun is highest. In the U.S.A., what we call Eastern

Figure 20-8. Passagemaker's *data board. To reduce glare, the entire forward part of the pilothouse was painted with green blackboard paint. This made a convenient surface on which to post data.*

Standard Time is the time of zone +5, while Eastern Daylight Time is the time of zone +4. But what happens when we leave our home boundaries to go out on the sea and disappear into the distance? What is the local time then?

Well, the answer is perfectly simple. The local time aboard a ship is what the captain says it is. This is literally true. In the old days, before accurate time pieces, when the captain observed the sun at its highest, he would say "Strike eight bells." This would be done and the hourglass turned over to start another cycle of watches.

So it ill behooves me to tell you, the captain of your vessel, what time to use. But let me respectfully suggest, as the result of my experience, that you do what we did on *Passagemaker:* Run your ship on zone time.

To handle this, the data board shows four things: the local time in the form of the presently used zone description; the local date, which means just that; the time of sunset; and the time of sunrise, which is for the next day.

Sunrise and sunset are useful for several reasons. They show when star sights will be taken when combined with the duration of twilight you experienced the previous day. (This is more accurate than the tables in the almanac.) And they show how the local time being used works in with the ship's routine. For example, steaming steadily eastward across the Atlantic, if you do not change your zone time, you will eventually find all the navigators on deck taking star sights just when the cook announces supper at the scheduled hour of 1800. And there is nothing madder than a cook who has fixed a gourmet masterpiece and finds no one ready to eat it! As one of the basic principles of cruising is to keep the cook happy, you are due for a time zone change, but quick!

Another thing to keep in mind is that it is desirable to arrive at your destination using the time zone there. For instance, in going from Bermuda to Horta you would change three hours on the way to be on Horta time. So as a practical matter you are limited to three changes of one hour each in a passage of about 10 days. The timing of the changes is arranged with consideration of the factors mentioned.

Figure 20-9. Passagemaker *leaving
Millwall Lock, Plymouth, England,
at the beginning of her transatlantic
passage to the United States.*

On vessels with varnished woodwork rather than *Passagemaker*'s blackboard paint, the data described above was kept on cards and posted near the wheel.

CONCLUSION

Writing these notes, and in fact writing the whole book, has forced me to review all that happened over a period of years in order to ensure that nothing of prime importance to successful passage-making in seagoing motorboats has been forgotten, or misstated, or is not found somewhere in the recommended reading. In the course of this review, both Linford and I had many nostalgic memories about our cruising. Like our first cruise with just the two of us in Greece, from Athens to Rhodes with the *meltemi* blowing furiously. And how Linford got seasick for the first and last time—bravely trying to brown slices of delicious Yugoslavian fillets in the galley below. And how our new stabilizer pennants began to unravel, and we took shelter briefly behind a rocky reef to put safety lines on the wires in case the pennants let go. And how we spent half a day making up new ones, with Linford learning to "pass the ball" as I served. And how the wind shifted and chased us out of our harbor before we swung onto the shore. And how we then took refuge in what was just a cleft in a sheer cliff on the south side of Nis Nikouria and got the anchor to hold after four attempts. And how Linford hoisted me up the mast so I could install the new pennants with the winds whistling down the gully, almost pushing us against the rocks, first one side then the other. And how these hectic-wonderful days are now just a note in Chapter 8, "Stabilizing Against Rolling."

The same thread runs through the whole book, of experiences shared and lessons learned. But one lesson is most important of all—we are glad we have done it and hope to do more. And so we will leave you with one simple thought: "Go!"

Revising author's note (1994): Bob Beebe and Bob Sutton helped bring *Passagemaker* home from Europe in 1976. Today, despite her 30-plus years of dependable service, she can still be seen cruising the Eastern Seaboard of the United States. So many routine passages, so many good times, so much adventure. A recent survey indicates she's capable of putting to sea again, and we hope to see more of her in the years to come.

HOW TO
OBTAIN
PLANS OF
PASSAGEMAKER

READERS OF THIS NEW EDITION of *Voyaging Under Power* will be pleased to learn that for the first time since the death of Captain Robert P. Beebe in August 1988, *Passagemaker* plans are again available to the public. As this book goes to press, a catalog is in preparation describing all the Beebe designs (including the small boats created during his years in the U.S. Navy). Anyone interested in Beebe *Passagemaker* plans should write to:

Beebe Plans Service
P.O. Box 881
Shelter Island Heights, NY 11965-0881

METRIC CONVERSION TABLE: LENGTHS

1 inch = 0.025 meters   2 inches = 0.051 meters

Ft.-In.	Meters	Ft.-In.	Meters	Ft.-In.	Meters	Ft.-In.	Meters	Ft.-In.	Meters
1-0	0.31	14-0	4.27	27-0	8.24	40-0	12.20	53-0	16.17
1-3	0.38	14-3	4.35	27-3	8.31	40-3	12.28	53-3	16.24
1-6	0.46	14-6	4.42	27-6	8.39	40-6	12.35	53-6	16.32
1-9	0.53	14-9	4.50	27-9	8.46	40-9	12.43	53-9	16.39
2-0	0.61	15-0	4.56	28-0	8.54	41-0	12.51	54-0	16.47
2-3	0.69	15-3	4.65	28-3	8.62	41-3	12.58	54-3	16.55
2-6	0.76	15-6	4.73	28-6	8.69	41-6	12.66	54-6	16.62
2-9	0.84	15-9	4.80	28-9	8.77	41-9	12.73	54-9	16.70
3-0	0.92	16-0	4.88	29-0	8.85	42-0	12.81	55-0	16.76
3-3	0.99	16-3	4.96	29-3	8.92	42-3	12.89	55-3	16.85
3-6	1.07	16-6	5.03	29-6	9.00	42-6	12.96	55-6	16.93
3-9	1.14	16-9	5.11	29-9	9.07	42-9	13.04	55-9	17.00
4-0	1.22	17-0	5.19	30-0	9.15	43-0	13.12	56-0	17.08
4-3	1.30	17-3	5.26	30-3	9.23	43-3	13.19	56-3	17.16
4-6	1.37	17-6	5.34	30-6	9.30	43-6	13.27	56-6	17.23
4-9	1.45	17-9	5.41	30-9	9.38	43-9	13.34	56-9	17.31
5-0	1.53	18-0	5.49	31-0	9.46	44-0	13.42	57-0	17.39
5-3	1.60	18-3	5.57	31-3	9.53	44-3	13.50	57-3	17.46
5-6	1.68	18-6	5.64	31-6	9.61	44-6	13.57	57-6	17.54
5-9	1.75	18-9	5.72	31-9	9.68	44-9	13.65	57-9	17.61
6-0	1.83	19-0	5.80	32-0	9.76	45-0	13.73	58-0	17.69
6-3	1.91	19-3	5.87	32-3	9.84	45-3	13.80	58-3	17.77
6-6	1.98	19-6	5.95	32-6	9.91	45-6	13.88	58-6	17.84
6-9	2.06	19-9	6.02	32-9	9.99	45-9	13.95	58-9	17.92
7-0	2.14	20-0	6.10	33-0	10.07	46-0	14.03	59-0	18.00
7-3	2.21	20-3	6.18	33-3	10.14	46-3	14.11	59-3	18.07
7-6	2.29	20-6	6.25	33-6	10.22	46-6	14.18	59-6	18.15
7-9	2.36	20-9	6.33	33-9	10.29	46-9	14.26	59-9	18.22
8-0	2.44	21-0	6.41	34-0	10.37	47-0	14.34	60-0	18.30
8-3	2.52	21-3	6.48	34-3	10.45	47-3	14.41	60-3	18.37
8-6	2.59	21-6	6.56	34-6	10.52	47-6	14.49	60-6	18.45
8-9	2.67	21-9	6.63	34-9	10.60	47-9	14.56	60-9	18.53
9-0	2.75	22-0	6.71	35-0	10.68	48-0	14.64	61-0	18.61
9-3	2.82	22-3	6.79	35-3	10.75	48-3	14.72	61-3	18.68
9-6	2.90	22-6	6.86	35-6	10.83	48-6	14.79	61-6	18.76
9-9	2.97	22-9	6.94	35-9	10.90	48-9	14.87	61-9	18.83
10-0	3.05	23-0	7.02	36-0	10.98	49-0	14.95	62-0	18.91
10-3	3.13	23-3	7.09	36-3	11.06	49-3	15.02	62-3	18.99
10-6	3.20	23-6	7.17	36-6	11.13	49-6	15.10	62-6	19.06
10-9	3.28	23-9	7.24	36-9	11.21	49-9	15.17	62-9	19.14
11-0	3.36	24-0	7.32	37-0	11.29	50-0	15.25	63-0	19.22
11-3	3.43	24-3	7.40	37-3	11.36	50-3	15.33	63-3	19.29
11-6	3.51	24-6	7.47	37-6	11.44	50-6	15.40	63-6	19.37
11-9	3.58	24-9	7.55	37-9	11.51	50-9	15.48	63-9	19.44
12-0	3.66	25-0	7.63	38-0	11.59	51-0	15.56	64-0	19.52
12-3	3.74	25-3	7.70	38-3	11.67	51-3	15.63	64-3	19.60
12-6	3.81	25-6	7.78	38-6	11.74	51-6	15.71	64-6	19.67
12-9	3.89	25-9	7.85	38-9	11.82	51-9	15.78	64-9	19.75
13-0	3.97	26-0	7.93	39-0	11.90	52-0	15.86	65-0	19.83
13-3	4.04	26-3	8.00	39-3	11.97	52-3	15.94	65-3	19.90
13-6	4.12	26-6	8.08	39-6	12.05	52-6	16.01	65-6	19.98
13-9	4.19	26-9	8.16	39-9	12.12	52-9	16.09	65-9	20.05

METRIC CONVERSION TABLE: WEIGHTS

Long Tons	=	Metric Tons	Long Tons	=	Metric Tons	Long Tons	=	Metric Tons
1.0	=	1.016	31.0	=	31.497	61.0	=	61.979
2.0	=	2.032	32.0	=	32.514	62.0	=	62.995
3.0	=	3.048	33.0	=	33.530	63.0	=	64.011
4.0	=	4.064	34.0	=	34.546	64.0	=	65.027
5.0	=	5.080	35.0	=	35.562	65.0	=	66.043
6.0	=	6.096	36.0	=	36.578	66.0	=	67.059
7.0	=	7.112	37.0	=	37.594	67.0	=	68.075
8.0	=	8.128	38.0	=	38.610	68.0	=	69.091
9.0	=	9.144	39.0	=	39.626	69.0	=	70.107
10.0	=	10.160	40.0	=	40.642	70.0	=	71.123
11.0	=	11.177	41.0	=	41.658	71.0	=	72.139
12.0	=	12.193	42.0	=	42.674	72.0	=	73.155
13.0	=	13.209	43.0	=	43.690	73.0	=	74.171
14.0	=	14.225	44.0	=	44.706	74.0	=	75.187
15.0	=	15.241	45.0	=	45.722	75.0	=	76.204
16.0	=	16.257	46.0	=	46.738	76.0	=	77.220
17.0	=	17.273	47.0	=	47.754	77.0	=	78.236
18.0	=	18.289	48.0	=	48.770	78.0	=	79.252
19.0	=	19.305	49.0	=	49.786	79.0	=	80.268
20.0	=	20.321	50.0	=	50.802	80.0	=	81.280
21.0	=	21.337	51.0	=	51.818	81.0	=	82.300
22.0	=	22.353	52.0	=	52.834	82.0	=	83.316
23.0	=	23.370	53.0	=	53.850	83.0	=	84.332
24.0	=	24.385	54.0	=	54.867	84.0	=	85.348
25.0	=	25.401	55.0	=	55.883	85.0	=	86.364
26.0	=	26.417	56.0	=	56.899	86.0	=	87.380
27.0	=	27.433	57.0	=	57.915	87.0	=	88.396
28.0	=	28.449	58.0	=	58.931	88.0	=	89.412
29.0	=	29.465	59.0	=	59.947	89.0	=	90.428
30.0	=	30.481	60.0	=	60.963	90.0	=	91.444

NOTE: To convert tenths of long tons into kilograms, add the following:

Tenths of Long Tons	0.1	0.2	0.3	0.4	0.5	0.6	0.7	0.8	0.9
Add Kilograms	101	203	305	406	508	610	711	713	914

METRIC CONVERSION TABLE: Inches to Centimeters

Inches:	1	2	3	4	5	6	7	8	9	10	11
Centimeters:	2.5	5.1	7.6	10.2	12.7	15.2	17.8	20.3	22.9	25.4	27.9

METRIC CONVERSION TABLE: Volume of Liquids

To convert U.S. Gals. to Liters, multiply U.S. Gals. $\times$ 3.785.

To convert U.S. Gals. to English (Imperial) Gals., multiply U.S. Gals. $\times$ 0.833.

INDEX

Note: Numbers in **boldface type** refer to illustrations.